# CON

# UNDERSTANDING THE

**Column 3 (Common Worship)**
**On Principal Feasts, Principal Holy Days, Sundays and Festivals** this gives the Principal Service Lectionary, intended for use at the main service of the day (in most churches the mid-morning service), whether or not it is a Eucharist.

**On other weekdays** this gives the Daily Eucharistic Lectionary for those wanting a semi-continuous pattern of readings and a psalm for Holy Communion. It is most useful in a church where there is a daily celebration and a core community that worships together day by day, though its use is not restricted to that.

**Column 4 (Common Worship)**
**On Principal Feasts, Principal Holy Days, Sundays and Festivals** this gives the Third Service Lectionary. Many churches will have no need of it, for it comes into use only if the Principal and Second Service Lectionaries have been used. Its most likely use is at Morning Prayer (when this is not the Principal Service). Where psalms are recommended for use in the morning, these also appear in this column.

**On other weekdays** this provides the psalmody and readings for Morning Prayer. Where two or more psalms are appointed, the psalm in bold italic may be used as the only psalm. Psalms printed in round brackets ( ) may be omitted if they are used as an opening canticle at Morning Prayer. Where † is printed after the psalm number, the psalm may be shortened if desired. For those wishing to follow the Ordinary Time psalm cycle throughout the year (except for the period between 19 December and the Epiphany and from the Monday of Holy Week to the Saturday of Easter Week), this is printed as an alternative to the seasonal provision.

**Column 1**
The date

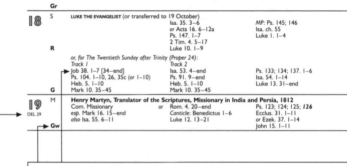

COMMON WORSHIP

## October 2015

| | | | Sunday Principal Service / Weekday Eucharist | Third Service / Morning Prayer |
|---|---|---|---|---|
| **17** | Sa | **Ignatius, Bishop of Antioch, Martyr, c. 107** Com. Martyr *also* Phil. 3. 7–12 John 6. 52–58 | *or* Rom. 4. 13, 16–18 Ps. 105. 6–10, 41–44 Luke 12. 8–12 | Ps. 120; *121*; 122 Ecclus. 28. 14–end *or* Ezek. 36. 16–36 John 14. 15–end |
| | Gr | | | |
| **18** | S | LUKE THE EVANGELIST (or transferred to 19 October) | Isa. 35. 3–6 *or* Acts 16. 6–12a Ps. 147. 1–7 2 Tim. 4. 5–17 Luke 10. 1–9 | MP: Ps. 145; 146 Isa. ch. 55 Luke 1. 1–4 |
| | R | | *or, for The Twentieth Sunday after Trinity (Proper 24):* | |
| | | | Track 1 Job 38. 1–7 [34–end] Ps. 104. 1–10, 26, 35c (*or* 1–10) Heb. 5. 1–10 Mark 10. 35–45 | Track 2 Isa. 53. 4–end Ps. 91. 9–end Heb. 5. 1–10 Mark 10. 35–45 |  Ps. 133; 134; 137. 1–6 Isa. 54. 1–14 Luke 13. 31–end |
| | G | | | |
| **19** DEL 29 | M | **Henry Martyn, Translator of the Scriptures, Missionary in India and Persia, 1812** Com. Missionary *esp.* Mark 16. 15–end *also* Isa. 55. 6–11 | *or* Rom. 4. 20–end *Canticle:* Benedictus 1–6 Luke 12. 13–21 | Ps. 123; 124; 125; *126* Ecclus. 31. 1–11 *or* Ezek. 37. 1–14 John 15. 1–11 |
| | Gw | | | |

**Column 2 provides for Common Worship:**
- the name of the Principal Holy Day, Sunday, Festival or Lesser Festival;
- a note of other Commemorations for mention in prayers;
- any general note that applies to the whole *Common Worship* provision for the day;
- one of the options where there are two options for readings at the Eucharist or Principal Service;
- an indication of the liturgical colour.

*Readings:* Readings occur in this column only in two circumstances. On Sundays after Trinity where there are two 'tracks' for the Principal Service readings (where there is a choice of first reading and psalm, but the second reading and Gospel are the same in both tracks), Track I appears in this column. On Lesser Festivals throughout the year, where there are readings for that festival that are alternative to the semi-continuous Daily Eucharistic Lectionary, these also appear in this column.

*Colour:* An upper-case letter indicates the liturgical colour of the day. A lower-case second colour indicates the colour for a Lesser Festival while the upper-case letter indicates the continuing seasonal colour.

**Column 1**
Week number of Daily Eucharistic Lectionary

# LECTIONARY

**Column 5 (Common Worship)**
**On Principal Feasts, Principal Holy Days, Sundays and Festivals** this gives the Second Service Lectionary, intended for use when a second set of readings is required. Its most likely use is in the evening, when the Principal Service Lectionary has been used in the morning. Sometimes it might be used at an evening Eucharist. Where the second reading is not a Gospel reading, an alternative to meet this need is provided. Where psalms are recommended for use in the evening, these also appear in this column.

**On other weekdays** this provides the psalmody and readings for Evening Prayer. Where two or more psalms are provided, the psalm may be omitted if they are used as an opening canticle at Evening Prayer. Where † is printed after the psalm number, the psalm may be shortened if desired. For those wishing to follow the Ordinary Time psalm cycle throughout the year (except for the period between 19 December and the Epiphany and from the Monday of Holy Week to the Saturday of Easter Week), this is printed as an alternative to the seasonal provision.

**Column 7 (Book of Common Prayer)**
This provides the readings for Morning Prayer, together with psalm provision where it varies from the BCP monthly cycle.

A letter to indicate liturgical colour in this column indicates a change of colour before Evening Prayer. The symbol in bold lower case, **ct**, indicates that the Collect at Evening Prayer should be that of the following day.

## BOOK OF COMMON PRAYER

| Second Service Evening Prayer | | Calendar and Holy Communion | Morning Prayer | Evening Prayer |
|---|---|---|---|---|
| | | **Etheldreda, Abbess of Ely, 679** | | |
| Ps. 118 | | Com. Abbess | Ecclus. 28. 14–end | 2 Kings ch. 20 |
| 2 Kings ch. 20 | | | or Ezek. 36. 16–36 | Phil. 4. 2–end |
| Phil. 4. 2–end | | | John 14. 15–end | ct |
| ct | | | | |
| or First EP of Luke | | | | or First EP of Luke |
| Ps. 33 | | | | (Ps. 33) |
| Hos. 6. 1–3 | | | | Hos. 6. 1–3 |
| 2 Tim. 3. 10–end | | | | 2 Tim. 3. 10–end |
| R ct | Gw | | | R ct |
| | | **LUKE THE EVANGELIST** (or transferred to 19 October) | | |
| EP: Ps. 103 | | Isa. 35. 3–6 | Ps. 145; 146 | Ps. 103 |
| Ecclus. 38. 1–14 | | Ps. 147. 1–6 | Isa. ch. 55 | Ecclus. 38. 1–14 |
| or Isa. 61. 1–6 | | 2 Tim. 4. 5–15 | Luke 1. 1–4 | or Isa. 61. 1–6 |
| Col. 4. 7–end | | Luke 10. 1–9 | | Col. 4. 7–end |
| | R | or Luke 7. 36–end | | |
| | | or, for The Twentieth Sunday after Trinity: | | |
| Ps. 141 | | Prov. 9. 1–6 | Ps. 133; 134; 137. 1–6 | Ps. 142 |
| Josh. 14. 6–14 | | Ps. 145. 15–end | Isa. 54. 1–14 | Josh. 14. 6–14 |
| Matt. 12. 1–21 | | Eph. 5. 15–21 | Luke 13. 31–end | Matt. 12. 1–21 |
| | R | Matt. 22. 1–14 | | |
| Ps. 127; 128; 129 | | | Ecclus. 31. 1–11 | 2 Kings 21. 1–18 |
| 2 Kings 21. 1–18 | | | or Ezek. 37. 1–14 | 1 Tim. 1. 1–17 |
| 1 Tim. 1. 1–17 | | | John 15. 1–11 | |
| | G | | | |

A letter to indicate liturgical colour in this column indicates a change of colour before Evening Prayer. The symbol in bold lower case, **ct**, indicates that the Collect at Evening Prayer should be that of the following day.

**Column 6** provides for Book of Common Prayer:
• the name of the Principal Holy Day, Sunday, Festival or Lesser Festival;
• any general note that applies to the whole Prayer Book provision for the day and an indication of points at which users may wish to draw on Common Worship material on the opposite page where the BCP has no provision;
• the Lectionary for the Eucharist on any day for which provision is made;
• an indication of liturgical colour (see column 2).

**Column 8 (Book of Common Prayer)**
This provides the readings for Evening Prayer, together with psalm provision where it varies from the BCP monthly cycle.

## Making Choices in *Common Worship*

*Common Worship* makes provision for a variety of pastoral and liturgical circumstances. It needs to, for it has to serve some church communities where Morning Prayer, Holy Communion and Evening Prayer are all celebrated every day, and yet be useful also in a church with only one service a week, and that service varying in form and time from week to week.

At the beginning of the year, some decisions in principle need to be taken.

In relation to the Calendar, a decision needs to be taken whether to keep The Epiphany on Tuesday 6 January or on Sunday 4 January, and whether to keep The Presentation of Christ (Candlemas) on Monday 2 February or on Sunday 1 February.

In relation to the Lectionary, the initial choices every year to decide in relation to Sundays are:

- which of the services on a Principal Feast, Principal Holy Day, Sunday or Festival constitutes the 'Principal Service'; then use the Principal Service Lectionary (column 3) consistently for that service through the year;
- during the Sundays after Trinity, whether to use Track 1 of the Principal Service Lectionary (column 2), where the first reading stays over several weeks with one Old Testament book read semi-continuously, or Track 2 (column 3), where the first reading is chosen for its relationship to the Gospel reading of the day;
- which, if any, service on a Principal Feast, Principal Holy Day, Sunday or Festival constitutes the 'Second Service'; then use the Second Service Lectionary (column 5) consistently for that service through the year;
- which, if any, service on a Principal Feast, Principal Holy Day, Sunday or Festival constitutes the 'Third Service'; then use the Third Service Lectionary (column 4) consistently for that service through the year.

And in relation to weekdays:

- whether to use the Daily Eucharistic Lectionary (column 3) consistently for weekday celebrations of Holy Communion (with the exception of Principal Feasts, Principal Holy Days and Festivals) or to make some use of the Lesser Festival provision;
- whether to follow the first psalm provision in column 4 (morning) and column 5 (evening), where psalms during the seasons have a seasonal flavour but in ordinary time follow a sequential pattern; or to follow the alternative provision in the same columns, where psalms follow the sequential pattern throughout the year, except for the period between 19 December and The Epiphany and from the Monday of Holy Week to the Saturday of Easter Week; or to follow the psalm cycle in the Book of Common Prayer, where they are nearly always used 'in course';
- whether to use the Additional Weekday Lectionary (which begins on page 92) for weekday services (other than Holy Communion). It provides a one-year cycle of two readings for each day (except for Sundays, Principal Feasts, Principal Holy Days, Festivals and during Holy Week). Since each of the readings is designed to 'stand alone' (that is, it is complete in itself and will make sense to the worshipper who has not attended on the previous day and who will not be present on the next day), it is intended particularly for use in those churches and cathedrals that attract occasional rather than regular congregations.

The flexibility of *Common Worship* is intended to enable the church and the minister to find the most helpful provision for them. But once a decision is made, it is advisable to stay with that decision through the year or at the very least through a complete season.

All Bible references (except to the psalms) are to the New Revised Standard Version (1995). Those who use other Bible translations should check the verse numbers against the NRSV. References to the psalms are to the *Common Worship* Psalter.

## Book of Common Prayer

A separate Lectionary for the Book of Common Prayer is no longer issued. Provision is made on the right-hand pages of this Lectionary for BCP worship on all Sundays in the year, for the major festivals and for Morning and Evening Prayer. The Epistles and Gospels for Holy Communion are those of 1662, with the additions and variations of 1928, now authorized under the *Common Worship* overall provision. The Old Testament readings and psalms for these services, formerly appended to the Series One Holy Communion service, may be used but are not mandatory with the 1662 order.

Readings for Morning and Evening Prayer, which are the same as those for *Common Worship*, are set out in the BCP section for Sundays and weekdays. The special psalm provision of the BCP is given; however, where the *Common Worship* psalm provision is used, verse numbering may occasionally differ slightly from that in the BCP Psalter, and appropriate adjustment will have to be made (a table of variations in verse numbering can be found at www.churchofengland.org/prayer-worship/worship/texts/daily2/psalter/psalterverses.aspx). Otherwise the Psalter is read in course daily through each month.

The Calendar observes BCP dates when these differ from those of *Common Worship*; for example, St Thomas on 21 December. Additional commemorations in the *Common Worship* Calendar are not included, but those who wish to observe them may use the *Collects and Post Communions in Traditional Language: Lesser Festivals, Common of the Saints, Special Occasions* (Church House Publishing).

The Lectionaries of 1871 and 1922, to be found in many copies of the BCP, are still authorized and may be used, but – with the exception of the psalms and readings for Holy Communion mentioned above – the Additional Alternative Lectionary (1961) is no longer authorized for public worship.

Although those who use the BCP, for private or public worship or both, are free to follow any of the authorized lectionaries, there is much to be said for common usage across the Church of England, so that the same passages are being read by all. It is of course appropriate that BCP readings should be taken from the Authorized or King James Version for harmony of style, with the daily recitation of the BCP Psalter.

The integrity of the BCP as the traditional source of worship in the Church of England is not in any way affected by the use of a common lectionary for the daily offices.

## CERTAIN DAYS AND OCCASIONS COMMONLY OBSERVED

**Plough Sunday** may be observed on 11 January 2015.
**The Week of Prayer for Christian Unity** may be observed from 18 to 25 January 2015.
**Education Sunday** may be observed on 1 February 2015.
**Rogation Sunday** may be observed on 10 May 2015.
**The Feast of Dedication** is observed on the anniversary of the dedication or consecration of a church, or, when the actual date is unknown, on 4 October 2015. In CW, 25 October 2015 is an alternative date.
**Ember Days.** CW encourages the bishop to set the Ember Days in each diocese in the week before the ordinations, whereas in BCP the dates are fixed.
**Days of Discipline and Self-Denial** in CW are the weekdays of Lent and all Fridays in the year, except all Principal Feasts and festivals outside Lent and Fridays between Easter Day and Pentecost. The eves of Principal Feasts are also appropriately kept as days of discipline and self-denial in preparation for the feast.
**Days of Fasting and Abstinence** according to the BCP are the forty days of Lent, the Ember Days at the four seasons, the three Rogation Days, and all Fridays in the year except Christmas Day. The BCP also orders the observance of the Evens or Vigils before The Nativity of our Lord, The Purification of the Blessed Virgin Mary, The Annunciation of the Blessed Virgin Mary, Easter Day, Ascension Day, Pentecost, and before the following saints' days: Matthias, John the Baptist, Peter, James, Bartholomew, Matthew, Simon and Jude, Andrew, Thomas, and All Saints. (If any of these days falls on Monday, the Vigil is to be kept on the previous Saturday.)

## KEY TO LITURGICAL COLOURS

*Common Worship* suggests appropriate liturgical colours. They are not mandatory, and traditional or local use may be followed.

For a detailed discussion of when colours may be used, see *Common Worship: Services and Prayers for the Church of England* (Church House Publishing), *New Handbook of Pastoral Liturgy* (SPCK) or *A Companion to Common Worship: Volume I* (SPCK).

W    White
ꟿ    Gold or white
R    Red
P    Purple (may vary from 'Roman purple' to violet, with blue as an alternative; a Lent array of sackcloth may be used in Lent, and rose pink on The Third Sunday of Advent and Fourth Sunday of Lent)
G    Green

When a lower-case letter accompanies an upper-case letter, the lower-case letter indicates the liturgical colour appropriate to the Lesser Festival of that day, while the upper-case letter indicates the continuing seasonal colour.

## PRINCIPAL FEASTS, HOLY DAYS AND FESTIVALS

Principal Feasts, and other Principal Holy Days (Ash Wednesday, Maundy Thursday, Good Friday) are printed in **LARGE BOLD CAPITALS** in the Lectionary.

There are no longer proper readings relating to the Holy Spirit on the six days after Pentecost. Instead they have been located on the nine days before Pentecost.

When Patronal and Dedication Festivals are kept as Principal Feasts, they may be transferred to the nearest Sunday, unless that day is already either a Principal Feast or The First Sunday of Advent, The Baptism of Christ, The First Sunday of Lent or Palm Sunday.

Festivals are printed in the Lectionary in SMALL BOLD CAPITALS.

For each day there is a full liturgical provision for the Holy Communion and for Morning and Evening Prayer. Most holy days that are in the category 'Festival' are provided with an optional First Evening Prayer. Its use is entirely at the discretion of the minister. Where it is used, the liturgical colour for the next day should be used at that First Evening Prayer, and this has been indicated in the provision on the following pages.

## LESSER FESTIVALS AND COMMEMORATIONS

Lesser Festivals (printed in **bold roman** typeface) are observed at the level appropriate to a particular church. The readings and psalms for The Common of the Saints are listed on page 9. In addition, there are special readings appropriate to the Festival listed in the first column. The daily psalms and readings at Morning and Evening Prayer are not usually superseded by those for Lesser Festivals, but the readings and psalms for Holy Communion may on occasion be used at Morning or Evening Prayer.

Commemorations are printed in the Lectionary in *italic* typeface. They do not have collect, psalm or readings, but may be observed by mention in prayers of intercession and thanksgiving. For local reasons, or where there is an established tradition in the wider Church, they may be kept as Lesser Festivals using the appropriate material from The Common of the Saints. Equally, it may be desirable to observe some Lesser Festivals as Commemorations.

If a Lesser Festival or a Commemoration falls on a Principal Feast, Principal Holy Day, Sunday or Festival, it is not normally observed that year, although it may be celebrated, where there is sufficient reason, on the nearest available day. Lesser Festivals and Commemorations which, for this reason, would not be celebrated in 2014–15 are listed on pages 7–8, so that, if desired, they may be mentioned in prayers of intercession and thanksgiving.

# LESSER FESTIVALS AND COMMEMORATIONS NOT OBSERVED IN 2014–15

**The Lesser Festivals and Commemorations (shown in italics) listed below fall on a Sunday or during Holy Week or Easter Week this year, and are thus not observed in this lectionary.**

*Common Worship*

## 2014

**December**

| | |
|---|---|
| 7 | Ambrose, Bishop of Milan, Teacher, 397 |
| 14 | John of the Cross, Poet, Teacher, 1591 |

## 2015

**January**

| | |
|---|---|
| 11 | *Mary Slessor, Missionary in West Africa, 1915* |
| 18 | *Amy Carmichael, Founder of the Dohnavur Fellowship, Spiritual Writer, 1951* |

**February**

| | |
|---|---|
| 1 | *Brigid, Abbess of Kildare, c. 525* |
| 15 | *Sigfrid, Bishop, Apostle of Sweden, 1045* |
| | *Thomas Bray, Priest, Founder of the SPCK and SPG, 1730* |

**March**

| | |
|---|---|
| 1 | David, Bishop of Menevia, Patron of Wales, c. 601 |
| 8 | Edward King, Bishop of Lincoln, 1910 |
| | *Felix, Bishop, Apostle to the East Angles, 647* |
| | *Geoffrey Studdert Kennedy, Priest, Poet, 1929* |
| 31 | *John Donne, Priest, Poet, 1631* |

**April**

| | |
|---|---|
| 1 | *Frederick Denison Maurice, Priest, Teacher, 1872* |
| 9 | *Dietrich Bonhoeffer, Lutheran Pastor, Martyr, 1945* |
| 10 | William Law, Priest, Spiritual Writer, 1761 |
| | *William of Ockham, Friar, Philosopher, Teacher, 1347* |
| 11 | *George Augustus Selwyn, first Bishop of New Zealand, 1878* |
| 19 | Alphege, Archbishop of Canterbury, Martyr, 1012 |

**May**

| | |
|---|---|
| 24 | John and Charles Wesley, Evangelists, Hymn Writers, 1791 and 1788 |

**June**

| | |
|---|---|
| 1 | Justin, Martyr at Rome, c. 165 |
| 14 | *Richard Baxter, Puritan Divine, 1691* |
| 28 | Irenaeus, Bishop of Lyons, Teacher, c. 200 |

**July**

| | |
|---|---|
| 19 | Gregory, Bishop of Nyssa, and his sister Macrina, Deaconess, Teachers, c. 394 and c. 379 |
| 26 | Anne and Joachim, Parents of the Blessed Virgin Mary |

**August**

| | |
|---|---|
| 9 | Mary Sumner, Founder of the Mothers' Union, 1921 |
| 30 | John Bunyan, Spiritual Writer, 1688 |

**September**

| | |
|---|---|
| 6 | *Allen Gardiner, Founder of the South American Mission Society, 1851* |
| 13 | John Chrysostom, Bishop of Constantinople, Teacher, 407 |
| 20 | John Coleridge Patteson, first Bishop of Melanesia, and his Companions, Martyrs, 1871 |
| 27 | Vincent de Paul, Founder of the Congregation of the Mission (Lazarists), 1660 |

**October**

| | |
|---|---|
| 4 | Francis of Assisi, Friar, Founder of the Friars Minor, 1226 |
| 11 | *Ethelburga, Abbess of Barking, 675* |
| | *James the Deacon, Companion of Paulinus, 7th century* |
| 25 | *Crispin and Crispinian, Martyrs at Rome, c. 287* |

**November**

| | |
|---|---|
| 8 | The Saints and Martyrs of England |
| 22 | *Cecilia, Martyr at Rome, c. 230* |
| 29 | Day of Intercession and Thanksgiving for the Missionary Work of the Church |

**December**

| | |
|---|---|
| 6 | Nicholas, Bishop of Myra, c. 326 |
| 13 | Lucy, Martyr at Syracuse, 304 |
| | *Samuel Johnson, Moralist, 1784* |

## Book of Common Prayer

### 2015

**January**

| | |
|---|---|
| 18 | Prisca, Martyr at Rome, c. 265 |

**March**

| | |
|---|---|
| 1 | David, Bishop of Menevia, Patron of Wales, c. 601 |

**April**

| | |
|---|---|
| 3 | Richard, Bishop of Chichester, 1253 |
| 4 | Ambrose, Bishop of Milan, 397 |
| 19 | Alphege, Archbishop of Canterbury, Martyr, 1012 |

**May**

| | |
|---|---|
| 3 | The Invention of the Cross |
| 26 | Augustine, first Archbishop of Canterbury, 605 |

**July**

| | |
|---|---|
| 26 | Anne, Mother of the Blessed Virgin Mary |

**October**

| | |
|---|---|
| 25 | Crispin, Martyr at Rome, c. 287 |

**November**

| | |
|---|---|
| 15 | Machutus, Bishop, Apostle of Brittany, c. 564 |
| 22 | Cecilia, Martyr at Rome, c. 230 |

**December**

| | |
|---|---|
| 13 | Lucy, Martyr at Syracuse, 304 |

# THE COMMON OF THE SAINTS

## The Blessed Virgin Mary

Genesis 3. 8–15, 20; Isaiah 7. 10–14; Micah 5. 1–4

Psalms 45. 10–17; 113; 131

Acts 1. 12–14; Romans 8. 18–30; Galatians 4. 4–7

Luke 1. 26–38; Luke 1. 39–47; John 19. 25–27

## Martyrs

2 Chronicles 24. 17–21; Isaiah 43. 1–7; Jeremiah 11. 18–20; Wisdom 4. 10–15

Psalms 3; 11; 31. 1–5; 44. 18–24; 126

Romans 8. 35–end; 2 Corinthians 4. 7–15; 2 Timothy 2. 3–7 [8–13]; Hebrews 11. 32–end; 1 Peter 4. 12–end; Revelation 12. 10–12a

Matthew 10. 16–22; Matthew 10. 28–39; Matthew 16. 24–26; John 12. 24–26; John 15. 18–21

## Teachers of the Faith and Spiritual Writers

1 Kings 3. [6–10] 11–14; Proverbs 4. 1–9; Wisdom 7. 7–10, 15–16; Ecclesiasticus 39. 1–10

Psalms 19. 7–10; 34. 11–17; 37. 31–35; 119. 89–96; 119. 97–104

1 Corinthians 1. 18–25; 1 Corinthians 2. 1–10; 1 Corinthians 2. 9–end;

Ephesians 3. 8–12; 2 Timothy 4. 1–8; Titus 2. 1–8

Matthew 5. 13–19; Matthew 13. 52–end; Matthew 23. 8–12; Mark 4. 1–9; John 16. 12–15

## Bishops and Other Pastors

1 Samuel 16. 1, 6–13; Isaiah 6. 1–8; Jeremiah 1. 4–10; Ezekiel 3. 16–21; Malachi 2. 5–7

Psalms 1; 15; 16. 5–end; 96; 110

Acts 20. 28–35; 1 Corinthians 4. 1–5; 2 Corinthians 4. 1–10 (or 1–2, 5–7); 2 Corinthians 5. 14–20; 1 Peter 5. 1–4

Matthew 11. 25–end; Matthew 24. 42–46; John 10. 11–16; John 15. 9–17; John 21. 15–17

## Members of Religious Communities

1 Kings 19. 9–18; Proverbs 10. 27–end; Song of Solomon 8. 6–7; Isaiah 61.10 – 62.5; Hosea 2. 14–15, 19–20

Psalms 34. 1–8; 112. 1–9; 119. 57–64; 123; 131

Acts 4. 32–35; 2 Corinthians 10.17 – 11.2; Philippians 3. 7–14; 1 John 2. 15–17; Revelation 19. 1, 5–9

Matthew 11. 25–end; Matthew 19. 3–12; Matthew 19. 23–end; Luke 9. 57–end; Luke 12. 32–37

## Missionaries

Isaiah 52. 7–10; Isaiah 61. 1–3a; Ezekiel 34. 11–16; Jonah 3. 1–5

Psalms 67; 87; 97; 100; 117

Acts 2. 14, 22–36; Acts 13. 46–49; Acts 16. 6–10; Acts 26. 19–23; Romans 15. 17–21; 2 Corinthians 5.11 – 6.2

Matthew 9. 35–end; Matthew 28. 16–end; Mark 16. 15–20; Luke 5. 1–11; Luke 10. 1–9

## Any Saint

Genesis 12. 1–4; Proverbs 8. 1–11; Micah 6. 6–8; Ecclesiasticus 2. 7–13 [14–end]

Psalms 32; 33. 1–5; 119. 1–8; 139. 1–4 [5–12]; 145. 8–14

Ephesians 3. 14–19; Ephesians 6. 11–18; Hebrews 13. 7–8, 15–16; James 2. 14–17; 1 John 4. 7–16; Revelation 21. [1–4] 5–7

Matthew 19. 16–21; Matthew 25. 1–13; Matthew 25. 14–30; John 15. 1–8; John 17. 20–end

## SPECIAL OCCASIONS

### The Guidance of the Holy Spirit
Proverbs 24. 3–7; Isaiah 30. 15–21; Wisdom 9. 13–17
Psalms 25. 1–9; 104. 26–33; 143. 8–10
Acts 15. 23–29; Romans 8. 22–27; 1 Corinthians 12. 4–13
Luke 14. 27–33; John 14. 23–26; John 16. 13–15

### The Commemoration of the Faithful Departed
Lamentations 3. 17–26, 31–33 or Wisdom 3. 1–9
Psalm 23 or Psalm 27. 1–6, 16–end
Romans 5. 5–11 or 1 Peter 1. 3–9
John 5. 19–25 or John 6. 37–40

### Rogation Days
Deuteronomy 8. 1–10; 1 Kings 8. 35–40; Job 28. 1–11
Psalms 104. 21–30; 107. 1–9; 121
Philippians 4. 4–7; 2 Thessalonians 3. 6–13; 1 John 5. 12–15
Matthew 6. 1–15; Mark 11. 22–24; Luke 11. 5–13

### Harvest Thanksgiving
#### Year A
Deuteronomy 8. 7–18 or Deuteronomy 28. 1–14
Psalm 65
2 Corinthians 9. 6–end
Luke 12. 16–30 or Luke 17. 11–19

#### Year B
Joel 2. 21–27
Psalm 126
1 Timothy 2. 1–7 or 1 Timothy 6. 6–10
Matthew 6. 25–33

#### Year C
Deuteronomy 26. 1–11
Psalm 100
Philippians 4. 4–9 or Revelation 14. 14–18
John 6. 25–35

### Mission and Evangelism
Isaiah 49. 1–6; Isaiah 52. 7–10; Micah 4. 1–5
Psalms 2; 46; 67
Acts 17. 12–end; 2 Corinthians 5.14 – 6.2; Ephesians 2. 13–end
Matthew 5. 13–16; Matthew 28. 16–end; John 17. 20–end

### The Unity of the Church
Jeremiah 33. 6–9a; Ezekiel 36. 23–28; Zephaniah 3. 16–end
Psalms 100; 122; 133
Ephesians 4. 1–6; Colossians 3. 9–17; 1 John 4. 9–15
Matthew 18. 19–22; John 11. 45–52; John 17. 11b–23

### The Peace of the World

Isaiah 9. 1–6; Isaiah 57. 15–19; Micah 4. 1–5
Psalms 40. 14–17; 72. 1–7; 85. 8–13
Philippians 4. 6–9; 1 Timothy 2. 1–6; James 3. 13–18
Matthew 5. 43–end; John 14. 23–29; John 15. 9–17

### Social Justice and Responsibility

Isaiah 32. 15–end; Amos 5. 21–24; Amos 8. 4–7; Acts 5. 1–11
Psalms 31. 21–24; 85. 1–7; 146. 5–10
Colossians 3. 12–15; James 2. 1–4
Matthew 5. 1–12; Matthew 25. 31–end; Luke 16. 19–end

### Ministry (including Ember Days)

Numbers 11. 16–17, 24–29; Numbers 27. 15–end; 1 Samuel 16. 1–13a
Isaiah 6. 1–8; Isaiah 61. 1–3; Jeremiah 1. 4–10
Psalms 40. 8–13; 84. 8–12; 89. 19–25; 101. 1–5, 7; 122
Acts 20. 28–35; 1 Corinthians 3. 3–11; Ephesians 4. 4–16; Philippians 3. 7–14
Luke 4. 16–21; Luke 12. 35–43; Luke 22. 24–27; John 4. 31–38; John 15. 5–17

### In Time of Trouble

Genesis 9. 8–17; Job 1. 13–end; Isaiah 38. 6–11
Psalms 86. 1–7; 107. 4–15; 142. 1–7
Romans 3. 21–26; Romans 8. 18–25; 2 Corinthians 8. 1–5, 9
Mark 4. 35–end; Luke 12. 1–7; John 16. 31–end

### For the Sovereign

Joshua 1. 1–9; Proverbs 8. 1–16
Psalms 20; 101; 121
Romans 13. 1–10; Revelation 21.22 – 22.4
Matthew 22. 16–22; Luke 22. 24–30

# November 2014

| | | Sunday Principal Service<br>Weekday Eucharist | Third Service<br>Morning Prayer |
|---|---|---|---|
| **30** | S<br><br>P | THE FIRST SUNDAY OF ADVENT (Andrew transferred to 1 December)<br>CW Year B begins<br><br>Isa. 64. 1–9<br>Ps. 80. 1–8, 18–20 (or 80. 1–8)<br>1 Cor. 1. 3–9<br>Mark 13. 24–end | Ps. 44<br>Isa. 2. 1–5<br>Luke 12. 35–48 |

# December 2014

| | | | Sunday Principal Service<br>Weekday Eucharist | Third Service<br>Morning Prayer |
|---|---|---|---|---|
| **1** | M<br><br>R | ANDREW THE APOSTLE | Isa. 52. 7–10<br>Ps. 19. 1–6<br>Rom. 10. 12–18<br>Matt. 4. 18–22 | MP: Ps. 47; 147. 1–12<br>Ezek. 47. 1–12<br>or Ecclus. 14. 20–end<br>John 12. 20–32 |
| **2** | Tu<br><br>P | Daily Eucharistic Lectionary<br>Year 1 begins | Isa. 11. 1–10<br>Ps. 72. 1–4, 18–19<br>Luke 10. 21–24 | Ps. **80**; 82<br>alt. Ps. **5**; 6; (8)<br>Isa. 43. 1–13<br>Rev. ch. 20 |
| **3** | W<br><br>P | Francis Xavier, Missionary, Apostle of the Indies, 1552 | Isa. 25. 6–10a<br>Ps. 23<br>Matt. 15. 29–37 | Ps. 5; **7**<br>alt. Ps. 119. 1–32<br>Isa. 43. 14–end<br>Rev. 21. 1–8 |
| **4** | Th<br><br>P | John of Damascus, Monk, Teacher, c. 749; Nicholas Ferrar, Deacon, Founder of the Little Gidding<br>Community, 1637 | Isa. 26. 1–6<br>Ps. 118. 18–27a<br>Matt. 7. 21, 24–27 | Ps. **42**; 43<br>alt. Ps. 14; **15**; 16<br>Isa. 44. 1–8<br>Rev. 21. 9–21 |
| **5** | F<br><br>P | | Isa. 29. 17–end<br>Ps. 27. 1–4, 16–17<br>Matt. 9. 27–31 | Ps. **25**; 26<br>alt. Ps. 17; **19**<br>Isa. 44. 9–23<br>Rev. 21.22 – 22.5 |
| **6** | Sa<br><br>Pw | Nicholas, Bishop of Myra, c. 326<br>Com. Bishop            or<br>also Isa. 61. 1–3<br>1 Tim. 6. 6–11<br>Mark 10. 13–16 | Isa. 30. 19–21, 23–26<br>Ps. 146. 4–9<br>Matt. 9.35 – 10.1, 6–8 | Ps. **9**; (10)<br>alt. Ps. 20; 21; **23**<br>Isa. 44.24 – 45.13<br>Rev. 22. 6–end |
| **7** | S<br><br>P | THE SECOND SUNDAY OF ADVENT | Isa. 40. 1–11<br>Ps. 85. 1–2, 8–end<br>(or 85. 8–end)<br>2 Pet. 3. 8–15a<br>Mark 1. 1–8 | Ps. 80<br>Baruch 5. 1–9<br>or Zeph. 3. 14–end<br>Luke 1. 5–20 |
| **8** | M<br><br>Pw | The Conception of the Blessed Virgin Mary<br>Com. BVM            or | Isa. ch. 35<br>Ps. 85. 7–end<br>Luke 5. 17–26 | Ps. 44<br>alt. Ps. 27; **30**<br>Isa. 45. 14–end<br>1 Thess. ch. 1 |
| **9** | Tu<br><br>P | | Isa. 40. 1–11<br>Ps. 96. 1, 10–end<br>Matt. 18. 12–14 | Ps. **56**; 57<br>alt. Ps. 32; **36**<br>Isa. ch. 46<br>1 Thess. 2. 1–12 |
| **10** | W<br><br>P | Ember Day* | Isa. 40. 25–end<br>Ps. 103. 8–13<br>Matt. 11. 28–end | Ps. **62**; 63<br>alt. Ps. 34<br>Isa. ch. 47<br>1 Thess. 2. 13–end |

*For Ember Day provision, see p. 11.

| Second Service Evening Prayer | | Calendar and Holy Communion | Morning Prayer | Evening Prayer |
|---|---|---|---|---|
| | | THE FIRST SUNDAY IN ADVENT (Andrew transferred to 1 December) | | |
| Ps. 25 (or 25. 1–9) Isa. 1. 1–20 Matt. 21. 1–13 or First EP of Andrew the Apostle Ps. 48 Isa. 49. 1–9a 1 Cor. 4. 9–16 **R ct** | **P** | Advent 1 Collect until Christmas Eve Mic. 4. 1–4, 6–7 Ps. 25. 1–9 Rom. 13. 8–14 Matt. 21. 1–13 | Ps. 44 Isa. 2. 1–5 Luke 12. 35–48 | Ps. 9 Isa. 1. 1–20 Mark 13. 24–end or First EP of Andrew the Apostle Ps. 48 Isa. 49. 1–9a 1 Cor. 4. 9–16 **R ct** |
| EP: Ps. 87; 96 Zech. 8. 20–end John 1. 35–42 | **R** | ANDREW THE APOSTLE Zech. 8. 20–end Ps. 92. 1–5 Rom. 10. 9–end Matt. 4. 18–22 | (Ps. 47; 147. 1–12) Ezek. 47. 1–12 or Ecclus. 14. 20–end John 12. 20–32 | (Ps. 87; 96) Isa. 52. 7–10 John 1. 35–42 |
| Ps. *74*; 75 *alt.* Ps. *9*; 10† Isa. 26. 1–13 Matt. 12. 22–37 | **P** | | Isa. 43. 1–13 Rev. ch. 20 | Isa. 26. 1–13 Matt. 12. 22–37 |
| Ps. 76; *77* *alt.* Ps. *11*; 12; 13 Isa. 28. 1–13 Matt. 12. 38–end | **P** | | Isa. 43. 14–end Rev. 21. 1–8 | Isa. 28. 1–13 Matt. 12. 38–end |
| Ps. *40*; 46 *alt.* Ps. 18† Isa. 28. 14–end Matt. 13. 1–23 | **P** | | Isa. 44. 1–8 Rev. 21. 9–21 | Isa. 28. 14–end Matt. 13. 1–23 |
| Ps. 16; *17* *alt.* Ps. 22 Isa. 29. 1–14 Matt. 13. 24–43 | **P** | | Isa. 44. 9–23 Rev. 21.22 – 22.5 | Isa. 29. 1–14 Matt. 13. 24–43 |
| Ps. *27*; 28 *alt.* Ps. *24*; 25 Isa. 29. 15–end Matt. 13. 44–end **ct** | **Pw** | Nicholas, Bishop of Myra, c. 326 Com. Bishop | Isa. 44.24 – 45.13 Rev. 22. 6–end | Isa. 29. 15–end Matt. 13. 44–end **ct** |
| Ps. 40 (or 40. 12–end) 1 Kings 22. 1–28 Rom. 15. 4–13 *Gospel:* Matt. 11. 2–11 | **P** | THE SECOND SUNDAY IN ADVENT 2 Kings 22. 8–10; 23. 1–3 Ps. 50. 1–6 Rom. 15. 4–13 Luke 21. 25–33 | Ps. 80 Baruch 5. 1–9 or Zeph. 3. 14–end Luke 1. 5–20 | Ps. 40 (or 40. 12–end) 1 Kings 22. 1–28 2 Peter 3. 8–15a |
| Ps. *144*; 146 *alt.* Ps. 26; *28*; 29 Isa. 30. 1–18 Matt. 14. 1–12 | **Pw** | The Conception of the Blessed Virgin Mary | Isa. 45. 14–end 1 Thess. ch. 1 | Isa. 30. 1–18 Matt. 14. 1–12 |
| Ps. *11*; 12; 13 *alt.* Ps. 33 Isa. 30. 19–end Matt. 14. 13–end | **P** | | Isa. ch. 46 1 Thess. 2. 1–12 | Isa. 30. 19–end Matt. 14. 13–end |
| Ps. *10*; 14 *alt.* Ps. 119. 33–56 Isa. ch. 31 Matt. 15. 1–20 | **P** | | Isa. ch. 47 1 Thess. 2. 13–end | Isa. ch. 31 Matt. 15. 1–20 |

# December 2014

| | | | Sunday Principal Service<br>Weekday Eucharist | Third Service<br>Morning Prayer |
|---|---|---|---|---|
| **11** | Th | | Isa. 41. 13–20<br>Ps. 145. 1, 8–13<br>Matt. 11. 11–15 | Ps. 53; *54*; 60<br>*alt.* Ps. 37†<br>Isa. 48. 1–11 |
| | P | | | 1 Thess. ch. 3 |
| **12** | F | Ember Day* | Isa. 48. 17–19<br>Ps. 1<br>Matt. 11. 16–19 | Ps. 85; *86*<br>*alt.* Ps. 31<br>Isa. 48. 12–end |
| | P | | | 1 Thess. 4. 1–12 |
| **13** | Sa | **Lucy, Martyr at Syracuse, 304**<br>Ember Day*<br>*Samuel Johnson, Moralist, 1784*<br>Com. Martyr              *or*<br>*also* Wisd. 3. 1–7<br>2 Cor. 4. 6–15 | Ecclus. 48. 1–4, 9–11<br>*or* 2 Kings 2. 9–12<br>Ps. 80. 1–4, 18–19<br>Matt. 17. 10–13 | Ps. 145<br>*alt.* Ps. 41; *42*; 43<br>Isa. 49. 1–13<br>1 Thess. 4. 13–end |
| | Pr | | | |
| **14** | S | THE THIRD SUNDAY OF ADVENT | Isa. 61. 1–4, 8–end<br>Ps. 126<br>*or Canticle:* Magnificat<br>1 Thess. 5. 16–24 | Ps. 50. 1–6; 62<br>Isa. ch. 12<br>Luke 1. 57–66 |
| | P | | John 1. 6–8, 19–28 | |
| **15** | M | | Num. 24. 2–7, 15–17<br>Ps. 25. 3–8<br>Matt. 21. 23–27 | Ps. 40<br>*alt.* Ps. 44<br>Isa. 49. 14–25 |
| | P | | | 1 Thess. 5. 1–11 |
| **16** | Tu | | Zeph. 3. 1–2, 9–13<br>Ps. 34. 1–6, 21–22<br>Matt. 21. 28–32 | Ps. *70*; 74<br>*alt.* Ps. *48*; 52<br>Isa. ch. 50 |
| | P | | | 1 Thess. 5. 12–end |
| **17** | W | O Sapientia**<br>*Eglantyne Jebb, Social Reformer, Founder of 'Save the Children', 1928* | Gen. 49. 2, 8–10<br>Ps. 72. 1–5, 18–19<br>Matt. 1. 1–17 | Ps. *75*; 96<br>*alt.* Ps. 119. 57–80<br>Isa. 51. 1–8 |
| | P | | | 2 Thess. ch. 1 |
| **18** | Th | | Jer. 23. 5–8<br>Ps. 72. 1–2, 12–13, 18–end<br>Matt. 1. 18–24 | Ps. *76*; 97<br>*alt.* Ps. 56; *57*; (63†)<br>Isa. 51. 9–16 |
| | P | | | 2 Thess. ch. 2 |
| **19** | F | | Judg. 13. 2–7, 24–end<br>Ps. 71. 3–8<br>Luke 1. 5–25 | Ps. 144; *146*<br>Isa. 51. 17–end<br>2 Thess. ch. 3 |
| | P | | | |
| **20** | Sa | | Isa. 7. 10–14<br>Ps. 24. 1–6<br>Luke 1. 26–38 | Ps. *46*; 95<br>Isa. 52. 1–12<br>Jude |
| | P | | | |
| **21** | S | THE FOURTH SUNDAY OF ADVENT | 2 Sam. 7. 1–11, 16<br>*Canticle:* Magnificat<br>*or* Ps. 89. 1–4, 19–26 (*or* 1–8)<br>Rom. 16. 25–end<br>Luke 1. 26–38 | Ps. 144<br>Isa. 7. 10–16<br>Rom. 1. 1–7 |
| | P | | | |

| Second Service Evening Prayer | | Calendar and Holy Communion | Morning Prayer | Evening Prayer |
|---|---|---|---|---|
| Ps. 73<br>*alt.* Ps. 39; **40**<br>Isa. ch. 32<br>Matt. 15. 21–28 | P | | Isa. 48. 1–11<br>1 Thess. ch. 3 | Isa. ch. 32<br>Matt. 15. 21–28 |
| Ps. 82; **90**<br>*alt.* Ps. 35<br>Isa. 33. 1–22<br>Matt. 15. 29–end | P | | Isa. 48. 12–end<br>1 Thess. 4. 1–12 | Isa. 33. 1–22<br>Matt. 15. 29–end |
| | | **Lucy, Martyr at Syracuse, 304**<br>Com. Virgin Martyr | | |
| Ps. 93; **94**<br>*alt.* Ps. 45; **46**<br>Isa. ch. 35<br>Matt. 16. 1–12<br>ct | Pr | | Isa. 49. 1–13<br>1 Thess. 4. 13–end | Isa. ch. 35<br>Matt. 16. 1–12<br><br>ct |
| Ps. 68. 1–19 (*or* 68. 1–8)<br>Mal. 3. 1–4; ch. 4<br>Phil. 4. 4–7<br>*Gospel:* Matt. 14. 1–12 | P | **THE THIRD SUNDAY IN ADVENT**<br>Isa. ch. 35<br>Ps. 80. 1–7<br>1 Cor. 4. 1–5<br>Matt. 11. 2–10 | Ps. 62<br>Isa. ch. 12<br>Luke 1. 57–66 | Ps. 68. 1–19<br>(*or* 68. 1–8)<br>Mal. 3. 1–4; ch. 4<br>Matt. 14. 1–12 |
| Ps. 25; **26**<br>*alt.* Ps. **47**; 49<br>Isa. 38. 1–8, 21–22<br>Matt. 16. 13–end | P | | Isa. 49. 14–25<br>1 Thess. 5. 1–11 | Isa. 38. 1–8, 21–22<br>Matt. 16. 13–end |
| Ps. **50**; 54<br>*alt.* Ps. 50<br>Isa. 38. 9–20<br>Matt. 17. 1–13 | P | O Sapientia | Isa. ch. 50<br>1 Thess. 5. 12–end | Isa. 38. 9–20<br>Matt. 17. 1–13 |
| Ps. 25; **82**<br>*alt.* Ps. **59**; 60; (67)<br>Isa. ch. 39<br>Matt. 17. 14–21 | P | Ember Day<br>Ember CEG | Isa. 51. 1–8<br>2 Thess. ch. 1 | Isa. ch. 39<br>Matt. 17. 14–21 |
| Ps. 44<br>*alt.* Ps. 61; **62**; 64<br>Zeph. 1.1 – 2.3<br>Matt. 17. 22–end | P | | Isa. 51. 9–16<br>2 Thess. ch. 2 | Zeph. 1.1 – 2.3<br>Matt. 17. 22–end |
| Ps. 10; **57**<br>Zeph. 3. 1–13<br>Matt. 18. 1–20 | P | Ember Day<br>Ember CEG | Isa. 51. 17–end<br>2 Thess. ch. 3 | Zeph. 3. 1–13<br>Matt. 18. 1–20 |
| Ps. **4**; 9<br>Zeph. 3. 14–end<br>Matt. 18. 21–end<br>ct | P | Ember Day<br>Ember CEG | Isa. 52. 1–12<br>Jude | Zeph. 3. 14–end<br>Matt. 18. 21–end<br><br>ct |
| Ps. 113; [131]<br>Zech. 2. 10–end<br>Luke 1. 39–55 | P | **THE FOURTH SUNDAY IN ADVENT**<br>(Thomas transferred to 22nd)<br>Isa. 40. 1–9<br>Ps. 145. 17–end<br>Phil. 4. 4–7<br>John 1. 19–28 | Ps. 144<br>Isa. 7. 10–16<br>Rom. 1. 1–7 | Ps. 113; [131]<br>Zech. 2. 10–end<br>Luke 1. 39–55<br>*or First EP of Thomas*<br>Ps. 27<br>Isa. ch. 35<br>Heb. 10.35 – 11.1<br>**R ct** |

# December 2014

| | | Sunday Principal Service Weekday Eucharist | Third Service Morning Prayer |
|---|---|---|---|

**22** M*

P

| I Sam. 1. 24–end | Ps. *124*; 125; 126; 127 |
|---|---|
| Ps. 113 | Isa. 52.13 – 53.end |
| Luke 1. 46–56 | 2 Pet. 1. 1–15 |

**23** Tu

P

| Mal. 3. 1–4; 4. 5–end | Ps. 128; 129; *130*; 131 |
|---|---|
| Ps. 25. 3–9 | Isa. ch. 54 |
| Luke 1. 57–66 | 2 Pet. 1.16 – 2.3 |

**24** W    CHRISTMAS EVE

P

| *Morning Eucharist* | Ps. *45*; 113 |
|---|---|
| 2 Sam. 7. 1–5, 8–11, 16 | Isa. ch. 55 |
| Ps. 89. 2, 19–27 | 2 Pet. 2. 4–end |
| Acts 13. 16–26 | |
| Luke 1. 67–79 | |

**25** Th    **CHRISTMAS DAY**

*Any of the following sets of readings may be used on the evening of Christmas Eve and on Christmas Day. Set III should be used at some service during the celebration.*

℣℣

| I | |
|---|---|
| Isa. 9. 2–7 | MP: Ps. *110*; 117 |
| Ps. 96 | Isa. 62. 1–5 |
| Titus 2. 11–14 | Matt. 1. 18–end |
| Luke 2. 1–14 [15–20] | |
| | |
| II | |
| Isa. 62. 6–end | |
| Ps. 97 | |
| Titus 3. 4–7 | |
| Luke 2. [1–7] 8–20 | |
| III | |
| Isa. 52. 7–10 | |
| Ps. 98 | |
| Heb. 1. 1–4 [5–12] | |
| John 1. 1–14 | |

**26** F    STEPHEN, DEACON, FIRST MARTYR

R

| 2 Chron. 24. 20–22 | MP: Ps. *13*; 31. 1–8; 150 |
|---|---|
| or Acts 7. 51–end | Jer. 26. 12–15 |
| Ps. 119. 161–168 | Acts ch. 6 |
| Acts 7. 51–end | |
| or Gal. 2. 16b–20 | |
| Matt. 10. 17–22 | |

**27** Sa    JOHN, APOSTLE AND EVANGELIST

W

| Exod. 33. 7–11a | MP: Ps. *21*; 147. 13–end |
|---|---|
| Ps. 117 | Exod. 33. 12–end |
| 1 John ch. 1 | 1 John 2. 1–11 |
| John 21. 19b–end | |

**28** S    THE HOLY INNOCENTS (or transferred to 29th)

R

| Jer. 31. 15–17 | MP: Ps. *36*; 146 |
|---|---|
| Ps. 124 | Baruch 4. 21–27 |
| 1 Cor. 1. 26–29 | or Gen. 37. 13–20 |
| Matt. 2. 13–18 | Matt. 18. 1–10 |

*or, for The First Sunday of Christmas:*

W

| Isa. 61.10 – 62.3 | Ps. 105. 1–11 |
|---|---|
| Ps. 148 (or 148. 7–end) | Isa. 63. 7–9 |
| Gal. 4. 4–7 | Eph. 3. 5–12 |
| Luke 2. 15–21 | |

*Thomas the Apostle may be celebrated on 22 December this year instead of 3 July.

| Second Service Evening Prayer | | Calendar and Holy Communion | Morning Prayer | Evening Prayer |
|---|---|---|---|---|
| | | **THOMAS THE APOSTLE** (transferred from 21st) | | |
| Ps. 24; **48** | | Job 42. 1–6 | (Ps. 92; 146) | (Ps. 139) |
| Mal. 1. 1, 6–end | | Ps. 139. 1–11 | 2 Sam. 15. 17–21 | Hab. 2. 1–4 |
| Matt. 19. 1–12 | | Eph. 2. 19–end | or Ecclus. ch. 2 | 1 Pet. 1. 3–12 |
| | R | John 20. 24–end | John 11. 1–16 | |
| Ps. 89. 1–37 | | | Isa. ch. 54 | Mal. 2. 1–16 |
| Mal. 2. 1–16 | | | 2 Pet. 1.16 – 2.3 | Matt. 19. 13–15 |
| Matt. 19. 13–15 | P | | | |
| | | **CHRISTMAS EVE** | | |
| Ps. 85 | | Collect | Isa. ch. 55 | Zech. ch. 2 |
| Zech. ch. 2 | | (1) Christmas Eve | 2 Pet. 2. 4–end | Rev. 1. 1–8 |
| Rev. 1. 1–8 | | (2) Advent 1 | | |
| | | Mic. 5. 2–5a | | |
| | | Ps. 24 | | |
| | | Titus 3. 3–7 | | |
| | P | Luke 2. 1–14 | | |
| | | **CHRISTMAS DAY** | | |
| EP: Ps. 8 | | Isa. 9. 2–7 | Ps. 110; 117 | Ps. 8 |
| Isa. 65. 17–25 | | Ps. 98 | Isa. 62. 1–5 | Isa. 65. 17–25 |
| Phil. 2. 5–11 | | Heb. 1. 1–12 | Matt. 1. 18–end | Phil. 2. 5–11 |
| or Luke 2. 1–20 | | John 1. 1–14 | | or Luke 2. 1–20 |
| *if it has not been used at the* | | | | |
| *principal service of the day* | | | | |
| | 𝔚 | | | |
| | | **STEPHEN, DEACON, FIRST MARTYR** | | |
| EP: Ps. 57; **86** | | Collect | (Ps. 13; 31. 1–8; 150) | (Ps. 57; 86) |
| Gen. 4. 1–10 | | (1) Stephen | Jer. 26. 12–15 | Gen. 4. 1–10 |
| Matt. 23. 34–end | | (2) Christmas | Acts ch. 6 | Matt. 10. 17–22 |
| | | 2 Chron. 24. 20–22 | | |
| | | Ps. 119. 161–168 | | |
| | | Acts 7. 55–end | | |
| | R | Matt. 23. 34–end | | |
| | | **JOHN, APOSTLE AND EVANGELIST** | | |
| EP: Ps. 97 | | Collect | (Ps. 21; 147. 13–end) | (Ps. 97) |
| Isa. 6. 1–8 | | (1) John | Exod. 33. 7–11a | Isa. 6. 1–8 |
| 1 John 5. 1–12 | | (2) Christmas | 1 John 2. 1–11 | 1 John 5. 1–12 |
| | | Exod. 33. 18–end | | |
| | | Ps. 92. 11–end | | |
| | | 1 John ch. 1 | | |
| | W | John 21. 19b–end | | |
| | | **THE HOLY INNOCENTS** | | |
| EP: Ps. 123; **128** | | Collect | Ps. 36; 146 | Ps. 124; 128 |
| Isa. 49. 14–25 | | (1) Innocents | Baruch 4. 21–27 | Isa. 49. 14–25 |
| Mark 10. 13–16 | | (2) Christmas | or Gen. 37. 13–20 | Mark 10. 13–16 |
| | | Jer. 31. 10–17 | Matt. 18. 1–10 | |
| | | Ps. 123 | | |
| | | Rev. 14. 1–5 | | |
| | R | Matt. 2. 13–18 | | |
| | | *or, for The Sunday after Christmas Day:* | | |
| Ps. 132 | | Isa. 62. 10–12 | Ps. 105. 1–11 | Ps. 132 |
| Isa. ch. 35 | | Ps. 45. 1–7 | Isa. 63. 7–9 | Isa. ch. 35 |
| Col. 1. 9–20 | | Gal. 4. 1–7 | Eph. 3. 5–12 | Col. 1. 9–20 |
| or Luke 2. 41–end | W | Matt. 1. 18–end | | or Luke 2. 41–end |

# December 2014

| | | | Sunday Principal Service<br>Weekday Eucharist | Third Service<br>Morning Prayer |
|---|---|---|---|---|
| **29** | M<br><br>Wr | **Thomas Becket, Archbishop of Canterbury, Martyr, 1170\*** <br> Com. Martyr <br> *esp.* Matt. 10. 28–33 <br> *also* Ecclus. 51. 1–8 | *or* | 1 John 2. 3–11 <br> Ps. 96. 1–4 <br> Luke 2. 22–35 | Ps. *19*; 20 <br> Isa. 57. 15–end <br> John 1. 1–18 |
| **30** | Tu<br><br>W | | | 1 John 2. 12–17 <br> Ps. 96. 7–10 <br> Luke 2. 36–40 | Ps. 111; 112; *113* <br> Isa. 59. 1–15a <br> John 1. 19–28 |
| **31** | W<br><br><br>W | *John Wyclif, Reformer, 1384* | | 1 John 2. 18–21 <br> Ps. 96. 1, 11–end <br> John 1. 1–18 | Ps. 102 <br> Isa. 59. 15b–end <br> John 1. 29–34 |

# January 2015

| | | | Sunday Principal Service<br>Weekday Eucharist | Third Service<br>Morning Prayer |
|---|---|---|---|---|
| **1** | Th<br><br><br><br><br>W | THE NAMING AND CIRCUMCISION OF JESUS | | Num. 6. 22–end <br> Ps. 8 <br> Gal. 4. 4–7 <br> Luke 2. 15–21 | *MP:* Ps. *103*; 150 <br> Gen. 17. 1–13 <br> Rom. 2. 17–end |
| **2** | F<br><br><br><br>W | **Basil the Great and Gregory of Nazianzus, Bishops, Teachers, 379 and 389** <br> *Seraphim, Monk of Sarov, Spiritual Guide, 1833; Vedanayagam Samuel Azariah, Bishop in South India, Evangelist, 1945* <br> Com. Teacher <br> *esp.* 2 Tim. 4. 1–8 <br> Matt. 5. 13–19 | *or* | 1 John 2. 22–28 <br> Ps. 98. 1–4 <br> John 1. 19–28 | Ps. 18. 1–30 <br> Isa. 60. 1–12 <br> John 1. 35–42 |
| **3** | Sa<br><br>W | | | 1 John 2.29 – 3.6 <br> Ps. 98. 2–7 <br> John 1. 29–34 | Ps. *127*; 128; 131 <br> Isa. 60. 13–end <br> John 1. 43–end |
| **4** | S<br><br><br><br><br><br>W | THE SECOND SUNDAY OF CHRISTMAS <br> *or* The Epiphany *(see provision on the 5th and 6th)* | | Jer. 31. 7–14 <br> Ps. 147. 13–end <br> *or* Ecclus. 24. 1–12 <br> *Canticle:* Wisd. of Sol. 10. 15–end <br> Eph. 1. 3–14 <br> John 1. [1–9] 10–18 | Ps. 87 <br> Zech. 8. 1–8 <br> Luke 2. 41–end |
| **5** | M | | | 1 John 3. 11–21 <br> Ps. 100 <br> John 1. 43–end | Ps. 8; *48* <br> Isa. ch. 62 <br> John 2. 13–end |
| | <br><br>W | *or, if The Epiphany is celebrated on 4 January:* | | 1 John 3.22 – 4.6 <br> Ps. 2. 7–end <br> Matt. 4. 12–17, 23–end | Ps. 8; *48* <br> *alt.* Ps. 71 <br> Isa. ch. 61 <br> John 2. 1–12 |

\*Thomas Becket may be celebrated on 7 July instead of 29 December.

| Second Service Evening Prayer | | Calendar and Holy Communion | Morning Prayer | Evening Prayer |
|---|---|---|---|---|
| Ps. 131; *132*<br>Jonah ch. 1<br>Col. 1. 1–14 | W | | Isa. 57. 15–end<br>John 1. 1–18 | Jonah ch. 1<br>Col. 1. 1–14 |
| Ps. *65*; 84<br>Jonah ch. 2<br>Col. 1. 15–23 | W | | Isa. 59. 1–15a<br>John 1. 19–28 | Jonah ch. 2<br>Col. 1. 15–23 |
| Ps. *90*; 148<br>Jonah chs 3 & 4<br>Col. 1.24 – 2.7<br>*or First EP of The Naming of Jesus*<br>Ps. 148<br>Jer. 23. 1–6<br>Col. 2. 8–15<br>ct | W | **Silvester, Bishop of Rome, 335**<br>Com. Bishop | Isa. 59. 15b–end<br>John 1. 29–34 | Jonah chs 3 & 4<br>Col. 1.24 – 2.7<br>*or First EP of The Circumcision of Christ*<br>(Ps. 148)<br>Jer. 23. 1–6<br>Col. 2. 8–15<br>ct |
| *EP:* Ps. 115<br>Deut. 30. [1–10] 11–end<br>Acts 3. 1–16 | W | **THE CIRCUMCISION OF CHRIST**<br>Additional collect<br>Gen. 17. 3b–10<br>Ps. 98<br>Rom. 4. 8–13<br>*or* Eph. 2. 11–18<br>Luke 2. 15–21 | (Ps. 103; 150)<br>Gen. 17. 1–13<br>Rom. 2. 17–end | (Ps. 115)<br>Deut. 30. [1–10] 11–end<br>Acts 3. 1–16 |
| Ps. 45; *46*<br>Ruth ch. 1<br>Col. 2. 8–end | W | | Isa. 60. 1–12<br>John 1. 35–42 | Ruth ch. 1<br>Col. 2. 8–end |
| Ps. *2*; 110<br>Ruth ch. 2<br>Col. 3. 1–11<br>ct | W | | Isa. 60. 13–end<br>John 1. 43–end | Ruth ch. 2<br>Col. 3. 1–11<br>ct |
| Ps. 135 (*or* 135. 1–14)<br>Isa. 46. 3–end<br>Rom. 12. 1–8<br>*Gospel:* Matt. 2. 13–end | W | **THE SECOND SUNDAY AFTER CHRISTMAS**<br>Exod. 24. 12–18<br>Ps. 93<br>2 Cor. 8. 9<br>John 1. 14–18 | Ps. 87<br>Zech. 8. 1–8<br>Eph. 1. 3–14 | Ps. 135 (*or* 135. 1–14)<br>Isa. 46. 3–end<br>Rom. 12. 1–8 |
| *First EP of The Epiphany*<br>Ps. 96; *97*<br>Isa. 49. 1–13<br>John 4. 7–26<br>℣ ct | | | Isa. ch. 62<br>John 2. 13–end | *First EP of The Epiphany*<br>Ps. 96; *97*<br>Isa. 49. 1–13<br>John 4. 7–26 |
| Ps. 96; *97*<br>*alt.* Ps. *72*; 75<br>Ruth ch. 3<br>Col. 3.12 – 4.1 | W | | | ℣ ct |

# January 2015

| | | Sunday Principal Service<br>Weekday Eucharist | Third Service<br>Morning Prayer |
|---|---|---|---|
| **6** | Tu | **THE EPIPHANY** | |
| | | Isa. 60. 1–6<br>Ps. 72 (or 72. 10–15)<br>Eph. 3. 1–12<br>Matt. 2. 1–12 | *MP*: Ps. *132*; 113<br>Jer. 31. 7–14<br>John 1. 29–34 |
| | | *or, if The Epiphany is celebrated on 4 January:* | |
| | | I John 4. 7–10<br>Ps. 72. 1–8<br>Mark 6. 34–44 | Ps. 89. 1–37<br>*alt.* Ps. 73<br>Isa. ch. 62<br>John 2. 13–end |
| | ☽ | | |
| **7** | W | I John 3.22 – 4.6<br>Ps. 2. 7–end<br>Matt. 4. 12–17, 23–end | *99*; 147. 1–12<br>*alt.* Ps. 77<br>Isa. 63. 7–end<br>I John ch. 3 |
| | | *or, if The Epiphany is celebrated on 4 January:* | |
| | | I John 4. 11–18<br>Ps. 72. 1, 10–13<br>Mark 6. 45–52 | Ps. *99*; 147. 1–12<br>*alt.* Ps. 77<br>Isa. 63. 7–end<br>I John ch. 3 |
| | W | | |
| **8** | Th | I John 4. 7–10<br>Ps. 72. 1–8<br>Mark 6. 34–44 | Ps. *46*; 147. 13–end<br>*alt.* Ps. 78. 1–39†<br>Isa. ch. 64<br>I John 4. 7–end |
| | | *or, if The Epiphany is celebrated on 4 January:* | |
| | | I John 4.19 – 5.4<br>Ps. 72. 1, 17–end<br>Luke 4. 14–22 | Ps. *46*; 147. 13–end<br>*alt.* Ps. 78. 1–39†<br>Isa. ch. 64<br>I John 4. 7–end |
| | W | | |
| **9** | F | I John 4. 11–18<br>Ps. 72. 1, 10–13<br>Mark 6. 45–52 | Ps. 2; *148*<br>*alt.* Ps. 55<br>Isa. 65. 1–16<br>I John 5. 1–12 |
| | | *or, if The Epiphany is celebrated on 4 January:* | |
| | | I John 5. 5–13<br>Ps. 147. 13–end<br>Luke 5. 12–16 | Ps. 2; *148*<br>*alt.* Ps. 55<br>Isa. 65. 1–16<br>I John 5. 1–12 |
| | W | | |
| **10** | Sa | *William Laud, Archbishop of Canterbury, 1645*<br>I John 4.19 – 5.4<br>Ps. 72. 1, 17–end<br>Luke 4. 14–22 | Ps. 97; *149*<br>*alt.* Ps. *76*; 79<br>Isa. 65. 17–end<br>I John 5. 13–end |
| | | *or, if The Epiphany is celebrated on 4 January:* | |
| | | I John 5. 14–end<br>Ps. 149. 1–5<br>John 3. 22–30 | Ps. 97; *149*<br>*alt.* Ps. *76*; 79<br>Isa. 65. 17–end<br>I John 5. 13–end |
| | W | | |

| Second Service Evening Prayer | Calendar and Holy Communion | Morning Prayer | Evening Prayer |
|---|---|---|---|
| *EP*: Ps. **98**; 100<br>Baruch 4.36 – 5.end<br>*or* Isa. 60. 1–9<br>John 2. 1–11 | **THE EPIPHANY**<br>Isa. 60. 1–9<br>Ps. 100<br>Eph. 3. 1–12<br>Matt. 2. 1–12 | Ps. 132; 113<br>Jer. 31. 7–14<br>John 1. 29–34 | Ps. 72; 98<br>Baruch 4.36 – 5.end<br>*or* Isa. 60. 1–9<br>John 2. 1–11 |
| Ps. 85; **87**<br>*alt.* Ps. 74<br>Ruth 4. 1–17<br>Col. 4. 2–end | ℬ | | |
| Ps. 118<br>*alt.* Ps. 119. 81–104<br>Baruch 1.15 – 2.10<br>*or* Jer. 23. 1–8<br>Matt. 20. 1–16 | | Isa. 63. 7–end<br>1 John ch. 3 | Baruch 1.15 – 2.10<br>*or* Jer. 23. 1–8<br>Matt. 20. 1–16 |
| Ps. 118<br>*alt.* Ps. 119. 81–104<br>Baruch 1.15 – 2.10<br>*or* Jer. 23. 1–8<br>Matt. 20. 1–16 | **W** *or* **G** | | |
| Ps. 145<br>*alt.* Ps. 78. 40–end†<br>Baruch 2. 11–end<br>*or* Jer. 30. 1–17<br>Matt. 20. 17–28 | **Lucian, Priest and Martyr, 290**<br>Com. Martyr | Isa. ch. 64<br>1 John 4. 7–end | Baruch 2. 11–end<br>*or* Jer. 30. 1–17<br>Matt. 20. 17–28 |
| Ps. 145<br>*alt.* Ps. 78. 40–end†<br>Baruch 2. 11–end<br>*or* Jer. 30. 1–17<br>Matt. 20. 17–28 | **Wr** *or* **Gr** | | |
| Ps. **67**; 72<br>*alt.* Ps. 69<br>Baruch 3. 1–8<br>*or* Jer. 30.18 – 31.9<br>Matt. 20. 29–end | | Isa. 65. 1–16<br>1 John 5. 1–12 | Baruch 3. 1–8<br>*or* Jer. 30.18 – 31.9<br>Matt. 20. 29–end |
| Ps. **67**; 72<br>*alt.* Ps. 69<br>Baruch 3. 1–8<br>*or* Jer. 30.18 – 31.9<br>Matt. 20. 29–end | **W** *or* **G** | | |
| Ps. 27; **29**<br>*alt.* Ps. 81; **84**<br>Baruch 3.9 – 4.4<br>*or* Jer. 31. 10–17<br>Matt. 23. 1–12<br>*or First EP of The Baptism*<br>Ps. 36<br>Isa. ch. 61<br>Titus 2. 11–14; 3. 4–7<br>ℬ **ct** | | Isa. 65. 17–end<br>1 John 5. 13–end | Baruch 3.9 – 4.4<br>*or* Jer. 31. 10–17<br>Matt. 23. 1–12 |
| Ps. 27; **29**<br>*alt.* Ps. 81; **84**<br>Baruch 3.9 – 4.4<br>*or* Jer. 31. 10–17<br>Matt. 23. 1–12<br>*or First EP of The Baptism*<br>Ps. 36<br>Isa. ch. 61<br>Titus 2. 11–14; 3. 4–7<br>ℬ **ct** | **W** *or* **G** | | **ct** |

# January 2015

| | Sunday Principal Service / Weekday Eucharist | Third Service / Morning Prayer |
|---|---|---|

**11 S** — THE BAPTISM OF CHRIST (THE FIRST SUNDAY OF EPIPHANY)

| | | |
|---|---|---|
| | Gen. 1. 1–5 | Ps. 89. 19–29 |
| | Ps. 29 | 1 Sam. 16. 1–3, 13 |
| | Acts 19. 1–7 | John 1. 29–34 |
| | Mark 1. 4–11 | |

ꟿ

**12 M**
**Aelred of Hexham, Abbot of Rievaulx, 1167**
*Benedict Biscop, Abbot of Wearmouth, Scholar, 689*

DEL 1

| | | |
|---|---|---|
| Com. Religious    *or* | Heb. 1. 1–6 | Ps. **2**; 110 |
| *also* Ecclus. 15. 1–6 | Ps. 97. 1–2, 6–10 | *alt.* Ps. **80**; 82 |
| | Mark 1. 14–20 | Amos ch. 1 |
| **W** | | 1 Cor. 1. 1–17 |

**13 Tu**
**Hilary, Bishop of Poitiers, Teacher, 367**
*Kentigern (Mungo), Missionary Bishop in Strathclyde and Cumbria, 603; George Fox, Founder of the Society of Friends (the Quakers), 1691*

| | | |
|---|---|---|
| Com. Teacher    *or* | Heb. 2. 5–12 | Ps. 8; **9** |
| *also* 1 John 2. 18–25 | Ps. 8 | *alt.* Ps. 87; **89. 1–18** |
| John 8. 25–32 | Mark 1. 21–28 | Amos ch. 2 |
| **W** | | 1 Cor. 1. 18–end |

**14 W**

| | | |
|---|---|---|
| | Heb. 2. 14–end | Ps. 19; **20** |
| | Ps. 105. 1–9 | *alt.* Ps. 119. 105–128 |
| | Mark 1. 29–39 | Amos ch. 3 |
| **W** | | 1 Cor. ch. 2 |

**15 Th**

| | | |
|---|---|---|
| | Heb. 3. 7–14 | Ps. **21**; 24 |
| | Ps. 95. 1, 8–end | *alt.* Ps. 90; **92** |
| | Mark 1. 40–end | Amos ch. 4 |
| **W** | | 1 Cor. ch. 3 |

**16 F**

| | | |
|---|---|---|
| | Heb. 4. 1–5, 11 | Ps. **67**; 72 |
| | Ps. 78. 3–8 | *alt.* Ps. **88**; (95) |
| | Mark 2. 1–12 | Amos 5. 1–17 |
| **W** | | 1 Cor. ch. 4 |

**17 Sa**
**Antony of Egypt, Hermit, Abbot, 356**
*Charles Gore, Bishop, Founder of the Community of the Resurrection, 1932*

| | | |
|---|---|---|
| Com. Religious    *or* | Heb. 4. 12–end | Ps. 29; **33** |
| *esp.* Phil. 3. 7–14 | Ps. 19. 7–end | *alt.* Ps. 96; **97**; 100 |
| *also* Matt. 19. 16–26 | Mark 2. 13–17 | Amos 5. 18–end |
| **W** | | 1 Cor. ch. 5 |

**18 S** — THE SECOND SUNDAY OF EPIPHANY
The Week of Prayer for Christian Unity until 25th

| | | |
|---|---|---|
| | 1 Sam. 3. 1–10 [11–20] | Ps. 145. 1–12 |
| | Ps. 139. 1–5, 12–18 (*or* 1–9) | Isa. 62. 1–5 |
| | Rev. 5. 1–10 | 1 Cor. 6. 11–end |
| | John 1. 43–end | |
| **W** | | |

**19 M**
**Wulfstan, Bishop of Worcester, 1095**

DEL 2

| | | |
|---|---|---|
| Com. Bishop    *or* | Heb. 5. 1–10 | Ps. 145; **146** |
| *esp.* Matt. 24. 42–46 | Ps. 110. 1–4 | *alt.* Ps. **98**; 99; 101 |
| | Mark 2. 18–22 | Amos ch. 6 |
| **W** | | 1 Cor. 6. 1–11 |

**20 Tu**
*Richard Rolle of Hampole, Spiritual Writer, 1349*

| | | |
|---|---|---|
| | Heb. 6. 10–end | Ps. **132**; 147. 1–12 |
| | Ps. 111 | *alt.* Ps. 106† (*or* Ps. 103) |
| | Mark 2. 23–end | Amos ch. 7 |
| **W** | | 1 Cor. 6. 12–end |

**21 W**
**Agnes, Child Martyr at Rome, 304**

| | | |
|---|---|---|
| Com. Martyr    *or* | Heb. 7. 1–3, 15–17 | Ps. **81**; 147. 13–end |
| *also* Rev. 7. 13–end | Ps. 110. 1–4 | *alt.* Ps. 110; **111**; 112 |
| | Mark 3. 1–6 | Amos ch. 8 |
| **Wr** | | 1 Cor. 7. 1–24 |

| Second Service / Evening Prayer | Calendar and Holy Communion | Morning Prayer | Evening Prayer |
|---|---|---|---|
| | **THE FIRST SUNDAY AFTER THE EPIPHANY**<br>To celebrate The Baptism of Christ, see *Common Worship* provision. | | |
| Ps. 46; [47]<br>Isa. 42. 1–9<br>Eph. 2. 1–10<br>*Gospel*: Matt. 3. 13–end | Zech. 8. 1–8<br>Ps. 72. 1–8<br>Rom. 12. 1–5<br>Luke 2. 41–end<br><br>**W** or **G** | Ps. 89. 19–29<br>1 Sam. 16. 1–3, 13<br>John 1. 29–34 | Ps. 46; [47]<br>Isa. 42. 1–9<br>Eph. 2. 1–10 |
| Ps. *34*; 36<br>*alt.* Ps. *85*; 86<br>Gen. 1. 1–19<br>Matt. 21. 1–17 | <br>**W** or **G** | Amos ch. 1<br>1 Cor. 1. 1–17 | Gen. 1. 1–19<br>Matt. 21. 1–17 |
| | **Hilary, Bishop of Poitiers, Teacher, 367** | | |
| Ps. *45*; 46<br>*alt.* Ps. 89. 19–end<br>Gen. 1.20 – 2.3<br>Matt. 21. 18–32 | Com. Doctor<br><br>**W** or **Gw** | Amos ch. 2<br>1 Cor. 1. 18–end | Gen. 1.20 – 2.3<br>Matt. 21. 18–32 |
| Ps. *47*; 48<br>*alt.* Ps. *91*; 93<br>Gen. 2. 4–end<br>Matt. 21. 33–end | <br>**W** or **G** | Amos ch. 3<br>1 Cor. ch. 2 | Gen. 2. 4–end<br>Matt. 21. 33–end |
| Ps. *61*; 65<br>*alt.* Ps. 94<br>Gen. ch. 3<br>Matt. 22. 1–14 | <br>**W** or **G** | Amos ch. 4<br>1 Cor. ch. 3 | Gen. ch. 3<br>Matt. 22. 1–14 |
| Ps. 68<br>*alt.* Ps. 102<br>Gen. 4. 1–16, 25–26<br>Matt. 22. 15–33 | <br>**W** or **G** | Amos 5. 1–17<br>1 Cor. ch. 4 | Gen. 4. 1–16, 25–26<br>Matt. 22. 15–33 |
| Ps. 84; *85*<br>*alt.* Ps. 104<br>Gen. 6. 1–10<br>Matt. 22. 34–end<br>ct | <br>**W** or **G** | Amos 5. 18–end<br>1 Cor. ch. 5 | Gen. 6. 1–10<br>Matt. 22. 34–end<br>ct |
| | **THE SECOND SUNDAY AFTER THE EPIPHANY**<br>For the Week of Prayer for Christian Unity, see *Common Worship* provision. | | |
| Ps. 96<br>Isa. 60. 9–end<br>Heb. 6.17 – 7.10<br>*Gospel*: Matt. 8. 5–13 | 2 Kings 4. 1–17<br>Ps. 107. 13–22<br>Rom. 12. 6–16a<br>John 2. 1–11<br><br>**W** or **G** | Ps. 145. 1–12<br>Isa. 62. 1–5<br>1 Cor. 6. 11–end | Ps. 96<br>Isa. 60. 9–end<br>Heb. 6.17 – 7.10 |
| Ps. 71<br>*alt.* Ps. 105† (*or* Ps. 103)<br>Gen. 6.11 – 7.10<br>Matt. 24. 1–14 | <br>**W** or **G** | Amos ch. 6<br>1 Cor. 6. 1–11 | Gen. 6.11 – 7.10<br>Matt. 24. 1–14 |
| Ps. 89. 1–37<br>*alt.* Ps. 107†<br>Gen. 7. 11–end<br>Matt. 24. 15–28 | **Fabian, Bishop of Rome, Martyr, 250**<br>Com. Martyr<br><br>**Wr** or **Gr** | Amos ch. 7<br>1 Cor. 6. 12–end | Gen. 7. 11–end<br>Matt. 24. 15–28 |
| Ps. *97*; 98<br>*alt.* Ps. 119. 129–152<br>Gen. 8. 1–14<br>Matt. 24. 29–end | **Agnes, Child Martyr at Rome, 304**<br>Com. Virgin Martyr<br><br>**Wr** or **Gr** | Amos ch. 8<br>1 Cor. 7. 1–24 | Gen. 8. 1–14<br>Matt. 24. 29–end |

# January 2015

| | | Sunday Principal Service / Weekday Eucharist | Third Service / Morning Prayer |
|---|---|---|---|

**22** Th — *Vincent of Saragossa, Deacon, first Martyr of Spain, 304*

| | Sunday Principal Service / Weekday Eucharist | Third Service / Morning Prayer |
|---|---|---|
| | Heb. 7.25 – 8.6 | Ps. *76*; 148 |
| | Ps. 40. 7–10, 17–end | *alt.* Ps. 113; *115* |
| | Mark 3. 7–12 | Amos ch. 9 |
| W | | 1 Cor. 7. 25–end |

**23** F

| | Heb. 8. 6–end | Ps. *27*; 149 |
|---|---|---|
| | Ps. 85. 7–end | *alt.* Ps. 139 |
| | Mark 3. 13–19 | Hos. 1.1 – 2.1 |
| W | | 1 Cor. ch. 8 |

**24** Sa — **Francis de Sales, Bishop of Geneva, Teacher, 1622**

| | Com. Teacher | *or* Heb. 9. 2–3, 11–14 | Ps. *122*; 128; 150 |
|---|---|---|---|
| | *also* Prov. 3. 13–18 | Ps. 47. 1–8 | *alt.* Ps. 120; *121*; 122 |
| | John 3. 17–21 | Mark 3. 20–21 | Hos. 2. 2–17 |
| | | | 1 Cor. 9. 1–14 |
| W | | | |

**25** S — THE CONVERSION OF PAUL

| | | Jer. 1. 4–10 | *MP*: Ps. 66; 147. 13–end |
|---|---|---|---|
| | | *or* Acts 9. 1–22 | Ezek. 3. 22–end |
| | | Ps. 67 | Phil. 3. 1–14 |
| | | Acts 9. 1–22 | |
| | | *or* Gal. 1. 11–16a | |
| W | | Matt. 19. 27–end | |

*or, for The Third Sunday of Epiphany*

| | | Gen. 14. 17–20 | Ps. 113 |
|---|---|---|---|
| | | Ps. 128 | Jonah 3. 1–5, 10 |
| | | Rev. 19. 6–10 | John 3. 16–21 |
| W | | John 2. 1–11 | |

**26** M  **DEL 3** — **Timothy and Titus, Companions of Paul**
(For Conversion of Paul, see provision on 25th)

| | Isa. 61. 1–3a | *or* Heb. 9. 15, 24–end | Ps. 40; *108* |
|---|---|---|---|
| | Ps. 100 | Ps. 98. 1–7 | *alt.* Ps. 123; 124; 125; *126* |
| | 2 Tim. 2. 1–8 | Mark 3. 22–30 | Hos. 2.18 – 3.end |
| | *or* Titus 1. 1–5 | | 1 Cor. 9. 15–end |
| W | Luke 10. 1–9 | | |

**27** Tu

| | Heb. 10. 1–10 | Ps. 34; *36* |
|---|---|---|
| | Ps. 40. 1–4, 7–10 | *alt.* Ps. *132*; 133 |
| | Mark 3. 31–end | Hos. 4. 1–16 |
| W | | 1 Cor. 10. 1–13 |

**28** W — **Thomas Aquinas, Priest, Philosopher, Teacher, 1274**

| | Com. Teacher | *or* Heb. 10. 11–18 | Ps. 45; *46* |
|---|---|---|---|
| | *esp.* Wisd. 7. 7–10, 15–16 | Ps. 110. 1–4 | *alt.* Ps. 119. 153–end |
| | 1 Cor. 2. 9–end | Mark 4. 1–20 | Hos. 5. 1–7 |
| W | John 16. 12–15 | | 1 Cor. 10.14 – 11.1 |

**29** Th

| | Heb. 10. 19–25 | Ps. *47*; 48 |
|---|---|---|
| | Ps. 24. 1–6 | *alt.* Ps. *143*; 146 |
| | Mark 4. 21–25 | Hos. 5.8 – 6.6 |
| W | | 1 Cor. 11. 2–16 |

**30** F — **Charles, King and Martyr, 1649**

| | Com. Martyr | *or* Heb. 10. 32–end | Ps. 61; *65* |
|---|---|---|---|
| | *also* Ecclus. 2. 12–17 | Ps. 37. 3–6, 40–end | *alt.* Ps. 142; *144* |
| | 1 Tim. 6. 12–16 | Mark 4. 26–34 | Hos. 6.7 – 7.2 |
| Wr | | | 1 Cor. 11. 17–end |

| Second Service Evening Prayer | Calendar and Holy Communion | Morning Prayer | Evening Prayer |
|---|---|---|---|
| | **Vincent of Saragossa, Deacon, first Martyr of Spain, 304** | | |
| Ps. 99; 100; *111* | Com. Martyr | Amos ch. 9 | Gen. 8.15 – 9.7 |
| *alt.* Ps. 114; *116*; 117 | | I Cor. 7. 25–end | Matt. 25. 1–13 |
| Gen. 8.15 – 9.7 | | | |
| Matt. 25. 1–13 | **Wr** *or* **Gr** | | |
| Ps. 73 | | Hos. 1.1 – 2.1 | Gen. 9. 8–19 |
| *alt.* Ps. *130*; 131; 137 | | I Cor. ch. 8 | Matt. 25. 14–30 |
| Gen. 9. 8–19 | | | |
| Matt. 25. 14–30 | **W** *or* **G** | | |
| Ps. *61*; 66 | | Hos. 2. 2–17 | Gen. 11. 1–9 |
| *alt.* Ps. 118 | | I Cor. 9. 1–14 | Matt. 25. 31–end |
| Gen. 11. 1–9 | | | ct |
| Matt. 25. 31–end | | | |
| ct | | | *or First EP of The* |
| *or First EP of The Conversion* | | | *Conversion of Paul* |
| *of Paul* | | | (Ps. 149) |
| Ps. 149 | | | Isa. 49. 1–13 |
| Isa. 49. 1–13 | | | Acts 22. 3–16 |
| Acts 22. 3–16 | | | |
| ct | **W** *or* **G** | | **W ct** |
| EP: Ps. 119. 41–56 | **THE CONVERSION OF PAUL** | Ps. 66; 147. 13–end | Ps. 119. 41–56 |
| Ecclus. 39. 1–10 | Josh. 5. 13–end | Ezek. 3. 22–end | Ecclus. 39. 1–10 |
| *or* Isa. 56. 1–8 | Ps. 67 | Phil. 3. 1–14 | *or* Isa. 56. 1–8 |
| Col. 1.24 – 2.7 | Acts 9. 1–22 | | Col. 1.24 – 2.7 |
| | Matt. 19. 27–end | | |
| Ps. 33 (*or* 33. 1–12) | | | |
| Jer. 3.21 – 4.2 | | | |
| Titus 2. 1–8, 11–14 | | | |
| *Gospel:* Matt. 4. 12–23 | **W** | | |
| Ps. *138*; 144 | | Hos. 2.18 – 3.end | Gen. 11.27 – 12.9 |
| *alt.* Ps. *127*; 128; 129 | | I Cor. 9. 15–end | Matt. 26. 1–16 |
| Gen. 11.27 – 12.9 | | | |
| Matt. 26. 1–16 | **W** *or* **G** | | |
| Ps. 145 | | Hos. 4. 1–16 | Gen. 13. 2–end |
| *alt.* Ps. (134); *135* | | I Cor. 10. 1–13 | Matt. 26. 17–35 |
| Gen. 13. 2–end | | | |
| Matt. 26. 17–35 | **W** *or* **G** | | |
| Ps. 21; *29* | | Hos. 5. 1–7 | Gen. ch. 14 |
| *alt.* Ps. 136 | | I Cor. 10.14 – 11.1 | Matt. 26. 36–46 |
| Gen. ch. 14 | | | |
| Matt. 26. 36–46 | **W** *or* **G** | | |
| Ps. *24*; 33 | | Hos. 5.8 – 6.6 | Gen. ch. 15 |
| *alt.* Ps. *138*; 140; 141 | | I Cor. 11. 2–16 | Matt. 26. 47–56 |
| Gen. ch. 15 | | | |
| Matt. 26. 47–56 | **W** *or* **G** | | |
| | **Charles, King and Martyr, 1649** | | |
| Ps. *67*; 77 | Com. Martyr | Hos. 6.7 – 7.2 | Gen. ch. 16 |
| *alt.* Ps. 145 | | I Cor. 11. 17–end | Matt. 26. 57–end |
| Gen. ch. 16 | | | |
| Matt. 26. 57–end | **Wr** *or* **Gr** | | |

# January 2015

| | | | Sunday Principal Service<br>Weekday Eucharist | Third Service<br>Morning Prayer |
|---|---|---|---|---|
| **31** | Sa | *John Bosco, Priest, Founder of the Salesian Teaching Order, 1888* | | |
| | | | Heb. 11. 1–2, 8–19 | Ps. 68 |
| | | | Canticle: Luke 1. 69–73 | *alt.* Ps. 147 |
| | | | Mark 4. 35–end | Hos. ch. 8 |
| | W | | | 1 Cor. 12. 1–11 |

# February 2015

| | | | | |
|---|---|---|---|---|
| **1** | S | **THE FOURTH SUNDAY OF EPIPHANY** | | |
| | | *or The Presentation of Christ in the* | Deut. 18. 15–20 | Ps. 71. 1–6, 15–17 |
| | | *Temple (Candlemas)** | Ps. 111 | Jer. 1. 4–10 |
| | | | Rev. 12. 1–5a | Mark 1. 40–end |
| | | | Mark 1. 21–28 | |
| | W | | | |

| | | | | |
|---|---|---|---|---|
| **2** | M | **THE PRESENTATION OF CHRIST IN THE TEMPLE (CANDLEMAS)** | | |
| DEL 4 | | | Mal. 3. 1–5 | MP: Ps. **48**; 146 |
| | | | Ps. 24 (*or* 24. 7–end) | Exod. 13. 1–16 |
| | ⅏ | | Heb. 2. 14–end | Rom. 12. 1–5 |
| | | | Luke 2. 22–40 | |
| | | *or, if The Presentation is observed on 1 February:* | | |
| | | | Heb. 11. 32–end | Ps. *1*; 2; 3 |
| | G | | Ps. 31. 19–end | Hos. ch. 9 |
| | | | Mark 5. 1–20 | 1 Cor. 12. 12–end |

| | | | | |
|---|---|---|---|---|
| **3** | Tu | **Anskar, Archbishop of Hamburg, Missionary in Denmark and Sweden, 865** | | |
| | | Ordinary Time starts today (or on 2 February if The Presentation is observed on 1 February) | | |
| | | Com. Missionary *or* | Heb. 12. 1–4 | Ps. *5*; 6; (8) |
| | | *esp.* Isa. 52. 7–10 | Ps. 22. 25b–end | Hos. ch. 10 |
| | Gw | *also* Rom. 10. 11–15 | Mark 5. 21–43 | 1 Cor. ch. 13 |

| | | | | |
|---|---|---|---|---|
| **4** | W | *Gilbert of Sempringham, Founder of the Gilbertine Order, 1189* | | |
| | | | Heb. 12. 4–7, 11–15 | Ps. 119. 1–32 |
| | | | Ps. 103. 1–2, 13–18 | Hos. 11. 1–11 |
| | G | | Mark 6. 1–6a | 1 Cor. 14. 1–19 |

| | | | | |
|---|---|---|---|---|
| **5** | Th | | | |
| | | | Heb. 12. 18–19, 21–24 | Ps. 14; *15*; 16 |
| | | | Ps. 48. 1–3, 8–10 | Hos. 11.12 – 12.end |
| | G | | Mark 6. 7–13 | 1 Cor. 14. 20–end |

| | | | | |
|---|---|---|---|---|
| **6** | F | *The Martyrs of Japan, 1597* | | |
| | | (The Accession of Queen Elizabeth II may be observed on 6 February, and Collect, Readings and | | |
| | | Post-Communion for the sovereign used.) | | |
| | | | Heb. 13. 1–8 | Ps. 17; *19* |
| | | | Ps. 27. 1–6, 9–12 | Hos. 13. 1–14 |
| | | | Mark 6. 14–29 | 1 Cor. 16. 1–9 |
| | G | | | |

| | | | | |
|---|---|---|---|---|
| **7** | Sa | | Heb. 13. 15–17, 20–21 | Ps. 20; 21; *23* |
| | | | Ps. 23 | Hos. ch. 14 |
| | G | | Mark 6. 30–34 | 1 Cor. 16. 10–end |

| | | | | |
|---|---|---|---|---|
| **8** | S | **THE SECOND SUNDAY BEFORE LENT** | | |
| | | | Prov. 8. 1, 22–31 | Ps. 29; 67 |
| | | | Ps. 104. 26–end | Deut. 8. 1–10 |
| | | | Col. 1. 15–20 | Matt. 6. 25–end |
| | G | | John 1. 1–14 | |

| | | | | |
|---|---|---|---|---|
| **9** | M | | Gen. 1. 1–19 | Ps. 27; *30* |
| | | | Ps. 104, 1–2, 6–13, 26 | 2 Chron. 9. 1–12 |
| DEL 5 | G | | Mark 6. 53–end | John 19. 1–16 |

*See provision for First EP on 1 February and throughout the day for The Presentation on 2 February.

| Second Service Evening Prayer | Calendar and Holy Communion | Morning Prayer | Evening Prayer |
|---|---|---|---|
| Ps. *72*; 76<br>alt. *148*; 149; 150<br>Gen. 17. 1–22<br>Matt. 27. 1–10<br>ct<br><br>W or G | | Hos. ch. 8<br>I Cor. 12. 1–11 | Gen. 17. 1–22<br>Matt. 27. 1–10<br><br>ct |
| *First EP of The Presentation*<br>Ps. 118<br>I Sam. 1. 19b–end<br>Heb. 4. 11–end<br><br>₩ ct | **SEPTUAGESIMA**<br>Gen. 1. 1–5<br>Ps. 9. 10–20<br>I Cor. 9. 24–end<br>Matt. 20. 1–16<br><br>W or G | Ps. 71. 1–6, 15–17<br>Jer. 1. 4–10<br>Mark 1. 40–end | *First EP of The Presentation*<br>Ps. 118<br>I Sam. 1. 19b–end<br>Heb. 4. 11–end<br>₩ ct |
| EP: Ps. 122; *132*<br>Hag. 2. 1–9<br>John 2. 18–22 | **THE PRESENTATION OF CHRIST IN THE TEMPLE**<br>Mal. 3. 1–5<br>Ps. 48. 1–7<br>Gal. 4. 1–7<br>Luke 2. 22–40 | Ps. 48; 146<br>Exod. 13. 1–16<br>Rom. 12. 1–5 | Ps. 122; 132<br>Hag. 2. 1–9<br>John 2. 18–22 |
| Ps. *4*; 7<br>Gen. 18. 1–15<br>Matt. 27. 11–26 | ₩ | | |
| Ps. *9*; 10†<br>Gen. 18. 16–end<br>Matt. 27. 27–44<br><br>Gr | **Blasius, Bishop of Sebastopol, Martyr, c. 316**<br>Com. Martyr<br><br>Gr | Hos. ch. 10<br>I Cor. ch. 13 | Gen. 18. 16–end<br>Matt. 27. 27–44 |
| Ps. *11*; 12; 13<br>Gen. 19. 1–3, 12–29<br>Matt. 27. 45–56<br>G | | Hos. 11. 1–11<br>I Cor. 14. 1–19 | Gen. 19. 1–3, 12–29<br>Matt. 27. 45–56 |
| Ps. 18†<br>Gen. 21. 1–21<br>Matt. 27. 57–end<br><br>Gr | **Agatha, Martyr in Sicily, 251**<br>Com. Virgin Martyr | Hos. 11.12 – 12.end<br>I Cor. 14. 20–end | Gen. 21. 1–21<br>Matt. 27. 57–end |
| Ps. 22<br>Gen. 22. 1–19<br>Matt. 28. 1–15 | **The Accession of Queen Elizabeth II, 1952**<br><br>*For Accession Service:* Ps. 20; 101; 121; Josh. 1. 1–9; Prov. 8. 1–16; Rom. 13. 1–10; Rev. 21.22 – 22.4<br>*For The Accession:*<br>I Pet. 2. 11–17<br>Matt. 22. 16–22<br>G | Hos. 13. 1–14<br>I Cor. 16. 1–9 | Gen. 22. 1–19<br>Matt. 28. 1–15 |
| Ps. *24*; 25<br>Gen. ch. 23<br>Matt. 28. 16–end<br>ct<br><br>G | | Hos. ch. 14<br>I Cor. 16. 10–end | Gen. ch. 23<br>Matt. 28. 16–end<br><br>ct |
| Ps. 65<br>Gen. 2. 4b–end<br>Luke 8. 22–35 | **SEXAGESIMA**<br>Gen. 3. 9–19<br>Ps. 83. 1–2, 13–end<br>2 Cor. 11. 19–31<br>Luke 8. 4–15<br>G | Ps. 29; 67<br>Deut. 8. 1–10<br>Matt. 6. 25–end | Ps. 65<br>Gen. 2. 4b–end<br>Luke 8. 22–35 |
| Ps. 26; *28*; 29<br>Gen. 29.31 – 30.24<br>2 Tim. 4. 1–8 | G | 2 Chron. 9. 1–12<br>John 19. 1–16 | Gen. 29.31 – 30.24<br>2 Tim. 4. 1–8 |

# February 2015

| | | | Sunday Principal Service<br>Weekday Eucharist | Third Service<br>Morning Prayer |
|---|---|---|---|---|
| **10** | Tu<br><br>G | *Scholastica, sister of Benedict, Abbess of Plombariola, c. 543* | Gen. 1.20 – 2.4a<br>Ps. 8<br>Mark 7. 1–13 | Ps. 32; **36**<br>2 Chron. 10.1 – 11.4<br>John 19. 17–30 |
| **11** | W<br><br>G | | Gen. 2. 4b–9, 15–17<br>Ps. 104. 11–12, 29–32<br>Mark 7. 14–23 | Ps. 34<br>2 Chron. ch. 12<br>John 19. 31–end |
| **12** | Th<br><br>G | | Gen. 2. 18–end<br>Ps. 128<br>Mark 7. 24–30 | Ps. 37†<br>2 Chron. 13.1 – 14.1<br>John 20. 1–10 |
| **13** | F<br><br>G | | Gen. 3. 1–8<br>Ps. 32. 1–8<br>Mark 7. 31–end | Ps. 31<br>2 Chron. 14. 2–end<br>John 20. 11–18 |
| **14** | Sa<br><br><br><br><br>Gw | **Cyril and Methodius, Missionaries to the Slavs, 869 and 885**<br>*Valentine, Martyr at Rome, c. 269*<br>Com. Missionaries     *or*<br>*esp.* Isa. 52. 7–10<br>*also* Rom. 10. 11–15 | Gen. 3. 9–end<br>Ps. 90. 1–12<br>Mark 8. 1–10 | Ps. 41; **42**; 43<br>2 Chron. 15. 1–15<br>John 20. 19–end |
| **15** | S<br><br><br>G | THE SUNDAY NEXT BEFORE LENT | 2 Kings 2. 1–12<br>Ps. 50. 1–6<br>2 Cor. 4. 3–6<br>Mark 9. 2–9 | Ps. 27; 150<br>Exod. 24. 12–end<br>2 Cor. 3. 12–end |
| **16**<br>DEL 6 | M<br><br>G | | Gen. 4. 1–15, 25<br>Ps. 50. 1, 8, 16–end<br>Mark 8. 11–13 | Ps. 44<br>Jer. ch. 1<br>John 3. 1–21 |
| **17** | Tu<br><br>Gr | **Janani Luwum, Archbishop of Uganda, Martyr, 1977**<br>Com. Martyr     *or*<br>*also* Ecclus. 4. 20–28<br>John 12. 24–32 | Gen. 6. 5–8; 7. 1–5, 10<br>Ps. 29<br>Mark 8. 14–21 | Ps. **48**; 52<br>Jer. 2. 1–13<br>John 3. 22–end |
| **18** | W<br><br><br><br><br>P | **ASH WEDNESDAY** | Joel 2. 1–2, 12–17<br>*or* Isa. 58. 1–12<br>Ps. 51. 1–18<br>2 Cor. 5.20b – 6.10<br>Matt. 6. 1–6, 16–21<br>*or* John 8. 1–11 | *MP:* Ps. 38<br>Dan. 9. 3–6, 17–19<br>1 Tim. 6. 6–19 |
| **19** | Th<br><br>P | | Deut. 30. 15–end<br>Ps. 1<br>Luke 9. 22–25 | Ps. 77<br>*alt.* Ps. 56; **57**; (63†)<br>Jer. 2. 14–32<br>John 4. 1–26 |
| **20** | F<br><br>P | | Isa. 58. 1–9a<br>Ps. 51. 1–5, 17–18<br>Matt. 9. 14–15 | Ps. **3**; 7<br>*alt.* Ps. **51**; 54<br>Jer. 3. 6–22<br>John 4. 27–42 |
| **21** | Sa<br><br>P | | Isa. 58. 9b–end<br>Ps. 86. 1–7<br>Luke 5. 27–32 | Ps. 71<br>*alt.* Ps. 68<br>Jer. 4. 1–18<br>John 4. 43–end |
| **22** | S<br><br><br><br>P | THE FIRST SUNDAY OF LENT | Gen. 9. 8–17<br>Ps. 25. 1–9<br>1 Pet. 3. 18–end<br>Mark 1. 9–15 | Ps. 77<br>Exod. 34. 1–10<br>Rom. 10. 8b–13 |

| Second Service Evening Prayer | | Calendar and Holy Communion | Morning Prayer | Evening Prayer |
|---|---|---|---|---|
| Ps. 33<br>Gen. 31. 1–24<br>2 Tim. 4. 9–end | G | | 2 Chron. 10.1 – 11.4<br>John 19. 17–30 | Gen. 31. 1–24<br>2 Tim. 4. 9–end |
| Ps. 119. 33–56<br>Gen. 31.25 – 32.2<br>Titus ch. 1 | G | | 2 Chron. ch. 12<br>John 19. 31–end | Gen. 31.25 – 32.2<br>Titus ch. 1 |
| Ps. 39; **40**<br>Gen. 32. 3–30<br>Titus ch. 2 | G | | 2 Chron. 13.1 – 14.1<br>John 20. 1–10 | Gen. 32. 3–30<br>Titus ch. 2 |
| Ps. 35<br>Gen. 33. 1–17<br>Titus ch. 3 | G | | 2 Chron. 14. 2–end<br>John 20. 11–18 | Gen. 33. 1–17<br>Titus ch. 3 |
| | | **Valentine, Martyr at Rome, c. 269** | | |
| Ps. 45; **46**<br>Gen. ch. 35<br>Philemon<br>ct | Gr | Com. Martyr | 2 Chron. 15. 1–15<br>John 20. 19–end | Gen. ch. 35<br>Philemon<br><br>ct |
| Ps. 2; [99]<br>1 Kings 19. 1–16<br>2 Pet. 1. 16–end<br>*Gospel:* Mark 9. [2–8] 9–13 | G | **QUINQUAGESIMA**<br>Gen. 9. 8–17<br>Ps. 77. 11–end<br>1 Cor. ch. 13<br>Luke 18. 31–43 | Ps. 27; 150<br>Exod. 24. 12–end<br>2 Cor. 3. 12–end | Ps. 2; [99]<br>1 Kings 19. 1–16<br>2 Pet. 1. 16–end |
| Ps. **47**; 49<br>Gen. 37. 1–11<br>Gal. ch. 1 | G | | Jer. ch. 1<br>John 3. 1–21 | Gen. 37. 1–11<br>Gal. ch. 1 |
| Ps. 50<br>Gen. 37. 12–end<br>Gal. 2. 1–10 | G | | Jer. 2. 1–13<br>John 3. 22–end | Gen. 37. 12–end<br>Gal. 2. 1–10 |
| *EP*: Ps. **51** or Ps. 102<br>(or 102. 1–18)<br>Isa. 1. 10–18<br>Luke 15. 11–end | P | **ASH WEDNESDAY**<br>Ash Wed. Collect until 4 April<br>Commination<br>Joel 2. 12–17<br>Ps. 57<br>James 4. 1–10<br>Matt. 6. 16–21 | Ps. 38<br>Dan. 9. 3–6, 17–19<br>1 Tim. 6. 6–19 | Ps. 51 or Ps. 102<br>(or 102. 1–18)<br>Isa. 1. 10–18<br>Luke 15. 11–end |
| Ps. 74<br>*alt*. Ps. 61; **62**; 64<br>Gen. ch. 39<br>Gal. 2. 11–end | P | Exod. 24. 12–end<br>Matt. 8. 5–13 | Jer. 2. 14–32<br>John 4. 1–26 | Gen. ch. 39<br>Gal. 2. 11–end |
| Ps. 31<br>*alt*. Ps. 38<br>Gen. ch. 40<br>Gal. 3. 1–14 | P | 1 Kings 19. 3b–8<br>Matt. 5.43 – 6.6 | Jer. 3. 6–22<br>John 4. 27–42 | Gen. ch. 40<br>Gal. 3. 1–14 |
| Ps. 73<br>*alt*. Ps. 65; **66**<br>Gen. 41. 1–24<br>Gal. 3. 15–22<br>ct | P | Isa. 38. 1–6a<br>Mark 6. 45–end | Jer. 4. 1–18<br>John 4. 43–end | Gen. 41. 1–24<br>Gal. 3. 15–22<br><br>ct |
| Ps. 119. 17–32<br>Gen. 2. 15–17; 3. 1–7<br>Rom. 5. 12–19<br>*or* Luke 13. 31–end | P | **THE FIRST SUNDAY IN LENT**<br>Collect<br>(1) Lent 1<br>(2) Ash Wednesday<br>Ember until 3 March<br>Gen. 3. 1–6<br>Ps. 91. 1–12<br>2 Cor. 6. 1–10<br>Matt. 4. 1–11 | Ps. 77<br>Exod. 34. 1–10<br>Rom. 10. 8b–13 | Ps. 119. 17–32<br>Gen. 2. 15–17; 3. 1–7<br>Rom. 5. 12–19<br>*or* Luke 13. 31–end |

# February 2015

| | | Sunday Principal Service<br>Weekday Eucharist | Third Service<br>Morning Prayer |
|---|---|---|---|

| **23** | M | **Polycarp, Bishop of Smyrna, Martyr, c. 155**<br>Com. Martyr                                  *or*<br>*also* Rev. 2. 8–11 | Lev. 19. 1–2, 11–18<br>Ps. 19. 7–end<br>Matt. 25. 31–end | Ps. 10; *11*<br>*alt.* Ps. 71<br>Jer. 4. 19–end<br>John 5. 1–18 |
|---|---|---|---|---|
| | **Pr** | | | |
| **24** | Tu* | | Isa. 55. 10–11<br>Ps. 34. 4–6, 21–22<br>Matt. 6. 7–15 | Ps. 44<br>*alt.* Ps. 73<br>Jer. 5. 1–19<br>John 5. 19–29 |
| | **P** | | | |
| **25** | W | Ember Day** | Jonah ch. 3<br>Ps. 51. 1–5, 17–18<br>Luke 11. 29–32 | Ps. **6**; 17<br>*alt.* Ps. 77<br>Jer. 5. 20–end<br>John 5. 30–end |
| | **P** | | | |
| **26** | Th | | Esther 14. 1–5, 12–14<br>*or* Isa. 55. 6–9<br>Ps. 138<br>Matt. 7. 7–12 | Ps. **42**; 43<br>*alt.* Ps. 78. 1–39†<br>Jer. 6. 9–21<br>John 6. 1–15 |
| | **P** | | | |
| **27** | F | **George Herbert, Priest, Poet, 1633**<br>Ember Day**<br>Com. Pastor                                *or*<br>*esp.* Mal. 2. 5–7<br>Matt. 11. 25–end | Ezek. 18. 21–28<br>Ps. 130<br>Matt. 5. 20–26 | Ps. 22<br>*alt.* Ps. 55<br>Jer. 6. 22–end<br>John 6. 16–27 |
| | **Pw** | *also* Rev. 19. 5–9 | | |
| **28** | Sa | Ember Day** | Deut. 26. 16–end<br>Ps. 119. 1–8<br>Matt. 5. 43–end | Ps. 59; **63**<br>*alt.* Ps. **76**; 79<br>Jer. 7. 1–20<br>John 6. 27–40 |
| | **P** | | | |

# March 2015

| **1** | S | THE SECOND SUNDAY OF LENT | Gen. 17. 1–7, 15–16<br>Ps. 22. 23–end<br>Rom. 4. 13–end<br>Mark 8. 31–end | Ps. 105. 1–6, 37–end<br>Isa. 51. 1–11<br>Gal. 3. 1–9, 23–end |
|---|---|---|---|---|
| | **P** | | | |
| **2** | M | **Chad, Bishop of Lichfield, Missionary, 672***<br>Com. Missionary                          *or*<br>*also* 1 Tim. 6. 11b–16 | Dan. 9. 4–10<br>Ps. 79. 8–9, 12, 14<br>Luke 6. 36–38 | Ps. 26; **32**<br>*alt.* Ps. **80**; 82<br>Jer. 7. 21–end<br>John 6. 41–51 |
| | **Pw** | | | |
| **3** | Tu | | Isa. 1. 10, 16–20<br>Ps. 50. 8, 16–end<br>Matt. 23. 1–12 | Ps. 50<br>*alt.* Ps. 87; **89. 1–18**<br>Jer. 8. 1–15<br>John 6. 52–59 |
| | **P** | | | |
| **4** | W | | Jer. 18. 18–20<br>Ps. 31. 4–5, 14–18<br>Matt. 20. 17–28 | Ps. 35<br>*alt.* Ps. 119. 105–128<br>Jer. 8.18 – 9.11<br>John 6. 60–end |
| | **P** | | | |
| **5** | Th | | Jer. 17. 5–10<br>Ps. 1<br>Luke 16. 19–end | Ps. 34<br>*alt.* Ps. 90; **92**<br>Jer. 9. 12–24<br>John 7. 1–13 |
| | **P** | | | |

*Matthias may be celebrated on 24 February instead of 15 May.
**For Ember Day provision, see p. 11.
***Chad may be celebrated with Cedd on 26 October instead of 2 March.

| Second Service Evening Prayer | | Calendar and Holy Communion | Morning Prayer | Evening Prayer |
|---|---|---|---|---|
| Ps. 12; *13*; 14<br>*alt.* Ps. *72*; 75<br>Gen. 41. 25–45<br>Gal. 3.23 – 4.7 | P | Ezek. 34. 11–16a<br>Matt. 25. 31–end | Jer. 4. 19–end<br>John 5. 1–18 | Gen. 41. 25–45<br>Gal. 3.23 – 4.7<br>*or First EP of Matthias*<br>(Ps. 147)<br>Isa. 22. 15–22<br>Phil. 3.13b – 4.1<br>**R ct** |
| Ps. 46; *49*<br>*alt.* Ps. 74<br>Gen. 41.46 – 42.5<br>Gal. 4. 8–20 | R | **MATTHIAS THE APOSTLE**<br>I Sam. 2. 27–35<br>Ps. 16. 1–7<br>Acts 1. 15–end<br>Matt. 1. 25–end | (Ps. 15)<br>Jonah 1. 1–9<br>Acts 2. 37–end | (Ps. 80)<br>I Sam. 16. 1–13a<br>Matt. 7. 15–27 |
| Ps. 9; *28*<br>*alt.* Ps. 119. 81–104<br>Gen. 42. 6–17<br>Gal. 4.21 – 5.1 | P | Ember Day<br>Ember CEG *or*<br>Isa. 58. 1–9a<br>Matt. 12. 38–end | Jer. 5. 20–end<br>John 5. 30–end | Gen. 42. 6–17<br>Gal. 4.21 – 5.1 |
| Ps. 137; 138; *142*<br>*alt.* Ps. 78. 40–end†<br>Gen. 42. 18–28<br>Gal. 5. 2–15 | P | Isa. 58. 9b–end<br>John 8. 31–45 | Jer. 6. 9–21<br>John 6. 1–15 | Gen. 42. 18–28<br>Gal. 5. 2–15 |
| Ps. 54; *55*<br>*alt.* Ps. 69<br>Gen. 42. 29–end<br>Gal. 5. 16–end | P | Ember Day<br>Ember CEG *or*<br>Ezek. 18. 20–25<br>John 5. 2–15 | Jer. 6. 22–end<br>John 6. 16–27 | Gen. 42. 29–end<br>Gal. 5. 16–end |
| Ps. *4*; 16<br>*alt.* Ps. 81; *84*<br>Gen. 43. 1–15<br>Gal. ch. 6<br>ct | P | Ember Day<br>Ember CEG *or*<br>Ezek. 18. 26–end<br>Matt. 17. 1–9<br>*or* Luke 4. 16–21<br>*or* John 10. 1–16 | Jer. 7. 1–20<br>John 6. 27–40 | Gen. 43. 1–15<br>Gal. ch. 6<br><br>ct |
| Ps. 135 (*or* 135. 1–14)<br>Gen. 12. 1–9<br>Heb. 11. 1–3, 8–16<br>*Gospel:* John 8. 51–end | P | **THE SECOND SUNDAY IN LENT**<br>Jer. 17. 5–10<br>Ps. 25. 13–end<br>I Thess. 4. 1–8<br>Matt. 15. 21–28 | Ps. 105. 1–6, 37–end<br>Isa. 51. 1–11<br>Gal. 3. 1–9, 23–end | Ps. 135 (*or* 135. 1–14)<br>Gen. 12. 1–9<br>Heb. 11. 1–3, 8–16 |
| Ps. 70; *74*<br>*alt.* Ps. *85*; 86<br>Gen. 43. 16–end<br>Heb. ch. 1 | Pw | **Chad, Bishop of Lichfield, Missionary, 672**<br>Com. Bishop *or*<br>Heb. 2. 1–10<br>John 8. 21–30 | Jer. 7. 21–end<br>John 6. 41–51 | Gen. 43. 16–end<br>Heb. ch. 1 |
| Ps. *52*; 53; 54<br>*alt.* Ps. 89. 19–end<br>Gen. 44. 1–17<br>Heb. 2. 1–9 | P | Heb. 2. 11–end<br>Matt. 23. 1–12 | Jer. 8. 1–15<br>John 6. 52–59 | Gen. 44. 1–17<br>Heb. 2. 1–9 |
| Ps. *3*; 51<br>*alt.* Ps. *91*; 93<br>Gen. 44. 18–end<br>Heb. 2. 10–end | P | Heb. 3. 1–6<br>Matt. 20. 17–28 | Jer. 8.18 – 9.11<br>John 6. 60–end | Gen. 44. 18–end<br>Heb. 2. 10–end |
| Ps. 71<br>*alt.* Ps. 94<br>Gen. 45. 1–15<br>Heb. 3. 1–6 | P | Heb. 3. 7–end<br>John 5. 30–end | Jer. 9. 12–24<br>John 7. 1–13 | Gen. 45. 1–15<br>Heb. 3. 1–6 |

# March 2015

| | | Sunday Principal Service<br>Weekday Eucharist | Third Service<br>Morning Prayer |
|---|---|---|---|
| **6** | F | Gen. 37. 3–4, 12–13, 17–28<br>Ps. 105. 16–22<br>Matt. 21. 33–43, 45–46 | Ps. 40; *41*<br>*alt.* Ps. *88*; (95)<br>Jer. 10. 1–16 |
| | P | | John 7. 14–24 |
| **7** | Sa | **Perpetua, Felicity and their Companions, Martyrs at Carthage, 203** | |
| | | Com. Martyr            *or*  Mic. 7. 14–15, 18–20<br>*esp.* Rev. 12. 10–12a       Ps. 103. 1–4, 9–12<br>*also* Wisd. 3. 1–7          Luke 15. 1–3, 11–end | Ps. 3; *25*<br>*alt.* Ps. 96; *97*; 100<br>Jer. 10. 17–24 |
| | Pr | | John 7. 25–36 |
| **8** | S | THE THIRD SUNDAY OF LENT | |
| | | Exod. 20. 1–17<br>Ps. 19 (*or* 19. 7–end)<br>1 Cor. 1. 18–25 | Ps. 18. 1–25<br>Jer. ch. 38<br>Phil. 1. 1–26 |
| | P | John 2. 13–22 | |
| **9** | M* | 2 Kings 5. 1–15<br>Ps. 42. 1–2; 43. 1–4<br>Luke 4. 24–30 | Ps. *5*; 7<br>*alt.* Ps. *98*; 99; 101<br>Jer. 11. 1–17 |
| | P | | John 7. 37–52 |
| **10** | Tu | Song of the Three 2, 11–20<br>*or* Dan. 2. 20–23<br>Ps. 25. 3–10<br>Matt. 18. 21–end | Ps. 6; *9*<br>*alt.* Ps. *106*† (*or* 103)<br>Jer. 11.18 – 12.6 |
| | P | | John 7.53 – 8.11 |
| **11** | W | Deut. 4. 1, 5–9<br>Ps. 147. 13–end<br>Matt. 5. 17–19 | Ps. 38<br>*alt.* Ps. 110; *111*; 112<br>Jer. 13. 1–11 |
| | P | | John 8. 12–30 |
| **12** | Th | Jer. 7. 23–28<br>Ps. 95. 1–2, 6–end<br>Luke 11. 14–23 | Ps. *56*; 57<br>*alt.* Ps. 113; *115*<br>Jer. ch. 14 |
| | P | | John 8. 31–47 |
| **13** | F | Hos. ch. 14<br>Ps. 81. 6–10, 13, 16<br>Mark 12. 28–34 | Ps. 22<br>*alt.* Ps. 139<br>Jer. 15. 10–end |
| | P | | John 8. 48–end |
| **14** | Sa | Hos. 5.15 – 6.6<br>Ps. 51. 1–2, 17–end<br>Luke 18. 9–14 | Ps. 31<br>*alt.* Ps. 120; *121*; 122<br>Jer. 16.10 – 17.4 |
| | P | | John 9. 1–17 |
| **15** | S | THE FOURTH SUNDAY OF LENT<br>(Mothering Sunday) | |
| | | Num. 21. 4–9<br>Ps. 107. 1–3, 17–22<br>(*or* 107. 1–9)<br>Eph. 2. 1–10<br>John 3. 14–21 | Ps. 27<br>1 Sam. 16. 1–13<br>John 9. 1–25 |
| | | *or, for Mothering Sunday:* | |
| | | Exod. 2. 1–10<br>*or* 1 Sam. 1. 20–end<br>Ps. 34. 11–20<br>*or* Ps. 127. 1–4<br>2 Cor. 1. 3–7<br>*or* Col. 3. 12–17<br>Luke 2. 33–35 | |
| | P | *or* John 19. 25b–27 | |

*The following readings may replace those provided for Holy Communion on any day during the Third Week of Lent: Exod. 17. 1–7; Ps. 95. 1–2, 6–end; John 4. 5–42.

| Second Service Evening Prayer | | Calendar and Holy Communion | Morning Prayer | Evening Prayer |
|---|---|---|---|---|
| Ps. *6*; 38<br>*alt.* Ps. 102<br>Gen. 45. 16–end<br>Heb. 3. 7–end | P | Heb. ch. 4<br>Matt. 21. 33–end | Jer. 10. 1–16<br>John 7. 14–24 | Gen. 45. 16–end<br>Heb. 3. 7–end |
| Ps. *23*; 27<br>*alt.* Ps. 104<br>Gen. 46. 1–7, 28–end<br>Heb. 4. 1–13<br>ct | Pr | **Perpetua, Felicity and their Companions, Martyrs at Carthage, 203**<br>Com. Martyr *or*<br>Heb. ch. 5<br>Luke 15. 11–end | Jer. 10. 17–24<br>John 7. 25–36 | Gen. 46. 1–7, 28–end<br>Heb. 4. 1–13<br><br>ct |
| Ps. 11; 12<br>Exod. 5.1 – 6.1<br>Phil. 3. 4b–14<br>*or* Matt. 10. 16–22 | P | **THE THIRD SUNDAY IN LENT**<br>Num. 22. 21–31<br>Ps. 9. 13–end<br>Eph. 5. 1–14<br>Luke 11. 14–28 | Ps. 18. 1–25<br>Jer. ch. 38<br>Phil. 1. 1–26 | Ps. 11; 12<br>Exod. 5.1 – 6.1<br>Phil. 3. 4b–14<br>*or* Matt. 10. 16–22 |
| Ps. 11; *17*<br>*alt.* Ps. *105*† (*or* 103)<br>Gen. 47. 1–27<br>Heb. 4.14 – 5.10 | P | Heb. 6. 1–10<br>Luke 4. 23–30 | Jer. 11. 1–17<br>John 7. 37–52 | Gen. 47. 1–27<br>Heb. 4.14 – 5.10 |
| Ps. 61; 62; *64*<br>*alt.* Ps. 107†<br>Gen. 47.28 – 48.end<br>Heb. 5.11 – 6.12 | P | Heb. 6. 11–end<br>Matt. 18. 15–22 | Jer. 11.18 – 12.6<br>John 7.53 – 8.11 | Gen. 47.28 – 48.end<br>Heb. 5.11 – 6.12 |
| Ps. 36; *39*<br>*alt.* Ps. 119. 129–152<br>Gen. 49. 1–32<br>Heb. 6. 13–end | P | Heb. 7. 1–10<br>Matt. 15. 1–20 | Jer. 13. 1–11<br>John 8. 12–30 | Gen. 49. 1–32<br>Heb. 6. 13–end |
| Ps. *59*; 60<br>*alt.* Ps. 114; *116*; 117<br>Gen. 49.33 – 50.end<br>Heb. 7. 1–10 | Pw | **Gregory the Great, Bishop of Rome, 604**<br>Com. Doctor *or*<br>Heb. 7. 11–25<br>John 6. 26–35 | Jer. ch. 14<br>John 8. 31–47 | Gen. 49.33 – 50.end<br>Heb. 7. 1–10 |
| Ps. 69<br>*alt.* Ps. *130*; 131; 137<br>Exod. 1. 1–14<br>Heb. 7. 11–end | P | Heb. 7. 26–end<br>John 4. 5–26 | Jer. 15. 10–end<br>John 8. 48–end | Exod. 1. 1–14<br>Heb. 7. 11–end |
| Ps. *116*; 130<br>*alt.* Ps. 118<br>Exod. 1.22 – 2.10<br>Heb. ch. 8<br>ct | P | Heb. 8. 1–6<br>John 8. 1–11 | Jer. 16.10 – 17.4<br>John 9. 1–17 | Exod. 1.22 – 2.10<br>Heb. ch. 8<br><br>ct |
| Ps. 13; 14<br>Exod. 6. 2–13<br>Rom. 5. 1–11<br>*Gospel:* John 12. 1–8<br>*If the Principal Service readings for The Fourth Sunday of Lent are displaced by Mothering Sunday provisions, they may be used at the Second Service.* | P | **THE FOURTH SUNDAY IN LENT**<br>To celebrate Mothering Sunday, see *Common Worship* provision.<br>Exod. 16. 2–7a<br>Ps. 122<br>Gal. 4. 21–end<br>*or* Heb. 12. 22–24<br>John 6. 1–14 | Ps. 27<br>1 Sam. 16. 1–13<br>John 9. 1–25 | Ps. 13; 14<br>Exod. 6. 2–13<br>Rom. 5. 1–11 |

# March 2015

| | | Sunday Principal Service<br>Weekday Eucharist | Third Service<br>Morning Prayer |
|---|---|---|---|

**16**  M*

Isa. 65. 17–21
Ps. 30. 1–5, 8, 11–end
John 4. 43–end

Ps. 70; **77**
*alt.* Ps. 123; 124; 125; **126**
Jer. 17. 5–18

P

John 9. 18–end

---

**17**  Tu  **Patrick, Bishop, Missionary, Patron of Ireland, c. 460**

Com. Missionary  or  Ezek. 47. 1–9, 12
*also* Ps. 91. 1–4, 13–end        Ps. 46. 1–8
Luke 10. 1–12, 17–20        John 5. 1–3, 5–16

Ps. 54; **79**
*alt.* Ps. **132**; 133
Jer. 18. 1–12

Pw

John 10. 1–10

---

**18**  W  *Cyril, Bishop of Jerusalem, Teacher, 386*

Isa. 49. 8–15
Ps. 145. 8–18
John 5. 17–30

Ps. **63**; 90
*alt.* Ps. 119. 153–end
Jer. 18. 13–end
John 10. 11–21

P

---

**19**  Th  JOSEPH OF NAZARETH

2 Sam. 7. 4–16
Ps. 89. 26–36
Rom. 4. 13–18

*MP*: Ps. 25; 147. 1–12
Isa. 11. 1–10
Matt. 13. 54–end

W

Matt. 1. 18–end

---

**20**  F  **Cuthbert, Bishop of Lindisfarne, Missionary, 687\*\***

Com. Missionary  or  Wisd. 2. 1, 12–22
*esp.* Ezek. 34. 11–16        *or* Jer. 26. 8–11
*also* Matt. 18. 12–14        Ps. 34. 15–end

Ps. 102
*alt.* Ps. 142; **144**
Jer. 19.14 – 20.6

Pw

John 7. 1–2, 10, 25–30

John 11. 1–16

---

**21**  Sa  **Thomas Cranmer, Archbishop of Canterbury, Reformation Martyr, 1556**

Com. Martyr  or  Jer. 11. 18–20
Ps. 7. 1–2, 8–10
John 7. 40–52

Ps. 32
*alt.* Ps. 147
Jer. 20. 7–end

Pr

John 11. 17–27

---

**22**  S  THE FIFTH SUNDAY OF LENT **(Passiontide begins)**

Jer. 31. 31–34
Ps. 51. 1–13
*or* Ps. 119. 9–16
Heb. 5. 5–10

Ps. 107. 1–22
Exod. 24. 3–8
Heb. 12. 18–end

P

John 12. 20–33

---

**23**  M\*\*\*

Susanna 1–9, 15–17, 19–30,
33–62 (or 41b–62)
*or* Josh. 2. 1–14
Ps. 23

Ps. **73**; 121
*alt.* Ps. **1**; 2; 3
Jer. 21. 1–10

P

John 8. 1–11

John 11. 28–44

---

**24**  Tu  *Walter Hilton of Thurgarton, Augustinian Canon, Mystic, 1396; Paul Couturier, Priest, Ecumenist, 1953;*
*Oscar Romero, Archbishop of San Salvador, Martyr, 1980*

Num. 21. 4–9
Ps. 102. 1–3, 16–23
John 8. 21–30

Ps. **35**; 123
*alt.* Ps. **5**; 6; (8)
Jer. 22. 1–5, 13–19
John 11. 45–end

P

---

\*The following readings may replace those provided for Holy Communion on any day (except St Joseph's Day) during the Fourth Week of Lent:
Mic. 7. 7–9; Ps. 27. 1, 9–10, 16–17; John ch. 9.
\*\*Cuthbert may be celebrated on 4 September instead of 20 March.
\*\*\*The following readings may replace those provided for Holy Communion on any day (except The Annunciation) during the Fifth Week of Lent:
2 Kings 4. 18–21, 32–37; Ps. 17. 1–8, 16; John 11. 1–45.

| Second Service<br>Evening Prayer | | Calendar and Holy Communion | Morning Prayer | Evening Prayer |
|---|---|---|---|---|
| Ps. *25*; 28<br>alt. Ps. *127*; 128; 129<br>Exod. 2. 11–22<br>Heb. 9. 1–14 | P | Heb. 11. 1–6<br>John 2. 13–end | Jer. 17. 5–18<br>John 9. 18–end | Exod. 2. 11–22<br>Heb. 9. 1–14 |
| Ps. *80*; 82<br>alt. Ps. (134); *135*<br>Exod. 2.23 – 3.20<br>Heb. 9. 15–end | P | Heb. 11. 13–16a<br>John 7. 14–24 | Jer. 18. 1–12<br>John 10. 1–10 | Exod. 2.23 – 3.20<br>Heb. 9. 15–end |
| Ps. 52; *91*<br>alt. Ps. 136<br>Exod. 4. 1–23<br>Heb. 10. 1–18<br>or First EP of Joseph<br>Ps. 132<br>Hos. 11. 1–9<br>Luke 2. 41–end<br>**W ct** | Pr | **Edward, King of the West Saxons, 978**<br>Com. Martyr *or*<br>Heb. 12. 1–11<br>John 9. 1–17 | Jer. 18. 13–end<br>John 10. 11–21 | Exod. 4. 1–23<br>Heb. 10. 1–18 |
| EP: Ps. 1; 112<br>Gen. 50. 22–end<br>Matt. 2. 13–end | P | To celebrate Joseph, see *Common Worship* provision.<br>Heb. 12. 12–17<br>John 5. 17–27 | Jer. 19. 1–13<br>John 10. 22–end | Exod. 4.27 – 6.1<br>Heb. 10. 19–25 |
| Ps. 13; *16*<br>alt. Ps. 145<br>Exod. 6. 2–13<br>Heb. 10. 26–end | P | Heb. 12. 22–end<br>John 11. 33–46 | Jer. 19.14 – 20.6<br>John 11. 1–16 | Exod. 6. 2–13<br>Heb. 10. 26–end |
| Ps. *140*; 141; 142<br>alt. Ps. *148*; 149; 150<br>Exod. 7. 8–end<br>Heb. 11. 1–16<br>ct | Pw | **Benedict, Abbot of Monte Cassino, c. 550**<br>Com. Abbot *or*<br>Heb. 13. 17–21<br>John 8. 12–20 | Jer. 20. 7–end<br>John 11. 17–27 | Exod. 7. 8–end<br>Heb. 11. 1–16<br><br>ct |
| Ps. 34 (*or* 34. 1–10)<br>Exod. 7. 8–24<br>Rom. 5. 12–end<br>*Gospel*: Luke 22. 1–13 | P | THE FIFTH SUNDAY IN LENT<br>Exod. 24. 4–8<br>Ps. 143<br>Heb. 9. 11–15<br>John 8. 46–end | Ps. 107. 1–22<br>Jer. 31. 31–34<br>Heb. 5. 5–10 | Ps. 34 (*or* 34. 1–10)<br>Exod. 7. 8–24<br>Rom. 5. 12–end |
| Ps. *26*; 27<br>alt. Ps. *4*; 7<br>Exod. 8. 1–19<br>Heb. 11. 17–31 | P | Col. 1. 13–23a<br>John 7. 1–13 | Jer. 21. 1–10<br>John 11. 28–44 | Exod. 8. 1–19<br>Heb. 11. 17–31 |
| *First EP of The Annunciation*<br>Ps. 85<br>Wisd. 9. 1–12<br>*or* Gen. 3. 8–15<br>Gal. 4. 1–5<br><br>℘ **ct** | P | Col. 2. 8–12<br>John 7. 32–39 | Jer. 22. 1–5, 13–19<br>John 11. 45–end | *First EP of The<br>Annunciation*<br>Ps. 85<br>Wisd. 9. 1–12<br>*or* Gen. 3. 8–15<br>Gal. 4. 1–5<br>℘ **ct** |

# March 2015

| | | | Sunday Principal Service<br>Weekday Eucharist | Third Service<br>Morning Prayer |
|---|---|---|---|---|

| | | | | |
|---|---|---|---|---|
| **25** | W | **THE ANNUNCIATION OF OUR LORD TO THE BLESSED VIRGIN MARY** | Isa. 7. 10–14<br>Ps. 40. 5–11<br>Heb. 10. 4–10<br>Luke 1. 26–38 | MP: Ps. 111; 113<br>1 Sam. 2. 1–10<br>Rom. 5. 12–end |
| | ⅏ | | | |
| **26** | Th | *Harriet Monsell, Founder of the Community of St John the Baptist, Clewer, 1883* | Gen. 17. 3–9<br>Ps. 105. 4–9<br>John 8. 51–end | Ps. *40*; 125<br>*alt.* Ps. 14; *15*; 16<br>Jer. 23. 9–32<br>John 12. 12–19 |
| | P | | | |
| **27** | F | | Jer. 20. 10–13<br>Ps. 18. 1–6<br>John 10. 31–end | Ps. *22*; 126<br>*alt.* Ps. 17; *19*<br>Jer. ch. 24<br>John 12. 20–36a |
| | P | | | |
| **28** | Sa | | Ezek. 37. 21–end<br>*Canticle:* Jer. 31. 10–13<br>*or* Ps. 121<br>John 11. 45–end | Ps. *23*; 127<br>*alt.* Ps. 20; 21; *23*<br>Jer. 25. 1–14<br>John 12. 36b–end |
| | P | | | |
| **29** | S | PALM SUNDAY<br>*Liturgy of the Palms*<br>Mark 11. 1–11<br>*or* John 12. 12–16<br>Ps. 118. 1–2, 19–end<br>(*or* 118. 19–end) | *Liturgy of the Passion*<br>Isa. 50. 4–9a<br>Ps. 31. 9–16 (*or* 31. 9–18)<br>Phil. 2. 5–11<br>Mark 14.1 – 15.end<br>*or* Mark 15. 1–39 [40–end] | Ps. 61; 62<br>Zech. 9. 9–12<br>1 Cor. 2. 1–12 |
| | R | | | |
| **30** | M | MONDAY OF HOLY WEEK | Isa. 42. 1–9<br>Ps. 36. 5–11<br>Heb. 9. 11–15<br>John 12. 1–11 | MP: Ps. 41<br>Lam. 1. 1–12a<br>Luke 22. 1–23 |
| | R | | | |
| **31** | Tu | TUESDAY OF HOLY WEEK | Isa. 49. 1–7<br>Ps. 71. 1–14 (*or* 71. 1–8)<br>1 Cor. 1. 18–31<br>John 12. 20–36 | MP: Ps. 27<br>Lam. 3. 1–18<br>Luke 22. [24–38] 39–53 |
| | R | | | |

# April 2015

| | | | | |
|---|---|---|---|---|
| **1** | W | WEDNESDAY OF HOLY WEEK | Isa. 50. 4–9a<br>Ps. 70<br>Heb. 12. 1–3<br>John 13. 21–32 | MP: Ps. 102 (*or* 102. 1–18)<br>Wisd. 1.16 – 2.1, 12–22<br>*or* Jer. 11. 18–20<br>Luke 22. 54–end |
| | R | | | |
| **2** | Th | **MAUNDY THURSDAY** | Exod. 12. 1–14<br>(*or* 12. 1–4, 11–14)<br>Ps. 116. 1, 10–end<br>(*or* 116. 9–end)<br>1 Cor. 11. 23–26<br>John 13. 1–17, 31b–35 | MP: Ps. 42; 43<br>Lev. 16. 2–24<br>Luke 23. 1–25 |
| | W (HC) R | | | |
| **3** | F | **GOOD FRIDAY** | Isa. 52.13 – 53.end<br>Ps. 22 (*or* 22. 1–11 *or* 22. 1–21)<br>Heb. 10. 16–25<br>*or* Heb. 4. 14–16; 5. 7–9<br>John 18.1 – 19.end | MP: Ps. 69<br>Gen. 22. 1–18<br>A part of John 18 – 19 if<br>not read at the Principal<br>Service<br>*or* Heb. 10. 1–10 |
| | R | | | |

| Second Service Evening Prayer | | Calendar and Holy Communion | Morning Prayer | Evening Prayer |
|---|---|---|---|---|
| | | **THE ANNUNCIATION OF THE BLESSED VIRGIN MARY** | | |
| EP: Ps. 131; 146 Isa. 52. 1–12 Heb. 2. 5–end | ℣ | Isa. 7. 10–14 [15] Ps. 113 Rom. 5. 12–19 Luke 1. 26–38 | Ps. 111 I Sam. 2. 1–10 Heb. 10. 4–10 | Ps. 131; 146 Isa. 52. 1–12 Heb. 2. 5–end |
| Ps. 42; *43* *alt.* Ps. 18† Exod. 9. 13–end Heb. 12. 14–end | P | Col. 3. 8–11 John 10. 22–38 | Jer. 23. 9–32 John 12. 12–19 | Exod. 9. 13–end Heb. 12. 14–end |
| Ps. 31 *alt.* Ps. 22 Exod. ch. 10 Heb. 13. 1–16 | P | Col. 3. 12–17 John 11. 47–54 | Jer. ch. 24 John 12. 20–36a | Exod. ch. 10 Heb. 13. 1–16 |
| Ps. 128; 129; *130* *alt.* Ps. *24*; 25 Exod. ch. 11 Heb. 13. 17–end ct | P | Col. 4. 2–6 John 6. 53–end | Jer. 25. 1–14 John 12. 36b–end | Exod. ch. 11 Heb. 13. 17–end ct |
| | | **THE SUNDAY NEXT BEFORE EASTER** (PALM SUNDAY) | | |
| Ps. 69. 1–20 Isa. 5. 1–7 Mark 12. 1–12 | R | Zech. 9. 9–12 Ps. 73. 22–end Phil. 2. 5–11 Passion acc. to Matthew Matt. 27. 1–54 *or* Matt. 26.1 – 27.61 *or* Matt. 21. 1–13 | Ps. 61; 62 Isa. 42. 1–9 I Cor. 2. 1–12 | Ps. 69. 1–20 Isa. 5. 1–7 Mark 12. 1–12 |
| | | **MONDAY IN HOLY WEEK** | | |
| EP: Ps. 25 Lam. 2. 8–19 Col. 1. 18–23 | R | Isa. 63. 1–19 Ps. 55. 1–8 Gal. 6. 1–11 Mark ch. 14 | Ps. 41 Lam. 1. 1–12a John 12. 1–11 | Ps. 25 Lam. 2. 8–19 Col. 1. 18–23 |
| | | **TUESDAY IN HOLY WEEK** | | |
| EP: Ps. 55. 13–24 Lam. 3. 40–51 Gal. 6. 11–end | R | Isa. 50. 5–11 Ps. 13 Rom. 5. 6–19 Mark 15. 1–39 | Ps. 27 Lam. 3. 1–18 John 12. 20–36 | Ps. 55. 13–24 Lam. 3. 40–51 Gal. 6. 11–end |
| | | **WEDNESDAY IN HOLY WEEK** | | |
| EP: Ps. 88 Isa. 63. 1–9 Rev. 14.18 – 15.4 | R | Isa. 49. 1–9a Ps. 54 Heb. 9. 16–end Luke ch. 22 | Ps. 102 (*or* 102. 1–18) Wisd. 1.16 – 2.1, 12–22 *or* Jer. 11. 18–20 John 13. 21–32 | Ps. 88 Isa. 63. 1–9 Rev. 14.18 – 15.4 |
| | | **MAUNDY THURSDAY** | | |
| EP: Ps. 39 Exod. ch. 11 Eph. 2. 11–18 | W (HC) R | Exod. 12. 1–11 Ps. 43 I Cor. 11. 17–end Luke 23. 1–49 | Ps. 42; 43 Lev. 16. 2–24 John 13. 1–17, 31b–35 | Ps. 39 Exod. ch. 11 Eph. 2. 11–18 |
| | | **GOOD FRIDAY** | | |
| EP: Ps. 130; 143 Lam. 5. 15–end A part of John 18 – 19 if not read at the Principal Service, especially John 19. 38–end *or* Col. 1. 18–23 | R | Alt. Collect Passion acc. to John Alt. Gospel, if Passion is read Num. 21. 4–9 Ps. 140. 1–9 Heb. 10. 1–25 John 19. 1–37 *or* John 19. 38–end | Ps. 69 Gen. 22. 1–18 John ch. 18 | Ps. 130; 143 Lam. 5. 15–end John 19. 38–end |

# April 2015

| | | | Sunday Principal Service<br>Weekday Eucharist | Third Service<br>Morning Prayer |
|---|---|---|---|---|
| **4** | Sa | **EASTER EVE**<br>*These readings are for use at services<br>other than the Easter Vigil.* | Job 14. 1–14<br>or Lam. 3. 1–9, 19–24<br>Ps. 31. 1–4, 15–16 (or 31. 1–5)<br>1 Pet. 4. 1–8<br>Matt. 27. 57–end<br>or John 19. 38–end | Ps. 142<br>Hos. 6. 1–6<br>John 2. 18–22 |
| **5** | S | **EASTER DAY**<br>*The following readings and psalms<br>(or canticles) are provided for use at<br>the Easter Vigil. A minimum of three<br>Old Testament readings should be<br>chosen. The reading from Exodus<br>ch. 14 should always be used.* | Gen. 1.1 – 2.4a & Ps. 136. 1–9,<br>23–end<br>Gen. 7. 1–5, 11–18; 8. 6–18;<br>9. 8–13 & Ps. 46<br>Gen. 22. 1–18 & Ps. 16<br>Exod. 14. 10–end; 15. 20–21 &<br>*Canticle:* Exod. 15. 1b–13, 17–18<br>Isa. 55. 1–11 & *Canticle:* Isa.<br>12. 2–end<br>Baruch 3.9–15, 32 – 4.4 &<br>Ps. 19 or<br>Prov. 8. 1–8, 19–21;<br>9. 4b–6 & Ps. 19<br>Ezek. 36. 24–28 & Ps. 42; 43<br>Ezek. 37. 1–14 & Ps. 143<br>Zeph. 3. 14–end & Ps. 98<br>Rom. 6. 3–11 & Ps. 114<br>Mark 16. 1–8 | |
| | | *Easter Day Services*<br>*The reading from Acts must be used<br>as either the first or second reading<br>at the Principal Service.* | Acts 10. 34–43<br>or Isa. 25. 6–9<br>Ps. 118. 1–2, 14–24<br>(or 118. 14–24)<br>1 Cor. 15. 1–11<br>or Acts 10. 34–43<br>John 20. 1–18<br>or Mark 16. 1–8 | MP: Ps. 114; 117<br>Gen. 1. 1–5, 26–end<br>2 Cor. 5.14 – 6.2 |
| **6** | M | MONDAY OF EASTER WEEK<br>W | Acts 2. 14, 22–32<br>Ps. 16. 1–2, 6–end<br>Matt. 28. 8–15 | Ps. *111*; 117; 146<br>Song of Sol. 1.9 – 2.7<br>Mark 16. 1–8 |
| **7** | Tu | TUESDAY OF EASTER WEEK<br>W | Acts 2. 36–41<br>Ps. 33. 4–5, 18–end<br>John 20. 11–18 | Ps. *112*; 147. 1–12<br>Song of Sol. 2. 8–end<br>Luke 24. 1–12 |
| **8** | W | WEDNESDAY OF EASTER WEEK<br>W | Acts 3. 1–10<br>Ps. 105. 1–9<br>Luke 24. 13–35 | Ps. *113*; 147. 13–end<br>Song of Sol. ch. 3<br>Matt. 28. 16–end |
| **9** | Th | THURSDAY OF EASTER WEEK<br>W | Acts 3. 11–end<br>Ps. 8<br>Luke 24. 35–48 | Ps. *114*; 148<br>Song of Sol. 5.2 – 6.3<br>Luke 7. 11–17 |
| **10** | F | FRIDAY OF EASTER WEEK<br>W | Acts 4. 1–12<br>Ps. 118. 1–4, 22–26<br>John 21. 1–14 | Ps. *115*; 149<br>Song of Sol. 7.10 – 8.4<br>Luke 8. 41–end |
| **11** | Sa | SATURDAY OF EASTER WEEK<br>W | Acts 4. 13–21<br>Ps. 118. 1–4, 14–21<br>Mark 16. 9–15 | Ps. *116*; 150<br>Song of Sol. 8. 5–7<br>John 11. 17–44 |

| Second Service Evening Prayer | | Calendar and Holy Communion | Morning Prayer | Evening Prayer |
|---|---|---|---|---|
| Ps. 116<br>Job 19. 21–27<br>1 John 5. 5–12 | | **EASTER EVE**<br>Job 14. 1–14<br>1 Pet. 3. 17–22<br>Matt. 27. 57–end | Ps. 142<br>Hos. 6. 1–6<br>John 2. 18–22 | Ps. 116<br>Job 19. 21–27<br>1 John 5. 5–12 |
| | | **EASTER DAY**<br>Exod. 12. 21–28<br>Ps. 111<br>Col. 3. 1–7<br>John 20. 1–10 | Ps. 114; 117<br>Gen. 1. 1–5, 26–end<br>2 Cor. 5.14 – 6.2 | Ps. 105<br>or Ps. 66. 1–11<br>Isa. 25. 6–9<br>Luke 24. 13–35 |
| *EP*: Ps. 105<br>or Ps. 66. 1–11<br>Ezek. 37. 1–14<br>Luke 24. 13–35 | | | | |
| | ℟ | | | |
| Ps. 135<br>Exod. 12. 1–14<br>1 Cor. 15. 1–11 | W | **MONDAY IN EASTER WEEK**<br>Hos. 6. 1–6<br>Easter Anthems<br>Acts 10. 34–43<br>Luke 24. 13–35 | Song of Sol. 1.9 – 2.7<br>Mark 16. 1–8 | Exod. 12. 1–14<br>1 Cor. 15. 1–11 |
| Ps. 136<br>Exod. 12. 14–36<br>1 Cor. 15. 12–19 | W | **TUESDAY IN EASTER WEEK**<br>1 Kings 17. 17–end<br>Ps. 16. 9–end<br>Acts 13. 26–41<br>Luke 24. 36b–48 | Song of Sol. 2. 8–end<br>Luke 24. 1–12 | Exod. 12. 14–36<br>1 Cor. 15. 12–19 |
| Ps. 105<br>Exod. 12. 37–end<br>1 Cor. 15. 20–28 | W | Isa. 42. 10–16<br>Ps. 111<br>Acts 3. 12–18<br>John 20. 11–18 | Song of Sol. ch. 3<br>Matt. 28. 16–end | Exod. 12. 37–end<br>1 Cor. 15. 20–28 |
| Ps. 106<br>Exod. 13. 1–16<br>1 Cor. 15. 29–34 | W | Isa. 43. 16–21<br>Ps. 113<br>Acts 8. 26–end<br>John 21. 1–14 | Song of Sol. 5.2 – 6.3<br>Luke 7. 11–17 | Exod. 13. 1–16<br>1 Cor. 15. 29–34 |
| Ps. 107<br>Exod. 13.17 – 14.14<br>1 Cor. 15. 35–50 | W | Ezek. 37. 1–14<br>Ps. 116. 1–9<br>1 Pet. 3. 18–end<br>Matt. 28. 16–end | Song of Sol. 7.10 – 8.4<br>Luke 8. 41–end | Exod. 13.17 – 14.14<br>1 Cor. 15. 35–50 |
| Ps. 145<br>Exod. 14. 15–end<br>1 Cor. 15. 51–end<br>ct | W | Zech. 8. 1–8<br>Ps. 118. 14–21<br>1 Pet. 2. 1–10<br>John 20. 24–end | Song of Sol. 8. 5–7<br>John 11. 17–44 | Exod. 14. 15–end<br>1 Cor. 15. 51–end<br><br>ct |

# April 2015

| | | | Sunday Principal Service<br>Weekday Eucharist | Third Service<br>Morning Prayer |
|---|---|---|---|---|
| **12** | S | **THE SECOND SUNDAY OF EASTER**<br>*The reading from Acts must be used<br>as either the first or second reading<br>at the Principal Service.* | Acts 4. 32–35<br>[or Exod. 14. 10–end;<br>15. 20–21]<br>Ps. 133<br>1 John 1.1 – 2.2 | Ps. 22. 20–31<br>Isa. 53. 6–12<br>Rom. 4. 13–25 |
| | W | | John 20. 19–end | |
| **13** | M | | Acts 4. 23–31<br>Ps. 2. 1–9<br>John 3. 1–8 | Ps. 2; *19*<br>*alt*. Ps. *1*; 2; 3<br>Deut. 1. 3–18 |
| | W | | | John 20. 1–10 |
| **14** | Tu | | Acts 4. 32–end<br>Ps. 93<br>John 3. 7–15 | Ps. *8*; 20; 21<br>*alt*. Ps. *5*; 6; (8)<br>Deut. 1. 19–40 |
| | W | | | John 20. 11–18 |
| **15** | W | | Acts 5. 17–26<br>Ps. 34. 1–8<br>John 3. 16–21 | Ps. 16; *30*<br>*alt*. Ps. 119. 1–32<br>Deut. 3. 18–end |
| | W | | | John 20. 19–end |
| **16** | Th | *Isabella Gilmore, Deaconess, 1923*<br><br>Acts 5. 27–33<br>Ps. 34. 1, 15–end<br>John 3. 31–end | | Ps. *28*; 29<br>*alt*. Ps. 14; *15*; 16<br>Deut. 4. 1–14 |
| | W | | | John 21. 1–14 |
| **17** | F | | Acts 5. 34–42<br>Ps. 27. 1–5, 16–17<br>John 6. 1–15 | Ps. 57; *61*<br>*alt*. Ps. 17; *19*<br>Deut. 4. 15–31 |
| | W | | | John 21. 15–19 |
| **18** | Sa | | Acts 6. 1–7<br>Ps. 33. 1–5, 18–19<br>John 6. 16–21 | Ps. 63; *84*<br>*alt*. Ps. 20; 21; *23*<br>Deut. 4. 32–40 |
| | W | | | John 21. 20–end |
| **19** | S | **THE THIRD SUNDAY OF EASTER**<br>*The reading from Acts must be used<br>as either the first or second reading<br>at the Principal Service.* | Acts 3. 12–19<br>[or Zeph. 3. 14–end]<br>Ps. 4<br>1 John 3. 1–7 | Ps. 77. 11–20<br>Isa. 63. 7–15<br>1 Cor. 10. 1–13 |
| | W | | Luke 24. 36b–48 | |
| **20** | M | | Acts 6. 8–15<br>Ps. 119. 17–24<br>John 6. 22–29 | Ps. *96*; 97<br>*alt*. Ps. 27; *30*<br>Deut. 5. 1–22 |
| | W | | | Eph. 1. 1–14 |
| **21** | Tu | **Anselm, Abbot of Le Bec, Archbishop of Canterbury, Teacher, 1109**<br>Com. Teacher           *or*   Acts 7.51 – 8.1a<br>*also* Wisd. 9. 13–end        Ps. 31. 1–5, 16<br>Rom. 5. 8–11           John 6. 30–35 | | Ps. *98*; 99; 100<br>*alt*. Ps. 32; *36*<br>Deut. 5. 22–end |
| | W | | | Eph. 1. 15–end |
| **22** | W | | Acts 8. 1b–8<br>Ps. 66. 1–6<br>John 6. 35–40 | Ps. 105<br>*alt*. Ps. 34<br>Deut. ch. 6 |
| | | | | Eph. 2. 1–10 |
| | W | | | |
| **23** | Th | **GEORGE, MARTYR, PATRON OF ENGLAND, c. 304**<br><br>1 Macc. 2. 59–64<br>or Rev. 12. 7–12<br>Ps. 126<br>2 Tim. 2. 3–13 | | MP: Ps. 5; 146<br>Josh. 1. 1–9<br>Eph. 6. 10–20 |
| | R | | John 15. 18–21 | |

| Second Service Evening Prayer | | Calendar and Holy Communion | Morning Prayer | Evening Prayer |
|---|---|---|---|---|
| Ps. 143. 1–11<br>Isa. 26. 1–9, 19<br>Luke 24. 1–12 | | **THE FIRST SUNDAY AFTER EASTER**<br>Ezek. 37. 1–10<br>Ps. 81. 1–4<br>1 John 5. 4–12<br>John 20. 19–23 | Ps. 22. 20–31<br>Isa. 53. 6–12<br>Rom. 4. 13–25 | Ps. 143. 1–11<br>Isa. 26. 1–9, 19<br>Luke 24. 1–12 |
| | W | | | |
| Ps. 139<br>alt. Ps. 4; 7<br>Exod. 15. 1–21<br>Col. 1. 1–14 | W | | Deut. 1. 3–18<br>John 20. 1–10 | Exod. 15. 1–21<br>Col. 1. 1–14 |
| Ps. 104<br>alt. Ps. 9; 10†<br>Exod. 15.22 – 16.10<br>Col. 1. 15–end | W | | Deut. 1. 19–40<br>John 20. 11–18 | Exod. 15.22 – 16.10<br>Col. 1. 15–end |
| Ps. 33<br>alt. Ps. 11; 12; 13<br>Exod. 16. 11–end<br>Col. 2. 1–15 | W | | Deut. 3. 18–end<br>John 20. 19–end | Exod. 16. 11–end<br>Col. 2. 1–15 |
| Ps. 34<br>alt. Ps. 18†<br>Exod. ch. 17<br>Col. 2.16 – 3.11 | W | | Deut. 4. 1–14<br>John 21. 1–14 | Exod. ch. 17<br>Col. 2.16 – 3.11 |
| Ps. 118<br>alt. Ps. 22<br>Exod. 18. 1–12<br>Col. 3.12 – 4.1 | W | | Deut. 4. 15–31<br>John 21. 15–19 | Exod. 18. 1–12<br>Col. 3.12 – 4.1 |
| Ps. 66<br>alt. Ps. 24; 25<br>Exod. 18. 13–end<br>Col. 4. 2–end<br>**ct** | W | | Deut. 4. 32–40<br>John 21. 20–end | Exod. 18. 13–end<br>Col. 4. 2–end<br>**ct** |
| Ps. 142<br>Deut. 7. 7–13<br>Rev. 2. 1–11<br>*Gospel:* Luke 16. 19–end | W | **THE SECOND SUNDAY AFTER EASTER**<br>Ezek. 34. 11–16a<br>Ps. 23<br>1 Pet. 2. 19–end<br>John 10. 11–16 | Ps. 77. 11–20<br>Isa. 63. 7–15<br>1 Cor. 10. 1–13 | Ps. 142<br>Deut. 7. 7–13<br>Rev. 2. 1–11 |
| Ps. 61; 65<br>alt. Ps. 26; 28; 29<br>Exod. ch. 19<br>Luke 1. 1–25 | W | | Deut. 5. 1–22<br>Eph. 1. 1–14 | Exod. ch. 19<br>Luke 1. 1–25 |
| Ps. 71<br>alt. Ps. 33<br>Exod. 20. 1–21<br>Luke 1. 26–38 | W | | Deut. 5. 22–end<br>Eph. 1. 15–end | Exod. 20. 1–21<br>Luke 1. 26–38 |
| Ps. 67; 72<br>alt. Ps. 119. 33–56<br>Exod. ch. 24<br>Luke 1. 39–56<br>*or First EP of George*<br>Ps. 111; 116<br>Jer. 15. 15–end<br>Heb. 11.32 – 12.2<br>**R ct** | W | | Deut. ch. 6<br>Eph. 2. 1–10 | Exod. ch. 24<br>Luke 1. 39–56 |
| | | To celebrate George, see *Common Worship* provision.<br>**George, Martyr, Patron of England, c. 304** | | |
| *EP*: Ps. 3; 11<br>Isa. 43. 1–7<br>John 15. 1–8 | Wr | Com. Martyr | Deut. 7. 1–11<br>Eph. 2. 11–end | Exod. 25. 1–22<br>Luke 1. 57–end |

# April 2015

| | | | Sunday Principal Service<br>Weekday Eucharist | Third Service<br>Morning Prayer |
|---|---|---|---|---|

| | | | |
|---|---|---|---|
| **24** | F | *Mellitus, Bishop of London, first Bishop at St Paul's, 624; The Seven Martyrs of the Melanesian Brotherhood, Solomon Islands, 2003* | |
| | | | Acts 9. 1–20<br>Ps. 117<br>John 6. 52–59 | Ps. 107<br>*alt.* Ps. 31<br>Deut. 7. 12–end<br>Eph. 3. 1–13 |
| | W | | | |
| **25** | Sa | MARK THE EVANGELIST | | |
| | | | Prov. 15. 28–end<br>*or* Acts 15. 35–end<br>Ps. 119. 9–16<br>Eph. 4. 7–16<br>Mark 13. 5–13 | MP: Ps. 37. 23–end; 148<br>Isa. 62. 6–10<br>*or* Ecclus. 51. 13–end<br>Acts 12.25 – 13.13 |
| | R | | | |
| **26** | S | THE FOURTH SUNDAY OF EASTER<br>*The reading from Acts must be used<br>as either the first or second reading<br>at the Principal Service.* | Acts 4. 5–12<br>[Gen. 7. 1–5, 11–18;<br>8. 6–18; 9. 8–13]<br>Ps. 23<br>1 John 3. 16–end<br>John 10. 11–18 | Ps. 119. 89–96<br>Neh. 7.73b – 8.12<br>Luke 24. 25–32 |
| | W | | | |
| **27** | M | *Christina Rossetti, Poet, 1894* | | |
| | | | Acts 11. 1–18<br>Ps. 42. 1–2; 43. 1–4<br>John 10. 1–10 (*or* 11–18) | Ps. 103<br>*alt.* Ps. 44<br>Deut. 9. 1–21<br>Eph. 4. 1–16 |
| | W | | | |
| **28** | Tu | *Peter Chanel, Missionary in the South Pacific, Martyr, 1841* | | |
| | | | Acts 11. 19–26<br>Ps. 87<br>John 10. 22–30 | Ps. 139<br>*alt.* Ps. *48*; 52<br>Deut. 9.23 – 10.5<br>Eph. 4. 17–end |
| | W | | | |
| **29** | W | **Catherine of Siena, Teacher, 1380**<br>Com. Teacher                *or*<br>*also* Prov. 8. 1, 6–11<br>John 17. 12–26 | Acts 12.24 – 13.5<br>Ps. 67<br>John 12. 44–end | Ps. 135<br>*alt.* Ps. 119. 57–80<br>Deut. 10. 12–end<br>Eph. 5. 1–14 |
| | W | | | |
| **30** | Th | *Pandita Mary Ramabai, Translator of the Scriptures, 1922* | | |
| | | | Acts 13. 13–25<br>Ps. 89. 1–2, 20–26<br>John 13. 16–20 | Ps. 118<br>*alt.* Ps. 56; **57**; (63†)<br>Deut. 11. 8–end<br>Eph. 5. 15–end |
| | W | | | |

# May 2015

| | | | | |
|---|---|---|---|---|
| **1** | F | PHILIP AND JAMES, APOSTLES | | |
| | | | Isa. 30. 15–21<br>Ps. 119. 1–8<br>Eph. 1. 3–10<br>John 14. 1–14 | MP: Ps. 139; 146<br>Prov. 4. 10–18<br>James 1. 1–12 |
| | R | | | |
| **2** | Sa | **Athanasius, Bishop of Alexandria, Teacher, 373**<br>Com. Teacher                *or*<br>*also* Ecclus. 4. 20–28<br>Matt. 10. 24–27 | Acts 13. 44–end<br>Ps. 98. 1–5<br>John 14. 7–14 | Ps. 34<br>*alt.* Ps. 68<br>Deut. 15. 1–18<br>Eph. 6. 10–end |
| | W | | | |

| Second Service Evening Prayer | | Calendar and Holy Communion | Morning Prayer | Evening Prayer |
|---|---|---|---|---|
| Ps. 77 *alt.* Ps. 35 Exod. 28. 1–4a, 29–38 Luke 2. 1–20 *or First EP of Mark:* Ps. 19 Isa. 52. 7–10 Mark 1. 1–15 **R ct** | W | | Deut. 7. 12–end Eph. 3. 1–13 | Exod. 28. 1–4a, 29–38 Luke 2. 1–20 *or First EP of Mark* (Ps. 19) Isa. 52. 7–10 Mark 1. 1–15 **R ct** |
| *EP:* Ps. 45 Ezek. 1. 4–14 2 Tim. 4. 1–11 | R | **MARK THE EVANGELIST** Prov. 15. 28–end Ps. 119. 9–16 Eph. 4. 7–16 John 15. 1–11 | (Ps. 37. 23–end; 148) Isa. 62. 6–10 *or* Ecclus. 51. 13–end Acts 12.25 – 13.13 | (Ps. 45) Ezek. 1. 4–14 2 Tim. 4. 1–11 |
| Ps. 81. 8–16 Exod. 16. 4–15 Rev. 2. 12–17 *Gospel:* John 6. 30–40 | W | **THE THIRD SUNDAY AFTER EASTER** Gen. 45. 3–10 Ps. 57 1 Pet. 2. 11–17 John 16. 16–22 | Ps. 119. 89–96 Neh. 7.73b – 8.12 Luke 24. 25–32 | Ps. 81. 8–16 Exod. 16. 4–15 Rev. 2. 12–17 |
| Ps. 112; 113; *114* *alt.* Ps. *47*; 49 Exod. 32. 1–14 Luke 2. 41–end | W | | Deut. 9. 1–21 Eph. 4. 1–16 | Exod. 32. 1–14 Luke 2. 41–end |
| Ps. 115; *116* *alt.* Ps. 50 Exod. 32. 15–34 Luke 3. 1–14 | W | | Deut. 9.23 – 10.5 Eph. 4. 17–end | Exod. 32. 15–34 Luke 3. 1–14 |
| Ps. *47*; 48 *alt.* Ps. *59*; 60 (67) Exod. ch. 33 Luke 3. 15–22 | W | | Deut. 10. 12–end Eph. 5. 1–14 | Exod. ch. 33 Luke 3. 15–22 |
| Ps. 81; *85* *alt.* Ps. 61; *62*; 64 Exod. 34. 1–10, 27–end Luke 4. 1–13 *or First EP of Philip and James:* Ps. 25 Isa. 40. 27–end John 12. 20–26 **R ct** | W | | Deut. 11. 8–end Eph. 5. 15–end | Exod. 34. 1–10, 27–end Luke 4. 1–13 *or First EP of Philip and James:* (Ps. 119. 1–8) Isa. 40. 27–end John 12. 20–26 **R ct** |
| *EP:* Ps. 149 Job 23. 1–12 John 1. 43–end | R | **PHILIP AND JAMES, APOSTLES** Prov. 4. 10–18 Ps. 25. 1–9 James 1. [1] 2–12 John 14. 1–14 | (Ps. 139; 146) Isa. 30. 1–5 John 12. 20–26 | (Ps. 149) Job 23. 1–12 John 1. 43–end |
| Ps. *84*; 86 *alt.* Ps. 65; *66* Exod. 40. 17–end Luke 4. 31–37 ct | W | | Deut. 15. 1–18 Eph. 6. 10–end | Exod. 40. 17–end Luke 4. 31–37 ct |

# May 2015

| | | Sunday Principal Service<br>Weekday Eucharist | Third Service<br>Morning Prayer |
|---|---|---|---|
| **3** | S<br><br><br><br><br>W | THE FIFTH SUNDAY OF EASTER<br>*The reading from Acts must be used<br>as either the first or second reading<br>at the Principal Service.* | Acts 8. 26–end<br>[Baruch 3.9–15, 32 – 4.4<br>or Gen. 22. 1–18]<br>Ps. 22. 25–end<br>1 John 4. 7–end<br>John 15. 1–8 | Ps. 44. 16–end<br>2 Macc. 7. 7–14<br>or Dan. 3. 16–28<br>Heb. 11.32 – 12.2 |
| **4** | M<br><br><br><br><br>W | **English Saints and Martyrs of the Reformation Era**<br>Isa. 43. 1–7        *or*<br>*or* Ecclus. 2. 10–17<br>Ps. 87<br>2 Cor. 4. 5–12<br>John 12. 20–26 | Acts 14. 5–18<br>Ps. 118. 1–3, 14–15<br>John 14. 21–26 | Ps. 145<br>*alt.* Ps. 71<br>Deut. 16. 1–20<br>1 Pet. 1. 1–12 |
| **5** | Tu<br><br><br>W | | Acts 14. 19–end<br>Ps. 145. 10–end<br>John 14. 27–end | Ps. *19*; 147. 1–12<br>*alt.* Ps. 73<br>Deut. 17. 8–end<br>1 Pet. 1. 13–end |
| **6** | W<br><br><br>W | | Acts 15. 1–6<br>Ps. 122. 1–5<br>John 15. 1–8 | Ps. *30*; 147. 13–end<br>*alt.* Ps. 77<br>Deut. 18. 9–end<br>1 Pet. 2. 1–10 |
| **7** | Th<br><br><br>W | | Acts 15. 7–21<br>Ps. 96. 1–3, 7–10<br>John 15. 9–11 | Ps. *57*; 148<br>*alt.* Ps. 78. 1–39†<br>Deut. ch. 19<br>1 Pet. 2. 11–end |
| **8** | F<br><br><br><br>W | **Julian of Norwich, Spiritual Writer, c. 1417**<br>Com. Religious    *or*<br>*also* 1 Cor. 13. 8–end<br>Matt. 5. 13–16 | Acts 15. 22–31<br>Ps. 57. 8–end<br>John 15. 12–17 | Ps. *138*; 149<br>*alt.* Ps. 55<br>Deut. 21.22 – 22.8<br>1 Pet. 3. 1–12 |
| **9** | Sa<br><br><br>W | | Acts 16. 1–10<br>Ps. 100<br>John 15. 18–21 | Ps. *146*; 150<br>*alt.* Ps. *76*; 79<br>Deut. 24. 5–end<br>1 Pet. 3. 13–end |
| **10** | S<br><br><br><br>W | THE SIXTH SUNDAY OF EASTER<br>*The reading from Acts must be used<br>as either the first or second reading<br>at the Principal Service.* | Acts 10. 44–end<br>[Isa. 55. 1–11]<br>Ps. 98<br>1 John 5. 1–6<br>John 15. 9–17 | Ps. 104. 26–32<br>Ezek. 47. 1–12<br>John 21. 1–19 |
| **11** | M<br><br><br>W | Rogation Day* | Acts 16. 11–15<br>Ps. 149. 1–5<br>John 15.26 – 16.4 | Ps. *65*; 67<br>*alt.* Ps. *80*; 82<br>Deut. ch. 26<br>1 Pet. 4. 1–11 |
| **12** | Tu<br><br><br>W | Rogation Day*<br>*Gregory Dix, Priest, Monk, Scholar,<br>1952* | Acts 16. 22–34<br>Ps. 138<br>John 16. 5–11 | Ps. 124; 125; *126*; 127<br>*alt.* Ps. 87; *89. 1–18*<br>Deut. 28. 1–14<br>1 Pet. 4. 12–end |
| **13** | W<br><br><br><br><br>W | Rogation Day* | Acts 17.15, 22 – 18.1<br>Ps. 148. 1–2, 11–end<br>John 16. 12–15 | Ps. *132*; 133<br>*alt.* Ps. 119. 105–128<br>Deut. 28. 58–end<br>1 Pet. ch. 5 |

*For Rogation Day provision, see p. 10.

| Second Service Evening Prayer | | Calendar and Holy Communion | Morning Prayer | Evening Prayer |
|---|---|---|---|---|
| Ps. 96<br>Isa. 60. 1–14<br>Rev. 3. 1–13<br>*Gospel*: Mark 16. 9–16 | | **THE FOURTH SUNDAY AFTER EASTER**<br>Job 19. 21–27a<br>Ps. 66. 14–end<br>James 1. 17–21<br>John 16. 5–15 | Ps. 44. 15–end<br>2 Macc. 7. 7–14<br>*or* Dan. 3. 16–28<br>Heb. 11.32 – 12.2 | Ps. 96<br>Isa. 60. 1–14<br>Rev. 3. 1–13 |
| | W | | | |
| Ps. 105<br>*alt*. Ps. **72**; 75<br>Num. 9. 15–end; 10. 33–end<br>Luke 4. 38–end | | | Deut. 16. 1–20<br>1 Pet. 1. 1–12 | Num. 9. 15–end;<br>10. 33–end<br>Luke 4. 38–end |
| | W | | | |
| Ps. 96; **97**<br>*alt*. Ps. 74<br>Num. 11. 1–33<br>Luke 5. 1–11 | | | Deut. 17. 8–end<br>1 Pet. 1. 13–end | Num. 11. 1–33<br>Luke 5. 1–11 |
| | W | | | |
| Ps. 98; **99**; 100<br>*alt*. Ps. 119. 81–104<br>Num. ch. 12<br>Luke 5. 12–26 | | **John the Evangelist, ante Portam Latinam**<br>CEG of 27 December | Deut. 18. 9–end<br>1 Pet. 2. 1–10 | Num. ch. 12<br>Luke 5. 12–26 |
| | W | | | |
| Ps. 104<br>*alt*. Ps. 78. 40–end†<br>Num. 13. 1–3, 17–end<br>Luke 5. 27–end | | | Deut. ch. 19<br>1 Pet. 2. 11–end | Num. 13. 1–3, 17–end<br>Luke 5. 27–end |
| | W | | | |
| Ps. 66<br>*alt*. Ps. 69<br>Num. 14. 1–25<br>Luke 6. 1–11 | | | Deut. 21.22 – 22.8<br>1 Pet. 3. 1–12 | Num. 14. 1–25<br>Luke 6. 1–11 |
| | W | | | |
| Ps. 118<br>*alt*. Ps. 81; **84**<br>Num. 14. 26–end<br>Luke 6. 12–26<br>ct | | | Deut. 24. 5–end<br>1 Pet. 3. 13–end | Num. 14. 26–end<br>Luke 6. 12–26<br>ct |
| | W | | | |
| Ps. 45<br>Song of Sol. 4.16 – 5.2;<br>8. 6–7<br>Rev. 3. 14–end<br>*Gospel*: Luke 22. 24–30 | | **THE FIFTH SUNDAY AFTER EASTER**<br>Rogation Sunday<br>Joel 2. 21–26<br>Ps. 66. 1–8<br>James 1. 22–end<br>John 16. 23b–end | Ps. 104. 26–32<br>Ezek. 47. 1–12<br>John 21. 1–19 | Ps. 45<br>Song of Sol. 4.16 – 5.2;<br>8. 6–7<br>Rev. 3. 14–end |
| | W | | | |
| Ps. **121**; 122; 123<br>*alt*. Ps. **85**; 86<br>Num. 16. 1–35<br>Luke 6. 27–38 | | Rogation Day<br>Job 28. 1–11<br>Ps. 107. 1–9<br>James 5. 7–11<br>Luke 6. 36–42 | Deut. ch. 26<br>1 Pet. 4. 1–11 | Num. 16. 1–35<br>Luke 6. 27–38 |
| | W | | | |
| Ps. **128**; 129; 130; 131<br>*alt*. Ps. 89. 19–end<br>Num. 16. 36–end<br>Luke 6. 39–end | | Rogation Day<br>Deut. 8. 1–10<br>Ps. 121<br>James 5. 16–end<br>Luke 11. 5–13 | Deut. 28. 1–14<br>1 Pet. 4. 12–end | Num. 16. 36–end<br>Luke 6. 39–end |
| | W | | | |
| *First EP of Ascension Day*<br>Ps. 15; 24<br>2 Sam. 23. 1–5<br>Col. 2.20 – 3.4<br><br>℣ ct | | Rogation Day<br>Deut. 34. 1–7<br>Ps. 108. 1–6<br>Eph. 4. 7–13<br>John 17. 1–11 | Deut. 28. 58–end<br>1 Pet. ch. 5 | *First EP of Ascension Day*<br>Ps. 15; 24<br>2 Sam. 23. 1–5<br>Col. 2.20 – 3.4<br><br>℣ ct |
| | W | | | |

# May 2015

| | | | Sunday Principal Service / Weekday Eucharist | Third Service / Morning Prayer |
|---|---|---|---|---|
| **14** | Th | **ASCENSION DAY** (Matthias transferred to 15th)<br>*The reading from Acts must be used*<br>*as either the first or second reading*<br>*at the Eucharist.* | Acts 1. 1–11<br>or Dan. 7. 9–14<br>Ps. 47 or Ps. 93<br>Eph. 1. 15–end<br>or Acts 1. 1–11 | MP: Ps. 110; 150<br>Isa. 52. 7–end<br>Heb. 7. [11–25] 26–end |
| | ໝ | | Luke 24. 44–end | |
| **15** | F | MATTHIAS THE APOSTLE* | Isa. 22. 15–end<br>or Acts 1. 15–end<br>Ps. 15<br>Acts 1. 15–end<br>or 1 Cor. 4. 1–7 | MP: Ps. 16; 147. 1–12<br>1 Sam. 2. 27–35<br>Acts 2. 37–end |
| | R | | John 15. 9–17 | |
| | | *or, if Matthias is celebrated on 24 February:* | Acts 18. 9–18<br>Ps. 47. 1–6<br>John 16. 20–23 | Ps. 20; *81*<br>alt. Ps. *88*; (95)<br>Deut. 29. 2–15<br>1 John 1.1 – 2.6<br>[Exod. 35.30 – 36.1 |
| | W | | | Gal. 5. 13–end]** |
| **16** | Sa | *Caroline Chisholm, Social Reformer, 1877* | Acts 18. 22–end<br>Ps. 47. 1–2, 7–end<br>John 16. 23–28 | Ps. 21; *47*<br>alt. Ps. 96; *97*; 100<br>Deut. ch. 30<br>1 John 2. 7–17<br>[Num. 11. 16–17, 24–29 |
| | W | | | 1 Cor. ch. 2] |
| **17** | S | THE SEVENTH SUNDAY OF EASTER (SUNDAY AFTER ASCENSION DAY)<br>*The reading from Acts must be used*<br>*as either the first or second reading*<br>*at the Principal Service.* | Acts 1. 15–17, 21–end<br>[Ezek. 36. 24–28]<br>Ps. 1<br>1 John 5. 9–13 | Ps. 76<br>Isa. 14. 3–15<br>Rev. 14. 1–13 |
| | W | | John 17. 6–19 | |
| **18** | M | | Acts 19. 1–8<br>Ps. 68. 1–6<br>John 16. 29–end | Ps. *93*; 96; 97<br>alt. Ps. *98*; 99; 101<br>Deut. 31. 1–13<br>1 John 2. 18–end<br>[Num. 27. 15–end |
| | W | | | 1 Cor. ch. 3] |
| **19** | Tu | **Dunstan, Archbishop of Canterbury, Restorer of Monastic Life, 988**<br>Com. Bishop                                        or<br>*esp.* Matt. 24. 42–46<br>*also* Exod. 31. 1–5 | Acts 20. 17–27<br>Ps. 68. 9–10, 18–19<br>John 17. 1–11 | Ps. 98; *99*; 100<br>alt. Ps. *106*† (or 103)<br>Deut. 31. 14–29<br>1 John 3. 1–10<br>[1 Sam. 10. 1–10 |
| | W | | | 1 Cor. 12. 1–13] |
| **20** | W | **Alcuin of York, Deacon, Abbot of Tours, 804**<br>Com. Religious                                    or<br>*also* Col. 3. 12–16<br>John 4. 19–24 | Acts 20. 28–end<br>Ps. 68. 27–28, 32–end<br>John 17. 11–19 | Ps. 2; *29*<br>alt. Ps. 110; *111*; 112<br>Deut. 31.30 – 32.14<br>1 John 3. 11–end<br>[1 Kings 19. 1–18 |
| | W | | | Matt. 3. 13–end] |
| **21** | Th | *Helena, Protector of the Holy Places, 330* | Acts 22. 30; 23. 6–11<br>Ps. 16. 1, 5–end<br>John 17. 20–end | Ps. *24*; 72<br>alt. Ps. 113; *115*<br>Deut. 32. 15–47<br>1 John 4. 1–6<br>[Ezek. 11. 14–20 |
| | W | | | Matt. 9.35 – 10.20] |

*Matthias may be celebrated on 24 February instead of 15 May.

**The alternative readings in square brackets may be used at one of the offices, in preparation for the Day of Pentecost.

| Second Service Evening Prayer | | Calendar and Holy Communion | Morning Prayer | Evening Prayer |
|---|---|---|---|---|
| *EP*: Ps. 8<br>Song of the Three 29–37<br>*or* 2 Kings 2. 1–15<br>Rev. ch. 5<br>*Gospel*: Matt. 28. 16–end | ℈ | **ASCENSION DAY**<br>Dan. 7. 13–14<br>Ps. 68. 1–6<br>Acts 1. 1–11<br>Mark 16. 14–end<br>*or* Luke 24. 44–end | Ps. 110; 150<br>Isa. 52. 7–end<br>Heb. 7. [11–25] 26–end | Ps. 8<br>Song of the Three 29–37<br>*or* 2 Kings 2. 1–15<br>Rev. ch. 5 |
| *EP*: Ps. 80<br>1 Sam. 16. 1–13a<br>Matt. 7. 15–27 | | Ascension CEG | Deut. 29. 2–15<br>1 John 1.1 – 2.6<br>[Exod. 35.30 – 36.1<br>Gal. 5. 13–end]\*\* | Num. 20. 1–13<br>Luke 7. 11–17 |
| Ps. 145<br>*alt.* Ps. 102<br>Num. 20. 1–13<br>Luke 7. 11–17 | W | | | |
| Ps. 84; **85**<br>*alt.* Ps. 104<br>Num. 21. 4–9<br>Luke 7. 18–35 | W | Ascension CEG | Deut. ch. 30<br>1 John 2. 7–17<br>[Num. 11. 16–17, 24–29<br>1 Cor. ch. 2] | Num. 21. 4–9<br>Luke 7. 18–35 |
| ct | | | | ct |
| Ps. 147. 1–12<br>Isa. ch. 61<br>Luke 4. 14–21 | W | **THE SUNDAY AFTER ASCENSION DAY**<br>2 Kings 2. 9–15<br>Ps. 68. 32–end<br>1 Pet. 4. 7–11<br>John 15.26 – 16.4a | Ps. 76<br>Isa. 14. 3–15<br>Rev. 14. 1–13 | Ps. 147. 1–12<br>Isa. ch. 61<br>Luke 4. 14–21 |
| Ps. 18<br>*alt.* Ps. **105**† *(or* 103)<br>Num. 22. 1–35<br>Luke 7. 36–end | W | | Deut. 31. 1–13<br>1 John 2. 18–end<br>[Num. 27. 15–end<br>1 Cor. ch. 3] | Num. 22. 1–35<br>Luke 7. 36–end |
| Ps. 68<br>*alt.* Ps. 107†<br>Num. 22.36 – 23.12<br>Luke 8. 1–15 | W | **Dunstan, Archbishop of Canterbury, Restorer of Monastic Life, 988**<br>Com. Bishop | Deut. 31. 14–29<br>1 John 3. 1–10<br>[1 Sam. 10. 1–10<br>1 Cor. 12. 1–13] | Num. 22.36 – 23.12<br>Luke 8. 1–15 |
| Ps. 36; **46**<br>*alt.* Ps. 119. 129–152<br>Num. 23. 13–end<br>Luke 8. 16–25 | W | | Deut. 31.30 – 32.14<br>1 John 3. 11–end<br>[1 Kings 19. 1–18<br>Matt. 3. 13–end] | Num. 23. 13–end<br>Luke 8. 16–25 |
| Ps. 139<br>*alt.* Ps. 114; **116**; 117<br>Num. ch. 24<br>Luke 8. 26–39 | W | | Deut. 32. 15–47<br>1 John 4. 1–6<br>[Ezek. 11. 14–20<br>Matt. 9.35 – 10.20] | Num. ch. 24<br>Luke 8. 26–39 |

# May 2015

| | | Sunday Principal Service<br>Weekday Eucharist | Third Service<br>Morning Prayer |
|---|---|---|---|
| **22** | F | Acts 25. 13–21<br>Ps. 103. 1–2, 11–12, 19–20<br>John 21. 15–19 | Ps. *28*; 30<br>*alt.* Ps. 139<br>Deut. ch. 33<br>1 John 4. 7–end<br>[Ezek. 36. 22–28 |
| | W | | Matt. 12. 22–32] |
| **23** | Sa | Acts 28. 16–20, 30–end<br>Ps. 11. 4–end<br>John 21. 20–end | Ps. 42; *43*<br>*alt.* Ps. 120; *121*; 122<br>Deut. 32. 48–end; ch. 34<br>1 John ch. 5<br>[Mic. 3. 1–8 |
| | W | | Eph. 6. 10–20] |
| **24** | S | **DAY OF PENTECOST (Whit Sunday)**<br>*The reading from Acts must be used as*<br>*either the first or second reading at the*<br>*Principal Service.* | MP: Ps. 145<br>Isa. 11. 1–9 |
| | | Acts 2. 1–21<br>*or* Ezek. 37. 1–14<br>Ps. 104. 26–36, 37b (*or* 26–end)<br>Rom. 8. 22–27<br>*or* Acts 2. 1–21 | *or* Wisd. 7. 15–23 [24–27]<br>1 Cor. 12. 4–13 |
| | R | John 15. 26–27; 16. 4b–15 | |
| **25**<br>DEL 8 | M | **The Venerable Bede, Monk at Jarrow, Scholar, Historian, 735**<br>*Aldhelm, Bishop of Sherborne, 709*<br>Ordinary Time resumes today<br>Com. Religious      *or*<br>*also* Ecclus. 39. 1–10 | Ecclus. 17. 24–29<br>*or* James 3. 13–end<br>Ps. 32. 1–8<br>*or* Ps. 19. 7–end | Ps. 123; 124; 125; *126*<br>2 Chron. 17. 1–12<br>Rom. 1. 1–17 |
| | Gw | | Mark 10. 17–27 | |
| **26** | Tu | **Augustine, first Archbishop of Canterbury, 605**<br>*John Calvin, Reformer, 1564; Philip Neri, Founder of the Oratorians, Spiritual Guide, 1595*<br>Com. Bishop      *or*<br>*also* 1 Thess. 2. 2b–8<br>Matt. 13. 31–33 | Ecclus. 35. 1–12<br>*or* James 4. 1–10<br>Ps. 50. 1–6<br>*or* Ps. 55. 7–9, 24 | Ps. *132*; 133<br>2 Chron. 18. 1–27<br>Rom. 1. 18–end |
| | Gw | | Mark 10. 28–31 | |
| **27** | W | | Ecclus. 36. 1–2, 4–5, 10–17<br>*or* James 4. 13–end<br>Ps. 79. 8–9, 12, 14<br>*or* Ps. 49. 1–2, 5–10 | Ps. 119. 153–end<br>2 Chron. 18.28 – 19.end<br>Rom. 2. 1–16 |
| | G | | Mark 10. 32–45 | |
| **28** | Th | *Lanfranc, Prior of Le Bec, Archbishop of Canterbury, Scholar, 1089*<br> | Ecclus. 42. 15–end<br>*or* James 5. 1–6<br>Ps. 33. 1–9<br>*or* Ps. 49. 12–20 | Ps. *143*; 146<br>2 Chron. 20. 1–23<br>Rom. 2. 17–end |
| | G | | Mark 10. 46–end | |
| **29** | F | | Ecclus. 44. 1, 9–13<br>*or* James 5. 9–12<br>Ps. 149. 1–5<br>*or* Ps. 103. 1–4, 8–13 | Ps. *142*; 144<br>2 Chron. 22.10 – 23.end<br>Rom. 3. 1–20 |
| | G | | Mark 11. 11–26 | |
| **30** | Sa | **Josephine Butler, Social Reformer, 1906**<br>*Joan of Arc, Visionary, 1431; Apolo Kivebulaya, Priest, Evangelist in Central Africa, 1933*<br>Com. Saint      *or*<br>*esp.* Isa. 58. 6–11<br>*also* 1 John 3. 18–23<br>Matt. 9. 10–13 | Ecclus. 51. 12b–20a<br>*or* James 5. 13–end<br>Ps. 19. 7–end<br>*or* Ps. 141. 1–4 | Ps. 147<br>2 Chron. 24. 1–22<br>Rom. 3. 21–end |
| | Gw | | Mark 11. 27–end | |

| Second Service Evening Prayer | | Calendar and Holy Communion | Morning Prayer | Evening Prayer |
|---|---|---|---|---|
| Ps. 147<br>*alt.* Ps. *130*; 131; 137<br>Num. 27. 12–end<br>Luke 8. 40–end<br><br>W | | | Deut. ch. 33<br>1 John 4. 7–end<br>[Ezek. 36. 22–28<br>Matt. 12. 22–32] | Num. 27. 12–end<br>Luke 8. 40–end |
| *First EP of Pentecost*<br>Ps. 48<br>Deut. 16. 9–15<br>John 7. 37–39<br><br>R ct | W | | Deut. 32. 48–end;<br>ch. 34<br>1 John ch. 5<br>[Mic. 3. 1–8<br>Eph. 6. 10–20] | *First EP of Whit Sunday*<br>Ps. 48<br>Deut. 16. 9–15<br>John 7. 37–39<br><br>R ct |
| *EP*: Ps. 139. 1–11, 13–18,<br>23–24 (or 139. 1–11)<br>Ezek. 36. 22–28<br>Acts 2. 22–38<br>*Gospel*: John 20. 19–23 | R | **WHIT SUNDAY**<br>Deut. 16. 9–12<br>Ps. 122<br>Acts 2. 1–11<br>John 14. 15–31a | Ps. 145<br>Isa. 11. 1–9<br>*or* Wisd. 7. 15–23 [24–27]<br>1 Cor. 12. 4–13 | Ps. 139. 1–11, 13–18,<br>23–24 (or 139. 1–11) Ezek. 36. 22–28<br>Acts 2. 22–38 |
| Ps. *127*; 128; 129<br>Josh. ch. 1<br>Luke 9. 18–27 | R | **Monday in Whitsun Week**<br><br>Acts 10. 34–end<br>John 3. 16–21 | Ezek. 11. 14–20<br>Acts 2. 12–36 | Ezek. 35.30 – 36.1<br>Acts 2.37–end |
| Ps. (134); *135*<br>Josh. ch. 2<br>Luke 9. 28–36 | R | **Tuesday in Whitsun Week**<br><br>Acts 8. 14–17<br>John 10. 1–10 | Ezek. 37. 1–14<br>1 Cor. 12. 1–13 | 2 Sam. 23. 1–5<br>1 Cor. 12.27 – 13.end |
| Ps. 136<br>Josh. ch. 3<br>Luke 9. 37–50 | Rw | **The Venerable Bede, Monk at Jarrow, Scholar, Historian, 735**<br>Ember Day<br>Com. Religious *or*<br>Ember CEG *or*<br>Acts 2. 14–21<br>John 6. 44–51 | 2 Chron. 18.28 – 19.end<br>Rom. 2. 1–16 | Josh. ch. 3<br>Luke 9. 37–50 |
| Ps. *138*; 140; 141<br>Josh. 4.1 – 5.1<br>Luke 9. 51–end | G | Acts 2. 22–28<br>Luke 9. 1–6 | 2 Chron. 20. 1–23<br>Rom. 2. 17–end | Josh. 4.1 – 5.1<br>Luke 9. 51–end |
| Ps. 145<br>Josh. 5. 2–end<br>Luke 10. 1–16 | R | Ember Day<br>Ember CEG *or*<br>Acts 8. 5–8<br>Luke 5. 17–26 | 2 Chron. 22.10 – 23.end<br>Rom. 3. 1–20 | Josh. 5. 2–end<br>Luke 10. 1–16 |
| *First EP of Trinity Sunday*<br>Ps. 97; 98<br>Isa. 40. 12–31<br>Mark 1. 1–13<br><br>𝔚 ct | R | Ember Day<br><br>Ember CEG *or*<br>Acts 13. 44–end<br>Matt. 20. 29–end | 2 Chron. 24. 1–22<br>Rom. 3. 21–end | *First EP of Trinity Sunday*<br>Ps. 97; 98<br>Isa. 40. 12–31<br>Mark 1. 1–13<br><br>𝔚 ct |

# May 2015

| | | Sunday Principal Service<br>Weekday Eucharist | Third Service<br>Morning Prayer |
|---|---|---|---|
| **31** | S | **TRINITY SUNDAY** (Visitation transferred to 1 June) | |
| | | Isa. 6. 1–8 | MP: Ps. 33. 1–12 |
| | | Ps. 29 | Prov. 8. 1–4, 22–31 |
| | | Rom. 8. 12–17 | 2 Cor. 13. [5–10] 11–end |
| | 𝕎 | John 3. 1–17 | |

# June 2015

| | | | | |
|---|---|---|---|---|
| **1**<br>DEL 9 | M | **THE VISIT OF THE BLESSED VIRGIN MARY TO ELIZABETH** (transferred from 31 May)* | | |
| | | | Zeph. 3. 14–18 | MP: Ps. 85; 150 |
| | | | Ps. 113 | 1 Sam. 2. 1–10 |
| | W | | Rom. 12. 9–16 | Mark 3. 31–end |
| | | | Luke 1. 39–49 [50–56] | |
| | | *or, if The Visitation is celebrated on 2 July:* | | |
| | | **Justin, Martyr at Rome, c. 165** | | |
| | | Com. Martyr *or* | Tob. 1. 1–2; 2. 1–8 | Ps. *1*; 2; 3 |
| | | *esp.* John 15. 18–21 | *or* 1 Pet. 1. 3–9 | 2 Chron. 26. 1–21 |
| | | *also* 1 Macc. 2. 15–22 | Ps. 15 | Rom. 4. 1–12 |
| | | 1 Cor. 1. 18–25 | *or* Ps. 111 | |
| | Gr | | Mark 12. 1–12 | |
| **2** | Tu | | Tob. 2. 9–end | Ps. *5*; 6; (8) |
| | | | *or* 1 Pet. 1. 10–16 | 2 Chron. ch. 28 |
| | | | Ps. 112 | Rom. 4. 13–end |
| | | | *or* Ps. 98. 1–5 | |
| | G | | Mark 12. 13–17 | |
| **3** | W | *The Martyrs of Uganda, 1885–87 and 1977* | | |
| | | | Tob. 3. 1–11, 16–end | Ps. 119. 1–32 |
| | | | *or* 1 Pet. 1, 18–25 | 2 Chron. 29. 1–19 |
| | | | Ps. 25. 1–8 | Rom. 5. 1–11 |
| | | | *or* Ps. 147. 13–end | |
| | | | Mark 12. 18–27 | |
| | G | | | |
| **4** | Th | **DAY OF THANKSGIVING FOR HOLY COMMUNION (CORPUS CHRISTI)** | | |
| | | *Petroc, Abbot of Padstow, 6th century* | Gen. 14. 18–20 | MP: Ps. 147 |
| | | | Ps. 116. 10–end | Deut. 8. 2–16 |
| | W | | 1 Cor. 11. 23–26 | 1 Cor. 10. 1–17 |
| | | | John 6. 51–58 | |
| | | *or, if Corpus Christi is not observed:* | | |
| | | | Tob. 6. 10–11; 7. 1–15; 8. 4–8 | Ps. 14; *15*; 16 |
| | | | *or* 1 Pet. 2. 2–5, 9–12 | 2 Chron. 29. 20–end |
| | | | Ps. 128 | Rom. 5. 12–end |
| | | | *or* Ps. 100 | |
| | G | | Mark 12. 28–34 | |
| **5** | F | **Boniface (Wynfrith) of Crediton, Bishop, Apostle of Germany, Martyr, 754** | | |
| | | Com. Martyr *or* | Tob. 11. 5–15 | Ps. 17; *19* |
| | | *also* Acts 20. 24–28 | *or* 1 Pet. 4. 7–13 | 2 Chron. ch. 30 |
| | | | Ps. 146 | Rom. 6. 1–14 |
| | | | *or* Ps. 96. 10–end | |
| | Gr | | Mark 12. 35–37 | |
| **6** | Sa | *Ini Kopuria, Founder of the Melanesian Brotherhood, 1945* | | |
| | | | Tob. 12. 1, 5–15, 20a | Ps. 20; 21; *23* |
| | | | *or* Jude 17, 20–25 | 2 Chron. 32. 1–22 |
| | | | Ps. 103. 1, 8–13 | Rom. 6. 15–end |
| | | | *or* Ps. 63. 1–6 | |
| | G | | Mark 12. 38–end | |
| **7** | S | **THE FIRST SUNDAY AFTER TRINITY (Proper 5)** | | |
| | | *Track 1* | *Track 2* | |
| | | 1 Sam. 8. 4–11 [12–15] 16–20; | Gen. 3. 8–15 | Ps. 36 |
| | | [11. 14–end] | Ps. 130 | Deut. 6. 10–end |
| | | Ps. 138 | 2 Cor. 4.13 – 5.1 | Acts 22.22 – 23.11 |
| | | 2 Cor. 4.13 – 5.1 | Mark 3. 20–end | |
| | G | Mark 3. 20–end | | |

*The Visit of the Blessed Virgin Mary to Elizabeth may be celebrated on 2 July instead of 1 June this year.

| Second Service Evening Prayer | | Calendar and Holy Communion | Morning Prayer | Evening Prayer |
|---|---|---|---|---|
| | | **TRINITY SUNDAY** | | |
| *EP*: Ps. 104. 1–10<br>Ezek. 1. 4–10, 22–28a<br>Rev. ch. 4<br>*Gospel*: Mark 1. 1–13 | ꟿ | Isa. 6. 1–8<br>Ps. 8<br>Rev. 4. 1–11<br>John 3. 1–15 | Ps. 33. 1–12<br>Prov. 8. 1–4, 22–31<br>2 Cor. 13. [5–10] 11–end | Ps. 104. 1–10<br>Ezek. 1. 4–10, 22–28a<br>Mark 1. 1–13 |
| | | **Nicomede, Priest and Martyr at Rome (date unknown)** | | |
| *EP*: Ps. 122; 127; 128<br>Zech. 2. 10–end<br>John 3. 25–30 | | Com. Martyr | 2 Chron. 26. 1–21<br>Rom. 4. 1–12 | Josh. 7. 1–15<br>Luke 10. 25–37 |
| Ps. *4*; 7<br>Josh. 7. 1–15<br>Luke 10. 25–37 | Gr | | | |
| Ps. *9*; 10†<br>Josh. 7. 16–end<br>Luke 10. 38–end | G | | 2 Chron. ch. 28<br>Rom. 4. 13–end | Josh. 7. 16–end<br>Luke 10. 38–end |
| Ps. *11*; 12; 13<br>Josh. 8. 1–29<br>Luke 11. 1–13<br>*or First EP of Corpus Christi*<br>Ps. 110; 111<br>Exod. 16. 2–15<br>John 6. 22–35<br>**W ct** | G | | 2 Chron. 29. 1–19<br>Rom. 5. 1–11 | Josh. 8. 1–29<br>Luke 11. 1–13 |
| | | To celebrate Corpus Christi, see *Common Worship* provision. | | |
| *EP*: Ps. 23; 42; 43<br>Prov. 9. 1–5<br>Luke 9. 11–17 | | | 2 Chron. 29. 20–end<br>Rom. 5. 12–end | Josh. 8. 30–end<br>Luke 11. 14–28 |
| Ps. 18†<br>Josh. 8. 30–end<br>Luke 11. 14–28 | G | | | |
| | | **Boniface (Wynfrith) of Crediton, Bishop, Apostle of Germany, Martyr, 754** | | |
| Ps. 22<br>Josh. 9. 3–26<br>Luke 11. 29–36 | | Com. Martyr | 2 Chron. ch. 30<br>Rom. 6. 1–14 | Josh. 9. 3–26<br>Luke 11. 29–36 |
| | Gr | | | |
| Ps. *24*; 25<br>Josh. 10. 1–15<br>Luke 11. 37–end | | | 2 Chron. 32. 1–22<br>Rom. 6. 15–end | Josh. 10. 1–15<br>Luke 11. 37–end |
| **ct** | G | | | **ct** |
| | | THE FIRST SUNDAY AFTER TRINITY | | |
| Ps. 37. 1–17 (*or* 37. 1–11)<br>Jer. 6. 16–21<br>Rom. 9. 1–13<br>*Gospel*: Luke 7. 11–17 | G | 2 Sam. 9. 6–end<br>Ps. 41. 1–4<br>1 John 4. 7–end<br>Luke 16. 19–31 | Ps. 36<br>Deut. 6. 10–end<br>Acts 22.22 – 23.11 | Ps. 37. 1–17<br>(*or* 37. 1–11)<br>Jer. 6. 16–21<br>Rom. 9. 1–13 |

# June 2015

| | | | Sunday Principal Service / Weekday Eucharist | Third Service / Morning Prayer |
|---|---|---|---|---|

**8**
DEL 10

| M | **Thomas Ken, Bishop of Bath and Wells, Nonjuror, Hymn Writer, 1711** | |
|---|---|---|
| | Com. Bishop | *or* 2 Cor. 1. 1–7 |
| | *esp.* 2 Cor. 4. 1–10 | Ps. 34. 1–8 |
| Gw | Matt. 24. 42–46 | Matt. 5. 1–12 |

Third Service: Ps. 27; **30** / 2 Chron. 33. 1–13 / Rom. 7. 1–6

**9**

| Tu | **Columba, Abbot of Iona, Missionary, 597** |
|---|---|
| | *Ephrem of Syria, Deacon, Hymn Writer, Teacher, 373* |
| | Com. Missionary    *or* 2 Cor. 1. 18–22 |
| | *also* Titus 2. 11–end    Ps. 119. 129–136 |
| Gw | Matt. 5. 13–16 |

Third Service: Ps. 32; **36** / 2 Chron. 34. 1–18 / Rom. 7. 7–end

**10**

| W | 2 Cor. 3. 4–11 |
|---|---|
| | Ps. 78. 1–4 |
| G | Matt. 5. 17–19 |

Third Service: Ps. 34 / 2 Chron. 34. 19–end / Rom. 8. 1–11

**11**

| Th | BARNABAS THE APOSTLE |
|---|---|
| | Job 29. 11–16 |
| | *or* Acts 11. 19–end |
| | Ps. 112 |
| | Acts 11. 19–end |
| | *or* Gal. 2. 1–10 |
| R | John 15. 12–17 |

Third Service: MP: Ps. 100; 101; 117 / Jer. 9. 23–24 / Acts 4. 32–end

**12**

| F | 2 Cor. 4. 7–15 |
|---|---|
| G | Ps. 99 |
| | Matt. 5. 27–32 |

Third Service: Ps. 31 / 2 Chron. 35.20 – 36.10 / Rom. 8. 18–30

**13**

| Sa | 2 Cor. 5. 14–end |
|---|---|
| | Ps. 103. 1–12 |
| G | Matt. 5. 33–37 |

Third Service: Ps. 41; **42**; 43 / 2 Chron. 36. 11–end / Rom. 8. 31–end

**14**

| S | THE SECOND SUNDAY AFTER TRINITY (Proper 6) | |
|---|---|---|
| | *Track 1* | *Track 2* |
| | 1 Sam. 15.34 – 16.13 | Ezek. 17. 22–end |
| | Ps. 20 | Ps. 92. 1–4, 12–end (*or* 1–8) |
| | 2 Cor. 5. 6–10 [11–13] 14–17 | 2 Cor. 5. 6–10 [11–13] 14–17 |
| G | Mark 4. 26–34 | Mark 4. 26–34 |

Third Service: Ps. 42; 43 / Deut. 10.12 – 11.1 / Acts 23. 12–35

**15**
DEL 11

| M | *Evelyn Underhill, Spiritual Writer, 1941* |
|---|---|
| | 2 Cor. 6. 1–10 |
| | Ps. 98 |
| G | Matt. 5. 38–42 |

Third Service: Ps. 44 / Ezra ch. 1 / Rom. 9. 1–18

**16**

| Tu | **Richard, Bishop of Chichester, 1253** |
|---|---|
| | *Joseph Butler, Bishop of Durham, Philosopher, 1752* |
| | Com. Bishop    *or* 2 Cor. 8. 1–9 |
| | *also* John 21. 15–19    Ps. 146 |
| Gw | Matt. 5. 43–end |

Third Service: Ps. **48**; 52 / Ezra ch. 3 / Rom. 9. 19–end

**17**

| W | *Samuel and Henrietta Barnett, Social Reformers, 1913 and 1936* |
|---|---|
| | 2 Cor. 9. 6–11 |
| | Ps. 112 |
| G | Matt. 6. 1–6, 16–18 |

Third Service: Ps. 119. 57–80 / Ezra 4. 1–5 / Rom. 10. 1–10

**18**

| Th | *Bernard Mizeki, Apostle of the MaShona, Martyr, 1896* |
|---|---|
| | 2 Cor. 11. 1–11 |
| | Ps. 111 |
| G | Matt. 6. 7–15 |

Third Service: Ps. 56; **57**; (63†) / Ezra 4. 7–end / Rom. 10. 11–end

**19**

| F | *Sundar Singh of India, Sadhu (holy man), Evangelist, Teacher, 1929* |
|---|---|
| | 2 Cor. 11. 18, 21b–30 |
| | Ps. 34. 1–6 |
| G | Matt. 6. 19–23 |

Third Service: Ps. **51**; 54 / Ezra ch. 5 / Rom. 11. 1–12

| Second Service Evening Prayer | Calendar and Holy Communion | Morning Prayer | Evening Prayer |
|---|---|---|---|
| Ps. 26; *28*; 29<br>Josh. ch. 14<br>Luke 12. 1–12 | G | 2 Chron. 33. 1–13<br>Rom. 7. 1–6 | Josh. ch. 14<br>Luke 12. 1–12 |
| Ps. 33<br>Josh. 21.43 – 22.8<br>Luke 12. 13–21 | G | 2 Chron. 34. 1–18<br>Rom. 7. 7–end | Josh. 21.43 – 22.8<br>Luke 12. 13–21 |
| Ps. 119. 33–56<br>Josh. 22. 9–end<br>Luke 12. 22–31<br>*or First EP of Barnabas*<br>Ps. 1; 15<br>Isa. 42. 5–12<br>Acts 14. 8–end<br>**R ct** | G | 2 Chron. 34. 19–end<br>Rom. 8. 1–11 | Josh. 22. 9–end<br>Luke 12. 22–31<br>*or First EP of Barnabas*<br>(Ps. 1; 15)<br>Isa. 42. 5–12<br>Acts 14. 8–end<br>**R ct** |
| EP: Ps. 147<br>Eccles. 12. 9–end<br>*or Tobit 4. 5–11*<br>Acts 9. 26–31 | **BARNABAS THE APOSTLE**<br>Job 29. 11–16<br>Ps. 112<br>Acts 11. 22–end<br>John 15. 12–16<br><br>R | (Ps. 100; 101; 117)<br>Jer. 9. 23–24<br>Acts 4. 32–end | (Ps. 147)<br>Eccles. 12. 9–end<br>*or Tobit 4. 5–11*<br>Acts 9. 26–31 |
| Ps. 35<br>Josh. 24. 1–28<br>Luke 12. 41–48 | G | 2 Chron. 35.20 – 36.10<br>Rom. 8. 18–30 | Josh. 24. 1–28<br>Luke 12. 41–48 |
| Ps. 45; *46*<br>Josh. 24. 29–end<br>Luke 12. 49–end<br>ct | G | 2 Chron. 36. 11–end<br>Rom. 8. 31–end | Josh. 24. 29–end<br>Luke 12. 49–end<br>ct |
| Ps. 39<br>Jer. 7. 1–16<br>Rom. 9. 14–26<br>*Gospel:* Luke 7.36 – 8.3 | **THE SECOND SUNDAY AFTER TRINITY**<br>Gen. 12. 1–4<br>Ps. 120<br>1 John 3. 13–end<br>Luke 14. 16–24<br>G | Ps. 42; 43<br>Deut. 10.12 – 11.1<br>Acts 23. 12–35 | Ps. 39<br>Jer. 7. 1–16<br>Rom. 9. 14–26 |
| Ps. *47*; 49<br>Judg. ch. 2<br>Luke 13. 1–9 | G | Ezra ch. 1<br>Rom. 9. 1–18 | Judg. ch. 2<br>Luke 13. 1–9 |
| Ps. 50<br>Judg. 4. 1–23<br>Luke 13. 10–21 | G | Ezra ch. 3<br>Rom. 9. 19–end | Judg. 4. 1–23<br>Luke 13. 10–21 |
| Ps. *59*; 60; (67)<br>Judg. ch. 5<br>Luke 13. 22–end | **Alban, first Martyr of Britain, c. 250**<br>Com. Martyr<br><br>Gr | Ezra 4. 1–5<br>Rom. 10. 1–10 | Judg. ch. 5<br>Luke 13. 22–end |
| Ps. 61; *62*; 64<br>Judg. 6. 1–24<br>Luke 14. 1–11 | G | Ezra 4. 7–end<br>Rom. 10. 11–end | Judg. 6. 1–24<br>Luke 14. 1–11 |
| Ps. 38<br>Judg. 6. 25–end<br>Luke 14. 12–24 | G | Ezra ch. 5<br>Rom. 11. 1–12 | Judg. 6. 25–end<br>Luke 14. 12–24 |

# June 2015

| | | Sunday Principal Service<br>Weekday Eucharist | Third Service<br>Morning Prayer |
|---|---|---|---|
| **20** | Sa | 2 Cor. 12. 1–10<br>Ps. 89. 20–33<br>Matt. 6. 24–end | Ps. 68<br>Ezra ch. 6<br>Rom. 11. 13–24 |
| | G | | |

| | | | | |
|---|---|---|---|---|
| **21** | S | **THE THIRD SUNDAY AFTER TRINITY (Proper 7)** | | |
| | | *Track 1* | *Track 2* | |
| | | 1 Sam. 17. [1a, 4–11, 19–23] 32–49 | Job 38. 1–11 | Ps. 48 |
| | | *and* Ps. 9. 9–end | Ps. 107. 1–3, 23–32 (or 23–32) | Deut. 11. 1–15 |
| | | *or* 1 Sam. 17.57 – 18.5, 10–16 | 2 Cor. 6. 1–13 | Acts 27. 1–12 |
| | | *and* Ps. 133 | Mark 4. 35–end | |
| | | 2 Cor. 6. 1–13 | | |
| | G | Mark 4. 35–end | | |

| | | | | |
|---|---|---|---|---|
| **22**<br>DEL 12 | M | **Alban, first Martyr of Britain, c. 250** | | |
| | | Com. Martyr | *or* Gen. 12. 1–9 | Ps. 71 |
| | | *esp.* 2 Tim. 2. 3–13 | Ps. 33. 12–end | Ezra ch. 7 |
| | Gr | John 12. 24–26 | Matt. 7. 1–5 | Rom. 11. 25–end |

| | | | | |
|---|---|---|---|---|
| **23** | Tu | **Etheldreda, Abbess of Ely, c. 678** | | |
| | | Com. Religious | *or* Gen. 13. 2, 5–end | Ps. 73 |
| | | *also* Matt. 25. 1–13 | Ps. 15 | Ezra 8. 15–end |
| | | | Matt. 7. 6, 12–14 | Rom. 12. 1–8 |
| | Gw | | | |

| | | | | |
|---|---|---|---|---|
| **24** | W | **THE BIRTH OF JOHN THE BAPTIST**<br>Ember Day* | | |
| | | | Isa. 40. 1–11 | MP: Ps. 50; 149 |
| | | | Ps. 85. 7–end | Ecclus. 48. 1–10 |
| | | | Acts 13. 14b–26 | or Mal. 3. 1–6 |
| | | | or Gal. 3. 23–end | Luke 3. 1–17 |
| | W | | Luke 1. 57–66, 80 | |

| | | | | |
|---|---|---|---|---|
| **25** | Th | | Gen. 16. 1–12, 15–16 | Ps. 78. 1–39† |
| | | | Ps. 106. 1–5 | Ezra 10. 1–7 |
| | G | | Matt. 7. 21–end | Rom. 13. 1–7 |

| | | | | |
|---|---|---|---|---|
| **26** | F | Ember Day* | | |
| | | | Gen. 17. 1, 9–10, 15–22 | Ps. 55 |
| | | | Ps. 128 | Neh. ch. 1 |
| | G *or* R | | Matt. 8. 1–4 | Rom. 13. 8–end |

| | | | | |
|---|---|---|---|---|
| **27** | Sa | Ember Day*<br>*Cyril, Bishop of Alexandria, Teacher, 444* | | |
| | | | Gen. 18. 1–15 | Ps. **76**; 79 |
| | | | *Canticle:* Luke 1. 46b–55 | Neh. ch. 2 |
| | G *or* R | | Matt. 8. 5–17 | Rom. 14. 1–12 |

| | | | | |
|---|---|---|---|---|
| **28** | S | **THE FOURTH SUNDAY AFTER TRINITY (Proper 8)** | | |
| | | *Track 1* | *Track 2* | |
| | | 1 Sam. 1. 1, 17–end | Wisd. of Sol. 1. 13–15; 2. 23–24 | Ps. 56 |
| | | Ps. 130 | *Canticle:* Lam. 3. 22–33 | Deut. 15. 1–11 |
| | | 2 Cor. 8. 7–end | *or* Ps. 30 | Acts 27. [13–32] 33–end |
| | | Mark 5. 21–end | 2 Cor. 8. 7–end | |
| | | | Mark 5. 21–end | |
| | G | | | |

*For Ember Day provision, see p. 11.

| Second Service Evening Prayer | Calendar and Holy Communion | Morning Prayer | Evening Prayer |
|---|---|---|---|
| | **Translation of Edward, King of the West Saxons, 979** | | |
| Ps. 65; **66** Judg. ch. 7 Luke 14. 25–end | Com. Martyr | Ezra ch. 6 Rom. 11. 13–24 | Judg. ch. 7 Luke 14. 25–end |
| ct | Gr | | ct |
| | THE THIRD SUNDAY AFTER TRINITY | | |
| Ps. 49 Jer. 10. 1–16 Rom. 11. 25–end *Gospel:* Luke 8. 26–39 | 2 Chron. 33. 9–13 Ps. 55. 17–23 1 Pet. 5. 5b–11 Luke 15. 1–10 | Ps. 48 Deut. 11. 1–15 Acts 27. 1–12 | Ps. 49 Jer. 10. 1–16 Rom. 11. 25–end |
| | G | | |
| Ps. **72**; 75 Judg. 8. 22–end Luke 15. 1–10 | | Ezra ch. 7 Rom. 11. 25–end | Judg. 8. 22–end Luke 15. 1–10 |
| | G | | |
| Ps. 74 Judg. 9. 1–21 Luke 15. 11–end *or First EP of The Birth of John the Baptist* Ps. 71 Judges 13. 2–7, 24–end Luke 1. 5–25 | | Ezra 8. 15–end Rom. 12. 1–8 | Judg. 9. 1–21 Luke 15. 11–end *or First EP of The Nativity of John the Baptist* (Ps. 71) Judges 13. 2–7, 24–end Luke 1. 5–25 |
| **W ct** | G | | **W ct** |
| | THE NATIVITY OF JOHN THE BAPTIST | | |
| *EP:* Ps. 80; 82 Mal. ch. 4 Matt. 11. 2–19 | Isa. 40. 1–11 Ps. 80. 1–7 Acts 13. 22–26 Luke 1. 57–80 | (Ps. 50; 149) Ecclus. 48. 1–10 *or* Mal. 3. 1–6 Luke 3. 1–17 | (Ps. 82) Mal. ch. 4 Matt. 11. 2–19 |
| | W | | |
| Ps. 78. 40–end† Judg. 11. 1–11 Luke 16. 19–end | | Ezra 10. 1–7 Rom. 13. 1–7 | Judg. 11. 1–11 Luke 16. 19–end |
| | G | | |
| Ps. 69 Judg. 11. 29–end Luke 17. 1–10 | | Neh. ch. 1 Rom. 13. 8–end | Judg. 11. 29–end Luke 17. 1–10 |
| | G | | |
| Ps. 81; **84** Judg. 12. 1–7 Luke 17. 11–19 | | Neh. ch. 2 Rom. 14. 1–12 | Judg. 12. 1–7 Luke 17. 11–19 |
| ct | G | | ct |
| | THE FOURTH SUNDAY AFTER TRINITY | | |
| Ps. [52]; 53 Jer. 11. 1–14 Rom. 13. 1–10 *Gospel:* Luke 9. 51–end *or First EP of Peter and Paul* Ps. 66; 67 Ezek. 3. 4–11 Gal. 1.13 – 2.8 *or, for Peter alone:* Acts 9. 32–end | Gen. 3. 17–19 Ps. 79. 8–10 Rom. 8. 18–23 Luke 6. 36–42 | Ps. 56 Deut. 15. 1–11 Acts 27. [13–32] 33–end | Ps. [52]; 53 Jer. 11. 1–14 Rom. 13. 1–10 *or First EP of Peter* (Ps. 66; 67) Ezek. 3. 4–11 Acts 9. 32–end |
| **R ct** | G | | **R ct** |

# June 2015

| | | | Sunday Principal Service<br>Weekday Eucharist | Third Service<br>Morning Prayer |
|---|---|---|---|---|
| **29**<br>DEL 13 | M | PETER AND PAUL, APOSTLES | Zech. 4. 1–6a, 10b–end<br>or Acts 12. 1–11<br>Ps. 125<br>Acts 12. 1–11<br>or 2 Tim. 4. 6–8, 17–18 | MP: Ps. 71; 113<br>Isa. 49. 1–6<br>Acts 11. 1–18 |
| | R | | Matt. 16. 13–19 | |
| | | or, if Peter is commemorated alone: | | |
| | | | Ezek. 3. 22–end<br>or Acts 12. 1–11<br>Ps. 125<br>Acts 12. 1–11<br>or 1 Pet. 2. 19–end | MP: Ps. 71; 113<br>Isa. 49. 1–6<br>Acts 11. 1–18 |
| | R | | Matt. 16. 13–19 | |
| **30** | Tu | | Gen. 19. 15–29<br>Ps. 26 | Ps. 87; **89. 1–18**<br>Neh. ch. 5 |
| | G | | Matt. 8. 23–27 | Rom. 15. 1–13 |

# July 2015

| | | | | |
|---|---|---|---|---|
| **1** | W | Henry, John and Henry Venn the Younger, Priests, Evangelical Divines, 1797, 1813 and 1873 | Gen. 21. 5, 8–20<br>Ps. 34. 1–12 | Ps. 119. 105–128<br>Neh. 6.1 – 7.4 |
| | G | | Matt. 8. 28–end | Rom. 15. 14–21 |
| **2** | Th | | Gen. 22. 1–19<br>Ps. 116. 1–7<br>Matt. 9. 1–8 | Ps. 90; **92**<br>Neh. 7.73b – 8.end<br>Rom. 15. 22–end |
| | G | | | |
| **3** | F | THOMAS THE APOSTLE** | Hab. 2. 1–4<br>Ps. 31. 1–6<br>Eph. 2. 19–end | MP: Ps. 92; 146<br>2 Sam. 15. 17–21<br>or Ecclus. ch. 2 |
| | R | | John 20. 24–29 | John 11. 1–16 |
| | | or, if Thomas is not celebrated: | | |
| | | | Gen. 23. 1–4, 19; 24. 1–8,<br>62–end<br>Ps. 106. 1–5 | Ps. **88**; (95)<br>Neh. 9. 1–23<br>Rom. 16. 1–16 |
| | G | | Matt. 9. 9–13 | |
| **4** | Sa | | Gen. 27. 1–5a, 15–29<br>Ps. 135. 1–6 | Ps. 96; **97**; 100<br>Neh. 9. 24–end |
| | G | | Matt. 9. 14–17 | Rom. 16. 17–end |
| **5** | S | THE FIFTH SUNDAY AFTER TRINITY **(Proper 9)**<br>*Track 1*<br>2 Sam. 5. 1–5, 9–10<br>Ps. 48<br>2 Cor. 12. 2–10 | *Track 2*<br>Ezek. 2. 1–5<br>Ps. 123<br>2 Cor. 12. 2–10 | Ps. 57<br>Deut. 24. 10–end<br>Acts 28. 1–16 |
| | G | | Mark 6. 1–13 | |
| **6**<br>DEL 14 | M | Thomas More, Scholar, and John Fisher, Bishop of Rochester, Reformation Martyrs, 1535 | Gen. 28. 10–end<br>Ps. 91. 1–10 | Ps. **98**; 99; 101<br>Neh. 12. 27–47 |
| | G | | Matt. 9. 18–26 | 2 Cor. 1. 1–14 |

*Common Worship Morning and Evening Prayer provision for 1 June may be used.
**Thomas the Apostle may be celebrated on 21 December instead of 3 July.

| Second Service<br>Evening Prayer | | Calendar and Holy Communion | Morning Prayer | Evening Prayer |
|---|---|---|---|---|
| *EP*: Ps. 124; 138<br>Ezek. 34. 11–16<br>John 21. 15–22 | | **PETER THE APOSTLE**<br>Ezek. 3. 4–11<br>Ps. 125<br>Acts 12. 1–11<br>Matt. 16. 13–19 | (Ps. 71; 113)<br>Isa. 49. 1–6<br>Acts 11. 1–18 | (Ps. 124; 138)<br>Ezek. 34. 11–16<br>John 21. 15–22 |
| *EP*: Ps. 124; 138<br>Ezek. 34. 11–16<br>John 21. 15–22 | | | | |
| | **R** | | | |
| Ps. 89. 19–end<br>Judg. ch. 14<br>Luke 18. 1–14 | **G** | | Neh. ch. 5<br>Rom. 15. 1–13 | Judg. ch. 14<br>Luke 18. 1–14 |
| | | | | |
| Ps. *91*; 93<br>Judg. 15.1 – 16.3<br>Luke 18. 15–30 | **G** | | Neh. 6.1 – 7.4<br>Rom. 15. 14–21 | Judg. 15.1 – 16.3<br>Luke 18. 15–30 |
| Ps. 94<br>Judg. 16. 4–end<br>Luke 18. 31–end<br>*or First EP of Thomas*<br>Ps. 27<br>Isa. ch. 35<br>Heb. 10.35 – 11.1<br>**R ct** | **Gw** | **The Visitation of the Blessed Virgin Mary***<br>1 Sam. 2. 1–3<br>Ps. 113<br>Gal. 4. 1–5<br>Luke 1. 39–45 | Neh. 7.73b – 8.end<br>Rom. 15. 22–end | Judg. 16. 4–end<br>Luke 18. 31–end |
| *EP*: Ps. 139<br>Job 42. 1–6<br>1 Pet. 1. 3–12 | | | Neh. 9. 1–23<br>Rom. 16. 1–16 | Judg. ch. 17<br>Luke 19. 1–10 |
| Ps. 102<br>Judg. ch. 17<br>Luke 19. 1–10 | **G** | | | |
| Ps. 104<br>Judg. 18. 1–20, 27–end<br>Luke 19. 11–27<br>**ct** | **Gw** | **Translation of Martin, Bishop of Tours, c. 397**<br>Com. Bishop | Neh. 9. 24–end<br>Rom. 16. 17–end | Judg. 18. 1–20,<br>27–end<br>Luke 19. 11–27<br>**ct** |
| Ps. [63]; 64<br>Jer. 20. 1–11a<br>Rom. 14. 1–17<br>*Gospel:* Luke 10. 1–11, 16–20 | **G** | **THE FIFTH SUNDAY AFTER TRINITY**<br>1 Kings 19. 19–21<br>Ps. 84. 8–end<br>1 Pet. 3. 8–15a<br>Luke 5. 1–11 | Ps. 57<br>Deut. 24. 10–end<br>Acts 28. 1–16 | Ps. [63]; 64<br>Jer. 20. 1–11a<br>Rom. 14. 1–17 |
| Ps. *105*† (*or* 103)<br>1 Sam. 1. 1–20<br>Luke 19. 28–40 | **G** | | Neh. 12. 27–47<br>2 Cor. 1. 1–14 | 1 Sam. 1. 1–20<br>Luke 19. 28–40 |

# July 2015

| | | | Sunday Principal Service / Weekday Eucharist | Third Service / Morning Prayer |
|---|---|---|---|---|

**7** Tu *    G

Gen. 32. 22–end
Ps. 17. 1–8
Matt. 9. 32–end

Ps. *106*† (or 103)
Neh. 13. 1–14
2 Cor. 1.15 – 2.4

**8** W    G

Gen. 41. 55–end; 42. 5–7, 17–end
Ps. 33. 1–4, 18–end
Matt. 10. 1–7

Ps. 110; *111*; 112
Neh. 13. 15–end
2 Cor. 2. 5–end

**9** Th    G

Gen. 44. 18–21, 23–29; 45. 1–5
Ps. 105. 11–17
Matt. 10. 7–15

Ps. 113; *115*
Esther ch. 1
2 Cor. ch. 3

**10** F    G

Gen. 46. 1–7, 28–30
Ps. 37. 3–6, 27–28
Matt. 10. 16–23

Ps. 139
Esther ch. 2
2 Cor. ch. 4

**11** Sa    Gw

**Benedict of Nursia, Abbot of Monte Cassino, Father of Western Monasticism, c. 550**
Com. Religious
*also* 1 Cor. 3. 10–11
Luke 18. 18–22

*or*   Gen. 49. 29–end; 50. 15–25
Ps. 105. 1–7
Matt. 10. 24–33

Ps. 120; *121*; 122
Esther ch. 3
2 Cor. ch. 5

**12** S    G

**THE SIXTH SUNDAY AFTER TRINITY (Proper 10)**

*Track 1*
2 Sam. 6. 1–5, 12b–19
Ps. 24
Eph. 1. 3–14
Mark 6. 14–29

*Track 2*
Amos 7. 7–15
Ps. 85. 8–end
Eph. 1. 3–14
Mark 6. 14–29

Ps. 65
Deut. 28. 1–14
Acts 28. 17–end

**13** M   DEL 15   G

Exod. 1. 8–14, 22
Ps. 124
Matt. 10.34 – 11.1

Ps. 123; 124; 125; *126*
Esther ch. 4
2 Cor. 6.1 – 7.1

**14** Tu    Gw

**John Keble, Priest, Tractarian, Poet, 1866**
Com. Pastor
*also* Lam. 3. 19–26
Matt. 5. 1–8

*or*   Exod. 2. 1–15
Ps. 69. 1–2, 31–end
Matt. 11. 20–24

Ps. *132*; 133
Esther ch. 5
2 Cor. 7. 2–end

**15** W    Gw

**Swithun, Bishop of Winchester, c. 862**
*Bonaventure, Friar, Bishop, Teacher, 1274*
Com. Bishop
*also* James 5. 7–11, 13–18

*or*   Exod. 3. 1–6, 9–12
Ps. 103. 1–7
Matt. 11. 25–27

Ps. 119. 153–end
Esther 6. 1–13
2 Cor. 8. 1–15

**16** Th    G

*Osmund, Bishop of Salisbury, 1099*

Exod. 3. 13–20
Ps. 105. 1, 5, 8–9, 24–27
Matt. 11. 28–end

Ps. *143*; 146
Esther 6.14 – 7.end
2 Cor. 8.16 – 9.5

**17** F    G

Exod. 11.10 – 12.14
Ps. 116. 10–end
Matt. 12. 1–8

Ps. 142; *144*
Esther ch. 8
2 Cor. 9. 6–end

**18** Sa    G

*Elizabeth Ferard, first deaconess of the Church of England, Founder of the Community of St Andrew, 1883*

Exod. 12. 37–42
Ps. 136. 1–4, 10–15
Matt. 12. 14–21

Ps. 147
Esther 9. 20–28
2 Cor. ch. 10

**19** S    G

**THE SEVENTH SUNDAY AFTER TRINITY (Proper 11)**

*Track 1*
2 Sam. 7. 1–14a
Ps. 89. 20–37
Eph. 2. 11–end
Mark 6. 30–34, 53–end

*Track 2*
Jer. 23. 1–6
Ps. 23
Eph. 2. 11–end
Mark 6. 30–34, 53–end

Ps. 67; 70
Deut. 30. 1–10
1 Pet. 3. 8–18

---

*Thomas Becket may be celebrated on 7 July instead of 29 December.

| Second Service Evening Prayer | | Calendar and Holy Communion | Morning Prayer | Evening Prayer |
|---|---|---|---|---|
| Ps. 107†<br>1 Sam. 1.21 – 2.11<br>Luke 19. 41–end | G | | Neh. 13. 1–14<br>2 Cor. 1.15 – 2.4 | 1 Sam. 1.21 – 2.11<br>Luke 19. 41–end |
| Ps. 119. 129–152<br>1 Sam. 2. 12–26<br>Luke 20. 1–8 | G | | Neh. 13. 15–end<br>2 Cor. 2. 5–end | 1 Sam. 2. 12–26<br>Luke 20. 1–8 |
| Ps. 114; *116*; 117<br>1 Sam. 2. 27–end<br>Luke 20. 9–19 | G | | Esther ch. 1<br>2 Cor. ch. 3 | 1 Sam. 2. 27–end<br>Luke 20. 9–19 |
| Ps. *130*; 131; 137<br>1 Sam. 3.1 – 4.1a<br>Luke 20. 20–26 | G | | Esther ch. 2<br>2 Cor. ch. 4 | 1 Sam. 3.1 – 4.1a<br>Luke 20. 20–26 |
| Ps. 118<br>1 Sam. 4. 1b–end<br>Luke 20. 27–40<br>ct | G | | Esther ch. 3<br>2 Cor. ch. 5 | 1 Sam. 4. 1b–end<br>Luke 20. 27–40<br>ct |
| | | **THE SIXTH SUNDAY AFTER TRINITY** | | |
| Ps. 66 (*or* 66. 1–8)<br>Job 4. 1; 5. 6–end<br>*or* Ecclus. 4. 11–end<br>Rom. 15. 14–29<br>*Gospel:* Luke 10. 25–37 | G | Gen. 4. 2b–15<br>Ps. 90. 12–end<br>Rom. 6. 3–11<br>Matt. 5. 20–26 | Ps. 65<br>Deut. 28. 1–14<br>Acts 28. 17–end | Ps. 66 (*or* 66. 1–8)<br>Job 4. 1; 5. 6–end<br>*or* Ecclus. 4. 11–end<br>Luke 10. 21–24 |
| Ps. *127*; 128; 129<br>1 Sam. ch. 5<br>Luke 20.41 – 21.4 | G | | Esther ch. 4<br>2 Cor. 6.1 – 7.1 | 1 Sam. ch. 5<br>Luke 20.41 – 21.4 |
| Ps. (134); *135*<br>1 Sam. 6. 1–16<br>Luke 21. 5–19 | G | | Esther ch. 5<br>2 Cor. 7. 2–end | 1 Sam. 6. 1–16<br>Luke 21. 5–19 |
| | | **Swithun, Bishop of Winchester, c. 862** | | |
| Ps. 136<br>1 Sam. ch. 7<br>Luke 21. 20–28 | Gw | Com. Bishop | Esther 6. 1–13<br>2 Cor. 8. 1–15 | 1 Sam. ch. 7<br>Luke 21. 20–28 |
| Ps. *138*; 140; 141<br>1 Sam. ch. 8<br>Luke 21. 29–end | G | | Esther 6.14 – 7.end<br>2 Cor. 8.16 – 9.5 | 1 Sam. ch. 8<br>Luke 21. 29–end |
| Ps. 145<br>1 Sam. 9. 1–14<br>Luke 22. 1–13 | G | | Esther ch. 8<br>2 Cor. 9. 6–end | 1 Sam. 9. 1–14<br>Luke 22. 1–13 |
| Ps. *148*; 149; 150<br>1 Sam. 9.15 – 10.1<br>Luke 22. 14–23<br>ct | G | | Esther 9. 20–28<br>2 Cor. ch. 10 | 1 Sam. 9.15 – 10.1<br>Luke 22. 14–23<br>ct |
| | | **THE SEVENTH SUNDAY AFTER TRINITY** | | |
| Ps. 73 (*or* 73. 21–end)<br>Job 13.13 – 14.6<br>*or* Ecclus. 18. 1–14<br>Heb. 2. 5–end<br>*Gospel:* Luke 10. 38–end | G | 1 Kings 17. 8–16<br>Ps. 34. 11–end<br>Rom. 6. 19–end<br>Mark 8. 1–10a | Ps. 67; 70<br>Deut. 30. 1–10<br>1 Pet. 3. 13–22 | Ps. 73 (*or* 73. 21–end)<br>Job 13.13 – 14.6<br>*or* Ecclus. 18. 1–14<br>Heb. 2. 5–end |

# July 2015

| | | | Sunday Principal Service<br>Weekday Eucharist | Third Service<br>Morning Prayer |
|---|---|---|---|---|

**20** M *Margaret of Antioch, Martyr, 4th century; Bartolomé de las Casas, Apostle to the Indies, 1566*

DEL 16

|  |  | Exod. 14. 5–18 | Ps. *1*; 2; 3 |
|---|---|---|---|
|  |  | Ps. 136. 1–4, 10–15 | Jer. ch. 26 |
|  |  | or Canticle: Exod. 15. 1–6 | 2 Cor. 11. 1–15 |
| G |  | Matt. 12. 38–42 |  |

**21** Tu

|  |  | Exod. 14.21 – 15.1 | Ps. *5*; 6; (8) |
|---|---|---|---|
|  |  | Ps. 105. 37–44 | Jer. ch. 28 |
|  |  | or Canticle: Exod. 15. 8–10, 12, 17 | 2 Cor. 11. 16–end |
|  |  | Matt. 12. 46–end |  |

G

**22** W    MARY MAGDALENE

|  |  | Song of Sol. 3. 1–4 | MP: Ps. 30; 32; 150 |
|---|---|---|---|
|  |  | Ps. 42. 1–10 | 1 Sam. 16. 14–end |
| W |  | 2 Cor. 5. 14–17 | Luke 8. 1–3 |
|  |  | John 20. 1–2, 11–18 |  |

**23** Th *Bridget of Sweden, Abbess of Vadstena, 1373*

|  |  | Exod. 19. 1–2, 9–11, 16–20 | Ps. 14; *15*; 16 |
|---|---|---|---|
|  |  | Canticle: Bless the Lord | Jer. 30. 1–11 |
| G |  | Matt. 13. 10–17 | 2 Cor. ch. 13 |

**24** F

|  |  | Exod. 20. 1–17 | Ps. 17; *19* |
|---|---|---|---|
|  |  | Ps. 19. 7–11 | Jer. 30. 12–22 |
|  |  | Matt. 13. 18–23 | James 1. 1–11 |

G

**25** Sa    JAMES THE APOSTLE

|  |  | Jer. 45. 1–5 | MP: Ps. 7; 29; 117 |
|---|---|---|---|
|  |  | or Acts 11.27 – 12.2 | 2 Kings 1. 9–15 |
|  |  | Ps. 126 | Luke 9. 46–56 |
|  |  | Acts 11.27 – 12.2 |  |
| R |  | or 2 Cor. 4. 7–15 |  |
|  |  | Matt. 20. 20–28 |  |

**26** S    THE EIGHTH SUNDAY AFTER TRINITY (**Proper 12**)

| | *Track 1* | *Track 2* | |
|---|---|---|---|
|  | 2 Sam. 11. 1–15 | 2 Kings 4. 42–end | Ps. 75 |
|  | Ps. 14 | Ps. 145. 10–19 | Song of Sol. ch. 2 |
|  | Eph. 3. 14–end | Eph. 3. 14–end | or 1 Macc. 2. [1–14] 15–22 |
| G | John 6. 1–21 | John 6. 1–21 | 1 Pet. 4. 7–14 |

**27** M *Brooke Foss Westcott, Bishop of Durham, Teacher, 1901*

DEL 17

|  |  | Exod. 32. 15–24, 30–34 | Ps. 27; *30* |
|---|---|---|---|
| G |  | Ps. 106. 19–23 | Jer. 31. 23–25, 27–37 |
|  |  | Matt. 13. 31–35 | James 2. 1–13 |

**28** Tu

|  |  | Exod. 33. 7–11; 34. 5–9, 28 | Ps. 32; *36* |
|---|---|---|---|
| G |  | Ps. 103. 8–12 | Jer. 32. 1–15 |
|  |  | Matt. 13. 36–43 | James 2. 14–end |

**29** W    **Mary, Martha and Lazarus, Companions of Our Lord**

|  | Isa. 25. 6–9 | *or* | Exod. 34. 29–end | Ps. 34 |
|---|---|---|---|---|
|  | Ps. 49. 1–10, 16 |  | Ps. 99 | Jer. 33. 1–13 |
|  | Heb. 2. 10–15 |  | Matt. 13. 44–46 | James ch. 3 |
| Gw | John 12. 1–8 |  |  |  |

**30** Th    **William Wilberforce, Social Reformer; Olaudah Equiano and Thomas Clarkson, Anti-Slavery Campaigners, 1833, 1797 and 1846**

|  | Com. Saint | *or* | Exod. 40. 16–21, 34–end | Ps. 37† |
|---|---|---|---|---|
|  | *also* Job 31. 16–23 |  | Ps. 84. 1–6 | Jer. 33. 14–end |
|  | Gal. 3. 26–end; 4. 6–7 |  | Matt. 13. 47–53 | James 4. 1–12 |
| Gw | Luke 4. 16–21 |  |  |  |

| Second Service Evening Prayer | Calendar and Holy Communion | Morning Prayer | Evening Prayer |
|---|---|---|---|
| | **Margaret of Antioch, Martyr, 4th century** | | |
| Ps. **4**; 7<br>1 Sam. 10. 1–16<br>Luke 22. 24–30 | Com. Virgin Martyr | Jer. ch. 26<br>2 Cor. 11. 1–15 | 1 Sam. 10. 1–16<br>Luke 22. 24–30 |
| | **Gr** | | |
| Ps. **9**; 10†<br>1 Sam. 10. 17–end<br>Luke 22. 31–38<br>*or First EP of Mary Magdalene*<br>Ps. 139<br>Isa. 25. 1–9<br>2 Cor. 1. 3–7<br>**W ct** | | Jer. ch. 28<br>2 Cor. 11. 16–end | 1 Sam. 10. 17–end<br>Luke 22. 31–38<br>*or First EP of Mary Magdalene*<br>(Ps. 139)<br>Isa. 25. 1–9<br>2 Cor. 1. 3–7<br>**W ct** |
| | **G** | | |
| | **MARY MAGDALENE** | | |
| *EP*: Ps. 63<br>Zeph. 3. 14–end<br>Mark 15.40 – 16.7 | Zeph. 3. 14–end<br>Ps. 30. 1–5<br>2 Cor. 5. 14–17<br>John 20. 11–18 | (Ps. 30; 32; 150)<br>1 Sam. 16. 14–end<br>Luke 8. 1–3 | (Ps. 63)<br>Song of Sol. 3. 1–4<br>Mark 15.40 – 16.7 |
| | **W** | | |
| Ps. 18†<br>1 Sam. ch. 12<br>Luke 22. 47–62 | | Jer. 30. 1–11<br>2 Cor. ch. 13 | 1 Sam. ch. 12<br>Luke 22. 47–62 |
| | **G** | | |
| Ps. 22<br>1 Sam. 13. 5–18<br>Luke 22. 63–end<br>*or First EP of James*<br>Ps. 144<br>Deut. 30. 11–end<br>Mark 5. 21–end<br>**R ct** | | Jer. 30. 12–22<br>James 1. 1–11 | 1 Sam. 13. 5–18<br>Luke 22. 63–end<br>*or First EP of James*<br>(Ps. 144)<br>Deut. 30. 11–end<br>Mark 5. 21–end<br>**R ct** |
| | **G** | | |
| | **JAMES THE APOSTLE** | | |
| *EP*: Ps. 94<br>Jer. 26. 1–15<br>Mark 1. 14–20 | 2 Kings 1. 9–15<br>Ps. 15<br>Acts 11.27 – 12.3a<br>Matt. 20. 20–28 | (Ps. 7; 29; 117)<br>Jer. 45. 1–5<br>Luke 9. 46–56 | (Ps. 94)<br>Jer. 26. 1–15<br>Mark 1. 14–20 |
| | **R** | | |
| | **THE EIGHTH SUNDAY AFTER TRINITY** | | |
| Ps. 74 (or 74. 11–16)<br>Job 19. 1–27a<br>*or Ecclus. 38. 24–end*<br>Heb. ch. 8<br>*Gospel:* Luke 11. 1–13 | Jer. 23. 16–24<br>Ps. 31. 1–6<br>Rom. 8. 12–17<br>Matt. 7. 15–21 | Ps. 75<br>Song of Sol. ch. 2<br>*or 1 Macc. 2. [1–14]*<br>15–22<br>1 Pet. 4. 7–14 | Ps. 74 (or 74. 11–16)<br>Job 19. 1–27a<br>*or Ecclus. 38. 24–end*<br>Heb. ch. 8 |
| | **G** | | |
| Ps. 26; **28**; 29<br>1 Sam. 14. 24–46<br>Luke 23. 13–25 | | Jer. 31. 23–25, 27–37<br>James 2. 1–13 | 1 Sam. 14. 24–46<br>Luke 23. 13–25 |
| | **G** | | |
| Ps. 33<br>1 Sam. 15. 1–23<br>Luke 23. 26–43 | | Jer. 32. 1–15<br>James 2. 14–end | 1 Sam. 15. 1–23<br>Luke 23. 26–43 |
| | **G** | | |
| Ps. 119. 33–56<br>1 Sam. ch. 16<br>Luke 23. 44–56a | | Jer. 33. 1–13<br>James ch. 3 | 1 Sam. ch. 16<br>Luke 23. 44–56a |
| | **G** | | |
| Ps. 39; **40**<br>1 Sam. 17. 1–30<br>Luke 23.56b – 24.12 | | Jer. 33. 14–end<br>James 4. 1–12 | 1 Sam. 17. 1–30<br>Luke 23.56b – 24.12 |
| | **G** | | |

# July 2015

| | | | Sunday Principal Service / Weekday Eucharist | Third Service / Morning Prayer |
|---|---|---|---|---|

**31**   F    *Ignatius of Loyola, Founder of the Society of Jesus, 1556*

|  |  |  |
|---|---|---|
| | Lev. 23. 1, 4–11, 15–16, 27, 34–37 | Ps. 31 / Jer. ch. 35 |
| G | Ps. 81. 1–8 / Matt. 13. 54–end | James 4.13 – 5.6 |

# August 2015

**1**   Sa

| | | |
|---|---|---|
| | Lev. 25. 1, 8–17 | Ps. 41; **42**; 43 |
| | Ps. 67 | Jer. 36. 1–18 |
| G | Matt. 14. 1–12 | James 5. 7–end |

**2**   S    **THE NINTH SUNDAY AFTER TRINITY (Proper 13)**

| Track 1 | Track 2 | |
|---|---|---|
| 2 Sam. 11.26 – 12.13a | Exod. 16. 2–4, 9–15 | |
| Ps. 51. 1–13 | Ps. 78. 23–29 | Ps. 86 |
| Eph. 4. 1–16 | Eph. 4. 1–16 | Song of Sol. 5. 2–end |
| John 6. 24–35 | John 6. 24–35 | or 1 Macc. 3. 1–12 |
| G | | 2 Pet. 1. 1–15 |

**3**   M    DEL 18   G

| | | |
|---|---|---|
| Num. 11. 4–15 | Ps. 44 | |
| Ps. 81. 11–end | Jer. 36. 19–end | |
| Matt. 14. 13–21 (or 14. 22–end) | Mark 1. 1–13 | |

**4**   Tu    *John-Baptiste Vianney, Curé d'Ars, Spiritual Guide, 1859*

| | | |
|---|---|---|
| | Num. 12. 1–13 | Ps. **48**; 52 |
| | Ps. 51. 1–8 | Jer. ch. 37 |
| G | Matt. 14. 22–end / or Matt. 15. 1–2, 10–14 | Mark 1. 14–20 |

**5**   W    **Oswald, King of Northumbria, Martyr, 642**

| Com. Martyr | or | Num. 13.1–2, 25 – 14.1, 26–35 | Ps. 119. 57–80 |
|---|---|---|---|
| esp. 1 Pet. 4. 12–end | | Ps. 106. 14–24 | Jer. 38. 1–13 |
| | | Matt. 15. 21–28 | Mark 1. 21–28 |

Gr

**6**   Th    **THE TRANSFIGURATION OF OUR LORD**

| | | |
|---|---|---|
| | Dan. 7. 9–10, 13–14 | MP: Ps. 27; 150 |
| | Ps. 97 | Ecclus. 48. 1–10 |
| ꟿ | 2 Pet. 1. 16–19 | or 1 Kings 19. 1–16 |
| | Luke 9. 28–36 | 1 John 3. 1–3 |

**7**   F    *John Mason Neale, Priest, Hymn Writer, 1866*

| | | |
|---|---|---|
| | Deut. 4. 32–40 | Ps. **51**; 54 |
| | Ps. 77. 11–end | Jer. ch. 39 |
| G | Matt. 16. 24–end | Mark 2. 1–12 |

**8**   Sa    **Dominic, Priest, Founder of the Order of Preachers, 1221**

| Com. Religious | or | Deut. 6. 4–13 | Ps. 68 |
|---|---|---|---|
| also Ecclus. 39. 1–10 | | Ps. 18. 1–2, 48–end | Jer. ch. 40 |
| Gw | | Matt. 17. 14–20 | Mark 2. 13–22 |

**9**   S    **THE TENTH SUNDAY AFTER TRINITY (Proper 14)**

| Track 1 | Track 2 | |
|---|---|---|
| 2 Sam. 18. 5–9, 15, 31–33 | 1 Kings 19. 4–8 | |
| Ps. 130 | Ps. 34. 1–8 | Ps. 90 |
| Eph. 4.25 – 5.2 | Eph. 4.25 – 5.2 | Song of Sol. 8. 5–7 |
| John 6. 35, 41–51 | John 6. 35, 41–51 | or 1 Macc. 14. 4–15 |
| G | | 2 Pet. 3. 8–13 |

**10**   M    **Laurence, Deacon at Rome, Martyr, 258**

| Com. Martyr | or | Deut. 10. 12–end | Ps. 71 |
|---|---|---|---|
| DEL 19   also 2 Cor. 9. 6–10 | | Ps. 147. 13–end | Jer. ch. 41 |
| Gr | | Matt. 17. 22–end | Mark 2.23 – 3.6 |

| Second Service Evening Prayer | | Calendar and Holy Communion | Morning Prayer | Evening Prayer |
|---|---|---|---|---|
| Ps. 35<br>1 Sam. 17. 31–54<br>Luke 24. 13–35 | G | | Jer. ch. 35<br>James 4.13 – 5.6 | 1 Sam. 17. 31–54<br>Luke 24. 13–35 |
| Ps. 45; *46*<br>1 Sam. 17.55 – 18.16<br>Luke 24. 36–end<br>ct | G | Lammas Day | Jer. 36. 1–18<br>James 5. 7–end | 1 Sam. 17.55 – 18.16<br>Luke 24. 36–end<br><br>ct |
| | | **THE NINTH SUNDAY AFTER TRINITY** | | |
| Ps. 88 (*or* 88. 1–10)<br>Job ch. 28<br>*or* Ecclus. 42. 15–end<br>Heb. 11. 17–31<br>Gospel: Luke 12. 13–21 | G | Num. 10.35 – 11.3<br>Ps. 95<br>1 Cor. 10. 1–13<br>Luke 16. 1–9<br>*or* Luke 15. 11–end | Ps. 86<br>Song of Sol. 5. 2–end<br>*or* 1 Macc. 3. 1–12<br>2 Pet. 1. 1–15 | Ps. 88 (*or* 88. 1–10)<br>Job ch. 28<br>*or* Ecclus. 42. 15–end<br>Heb. 11. 17–31 |
| Ps. *47*; 49<br>1 Sam. 19. 1–18<br>Acts 1. 1–14 | G | | Jer. 36. 19–end<br>Mark 1. 1–13 | 1 Sam. 19. 1–18<br>Acts 1. 1–14 |
| Ps. 50<br>1 Sam. 20. 1–17<br>Acts 1. 15–end | G | | Jer. ch. 37<br>Mark 1. 14–20 | 1 Sam. 20. 1–17<br>Acts 1. 15–end |
| Ps. *59*; 60; (67)<br>1 Sam. 20. 18–end<br>Acts 2. 1–21<br>*or First EP of The Transfiguration*<br>Ps. 99; 110<br>Exod. 24. 12–end<br>John 12. 27–36a<br>𝕎 ct | G | | Jer. 38. 1–13<br>Mark 1. 21–28 | 1 Sam. 20. 18–end<br>Acts 2. 1–21<br>*or First EP of The Transfiguration*<br>(Ps. 99; 110)<br>Exod. 24. 12–end<br>John 12. 27–36a<br><br>𝕎 ct |
| | | **THE TRANSFIGURATION OF OUR LORD** | | |
| EP: Ps. 72<br>Exod. 34. 29–end<br>2 Cor. ch. 3 | 𝕎 | Exod. 24. 12–end<br>Ps. 84. 1–7<br>1 John 3. 1–3<br>Mark 9. 2–7 | (Ps. 27; 150)<br>Ecclus. 48. 1–10<br>*or* 1 Kings 19. 1–16<br>2 Pet. 1. 16–19 | (Ps. 72)<br>Exod. 34. 29–end<br>2 Cor. ch. 3 |
| Ps. 38<br>1 Sam. 22. 6–end<br>Acts 2. 37–end | Gw | **The Name of Jesus**<br>Jer. 14. 7–9<br>Ps. 8<br>Acts 4. 8–12<br>Matt. 1. 20–23 | Jer. ch. 39<br>Mark 2. 1–12 | 1 Sam. 22. 6–end<br>Acts 2. 37–end |
| Ps. 65; *66*<br>1 Sam. ch. 23<br>Acts 3. 1–10<br>ct | G | | Jer. ch. 40<br>Mark 2. 13–22 | 1 Sam. ch. 23<br>Acts 3. 1–10<br><br>ct |
| | | **THE TENTH SUNDAY AFTER TRINITY** | | |
| Ps. 91 (*or* 91. 1–12)<br>Job 39.1 – 40.4<br>*or* Ecclus. 43. 13–end<br>Heb. 12. 1–17<br>Gospel: Luke 12. 32–40 | G | Jer. 7. 9–15<br>Ps. 17. 1–8<br>1 Cor. 12. 1–11<br>Luke 19. 41–47a | Ps. 89. 1–18<br>Song of Sol. 8. 5–7<br>*or* 1 Macc. 14. 4–15<br>2 Pet. 3. 8–13 | Ps. 91 (*or* 91. 1–12)<br>Job 39.1 – 40.4<br>*or* Ecclus. 43. 13–end<br>Heb. 12. 1–17 |
| Ps. *72*; 75<br>1 Sam. ch. 24<br>Acts 3. 11–end | Gr | **Laurence, Deacon at Rome, Martyr, 258**<br>Com. Martyr | Jer. ch. 41<br>Mark 2.23 – 3.6 | 1 Sam. ch. 24<br>Acts 3. 11–end |

# August 2015

| | | Sunday Principal Service / Weekday Eucharist | Third Service / Morning Prayer |
|---|---|---|---|

**11** Tu

**Clare of Assisi, Founder of the Minoresses (Poor Clares), 1253**
*John Henry Newman, Priest, Tractarian, 1890*

Com. Religious      *or*
*esp.* Song of Sol. 8. 6–7

Gw

| Sunday Principal Service / Weekday Eucharist | Third Service / Morning Prayer |
|---|---|
| Deut. 31. 1–8 | Ps. 73 |
| Ps. 107. 1–3, 42–end | Jer. ch. 42 |
| *or Canticle*: Deut. 32. 3–4, 7–9 | Mark 3. 7–19a |
| Matt. 18. 1–5, 10, 12–14 | |

**12** W / G

| | |
|---|---|
| Deut. ch. 34 | Ps. 77 |
| Ps. 66. 14–end | Jer. ch. 43 |
| Matt. 18. 15–20 | Mark 3. 19b–end |

**13** Th

**Jeremy Taylor, Bishop of Down and Connor, Teacher, 1667**
*Florence Nightingale, Nurse, Social Reformer, 1910; Octavia Hill, Social Reformer, 1912*

Com. Teacher      *or*
*also* Titus 2. 7–8, 11–14

Gw

| | |
|---|---|
| Josh. 3. 7–11, 13–17 | Ps. 78. 1–39† |
| Ps. 114 | Jer. 44. 1–14 |
| Matt. 18.21 – 19.1 | Mark 4. 1–20 |

**14** F

*Maximilian Kolbe, Friar, Martyr, 1941*

| | |
|---|---|
| Josh. 24. 1–13 | Ps. 55 |
| Ps. 136. 1–3, 16–22 | Jer. 44. 15–end |
| Matt. 19. 3–12 | Mark 4. 21–34 |

G

**15** Sa

THE BLESSED VIRGIN MARY*

W

| | |
|---|---|
| Isa. 61. 10–end | MP: Ps. 98; 138; 147. 1–12 |
| *or* Rev. 11.19 – 12.6, 10 | Isa. 7. 10–15 |
| Ps. 45. 10–end | Luke 11. 27–28 |
| Gal. 4. 4–7 | |
| Luke 1. 46–55 | |

*or, if The Blessed Virgin Mary is
celebrated on 8 September:*

G

| | |
|---|---|
| Josh. 24. 14–29 | Ps. 76; 79 |
| Ps. 16. 1, 5–end | Jer. ch. 45 |
| Matt. 19. 13–15 | Mark 4. 35–end |

**16** S

THE ELEVENTH SUNDAY AFTER TRINITY **(Proper 15)**

Track 1
1 Kings 2. 10–12; 3. 3–14
Ps. 111
Eph. 5. 15–20
G   John 6. 51–58

| Track 2 | Third Service / Morning Prayer |
|---|---|
| Prov. 9. 1–6 | Ps. 106. 1–10 |
| Ps. 34. 9–14 | Jonah ch. 1 |
| Eph. 5. 15–20 | *or* Ecclus. 3. 1–15 |
| John 6. 51–58 | 2 Pet. 3. 14–end |

**17** M
DEL 20   G

| | |
|---|---|
| Judg. 2. 11–19 | Ps. 80; 82 |
| Ps. 106. 34–42 | Mic. 1. 1–9 |
| Matt. 19. 16–22 | Mark 5. 1–20 |

**18** Tu / G

| | |
|---|---|
| Judg. 6. 11–24 | Ps. 87; 89. 1–18 |
| Ps. 85. 8–end | Mic. ch. 2 |
| Matt. 19. 23–end | Mark 5. 21–34 |

**19** W / G

| | |
|---|---|
| Judg. 9. 6–15 | Ps. 119. 105–128 |
| Ps. 21. 1–6 | Mic. ch. 3 |
| Matt. 20. 1–16 | Mark 5. 35–end |

**20** Th

**Bernard, Abbot of Clairvaux, Teacher, 1153**
*William and Catherine Booth, Founders of the Salvation Army, 1912 and 1890*

Com. Religious      *or*
*esp.* Rev. 19. 5–9

Gw

| | |
|---|---|
| Judg. 11. 29–end | Ps. 90; 92 |
| Ps. 40. 4–11 | Mic. 4.1 – 5.1 |
| Matt. 22. 1–14 | Mark 6. 1–13 |

**21** F / G

| | |
|---|---|
| Ruth 1. 1, 3–6, 14–16, 22 | Ps. 88; (95) |
| Ps. 146 | Mic. 5. 2–end |
| Matt. 22. 34–40 | Mark 6. 14–29 |

**22** Sa / G

| | |
|---|---|
| Ruth 2. 1–3, 8–11; 4. 13–17 | Ps. 96; 97; 100 |
| Ps. 128 | Mic. ch. 6 |
| Matt. 23. 1–12 | Mark 6. 30–44 |

*The Blessed Virgin Mary may be celebrated on 8 September instead of 15 August.

| Second Service<br>Evening Prayer | Calendar and Holy Communion | Morning Prayer | Evening Prayer |
|---|---|---|---|
| Ps. 74<br>1 Sam. ch. 26<br>Acts 4. 1–12 | G | Jer. ch. 42<br>Mark 3. 7–19a | 1 Sam. ch. 26<br>Acts 4. 1–12 |
| Ps. 119. 81–104<br>1 Sam. 28. 3–end<br>Acts 4. 13–31 | G | Jer. ch. 43<br>Mark 3. 19b–end | 1 Sam. 28. 3–end<br>Acts 4. 13–31 |
| Ps. 78. 40–end†<br>1 Sam. ch. 31<br>Acts 4.32 – 5.11 | G | Jer. 44. 1–14<br>Mark 4. 1–20 | 1 Sam. ch. 31<br>Acts 4.32 – 5.11 |
| Ps. 69<br>2 Sam. ch. 1<br>Acts 5. 12–26<br>*or First EP of The Blessed Virgin Mary*<br>Ps. 72<br>Prov. 8. 22–31<br>John 19. 23–27<br>**W ct** | G | Jer. 44. 15–end<br>Mark 4. 21–34 | 2 Sam. ch. 1<br>Acts 5. 12–26 |
| *EP*: Ps. 132<br>Song of Sol. 2. 1–7<br>Acts 1. 6–14 | To celebrate The Blessed Virgin Mary, see *Common Worship* provision.<br>Jer. ch. 45<br>Mark 4. 35–end | | 2 Sam. 2. 1–11<br>Acts 5. 27–end |
| Ps. 81; **84**<br>2 Sam. 2. 1–11<br>Acts 5. 27–end<br>ct | G | | ct |
| | **THE ELEVENTH SUNDAY AFTER TRINITY** | | |
| Ps. [92]; 100<br>Exod. 2.23 – 3.10<br>Heb. 13. 1–15<br>*Gospel*: Luke 12. 49–56 | 1 Kings 3. 5–15<br>Ps. 28<br>1 Cor. 15. 1–11<br>Luke 18. 9–14  G | Ps. 106. 1–10<br>Jonah ch. 1<br>*or* Ecclus. 3. 1–15<br>2 Pet. 3. 14–end | Ps. [92]; 100<br>Exod. 2.23 – 3.10<br>Heb. 13. 1–15 |
| Ps. **85**; 86<br>2 Sam. 3. 12–end<br>Acts ch. 6 | G | Mic. 1. 1–9<br>Mark 5. 1–20 | 2 Sam. 3. 12–end<br>Acts ch. 6 |
| Ps. 89. 19–end<br>2 Sam. 5. 1–12<br>Acts 7. 1–16 | G | Mic. ch. 2<br>Mark 5. 21–34 | 2 Sam. 5. 1–12<br>Acts 7. 1–16 |
| Ps. **91**; 93<br>2 Sam. 6. 1–19<br>Acts 7. 17–43 | G | Mic. ch. 3<br>Mark 5. 35–end | 2 Sam. 6. 1–19<br>Acts 7. 17–43 |
| Ps. 94<br>2 Sam. 7. 1–17<br>Acts 7. 44–53 | G | Mic. 4.1 – 5.1<br>Mark 6. 1–13 | 2 Sam. 7. 1–17<br>Acts 7. 44–53 |
| Ps. 102<br>2 Sam. 7. 18–end<br>Acts 7.54 – 8.3 | G | Mic. 5. 2–end<br>Mark 6. 14–29 | 2 Sam. 7. 18–end<br>Acts 7.54 – 8.3 |
| Ps. 104<br>2 Sam. ch. 9<br>Acts 8. 4–25<br>ct | G | Mic. ch. 6<br>Mark 6. 30–44 | 2 Sam. ch. 9<br>Acts 8. 4–25<br>ct |

# August 2015

|  |  |  | Sunday Principal Service<br>Weekday Eucharist | Third Service<br>Morning Prayer |
|---|---|---|---|---|

| | | | Sunday Principal Service / Weekday Eucharist | Third Service / Morning Prayer |
|---|---|---|---|---|
| **23** | S | THE TWELFTH SUNDAY AFTER TRINITY **(Proper 16)**<br>*Track 1*<br>1 Kings 8. [1, 6, 10–11] 22–30,<br>41–43<br>Ps. 84<br>Eph. 6. 10–20<br>John 6. 56–69 | *Track 2*<br>Josh. 24. 1–2a, 14–18<br>Ps. 34. 15–end<br>Eph. 6. 10–20<br>John 6. 56–69 | Ps. 115<br>Jonah ch. 2<br>or Ecclus. 3. 17–29<br>Rev. ch. 1 |
| | G | | | |
| **24**<br>DEL 21 | M | BARTHOLOMEW THE APOSTLE | Isa. 43. 8–13<br>or Acts 5. 12–16<br>Ps. 145. 1–7<br>Acts 5. 12–16<br>or 1 Cor. 4. 9–15<br>Luke 22. 24–30 | MP: Ps. 86; 117<br>Gen. 28. 10–17<br>John 1. 43–end |
| | R | | | |
| **25** | Tu | | 1 Thess. 2. 1–8<br>Ps. 139. 1–9<br>Matt. 23. 23–26 | Ps. 106† (or Ps. 103)<br>Mic. 7. 8–end<br>Mark 7. 1–13 |
| | G | | | |
| **26** | W | | 1 Thess. 2. 9–13<br>Ps. 126<br>Matt. 23. 27–32 | Ps. 110; *111*; 112<br>Hab. 1. 1–11<br>Mark 7. 14–23 |
| | G | | | |
| **27** | Th | Monica, Mother of Augustine of Hippo, 387<br>Com. Saint            *or*<br>*also* Ecclus. 26. 1–3, 13–16 | 1 Thess. 3. 7–end<br>Ps. 90. 13–end<br>Matt. 24. 42–end | Ps. 113; *115*<br>Hab. 1.12 – 2.5<br>Mark 7. 24–30 |
| | Gw | | | |
| **28** | F | Augustine, Bishop of Hippo, Teacher, 430<br>Com. Teacher          *or*<br>*esp.* Ecclus. 39. 1–10<br>*also* Rom. 13. 11–13 | 1 Thess. 4. 1–8<br>Ps. 97<br>Matt. 25. 1–13 | Ps. 139<br>Hab. 2. 6–end<br>Mark 7. 31–end |
| | Gw | | | |
| **29** | Sa | The Beheading of John the Baptist<br>Jer. 1. 4–10            *or*<br>Ps. 11<br>Heb. 11.32 – 12.2<br>Matt. 14. 1–12 | 1 Thess. 4. 9–12<br>Ps. 98. 1–2, 8–end<br>Matt. 25. 14–30 | Ps. 120; *121*; 122<br>Hab. 3. 2–19a<br>Mark 8. 1–10 |
| | Gr | | | |
| **30** | S | THE THIRTEENTH SUNDAY AFTER TRINITY **(Proper 17)**<br>*Track 1*<br>Song of Sol. 2. 8–13<br>Ps. 45. 1–2, 6–9 (or 1–7)<br>James 1. 17–end<br>Mark 7. 1–8, 14–15, 21–23 | *Track 2*<br>Deut. 4. 1–2, 6–9<br>Ps. 15<br>James 1. 17–end<br>Mark 7. 1–8, 14–15, 21–23 | Ps. 119. 17–40<br>Jonah 3. 1–9<br>or Ecclus. 11. [7–18] 19–28<br>Rev. 3. 14–end |
| | G | | | |
| **31**<br>DEL 22 | M | Aidan, Bishop of Lindisfarne, Missionary, 651<br>Com. Missionary      *or*<br>*also* 1 Cor. 9. 16–19 | 1 Thess. 4. 13–end<br>Ps. 96<br>Luke 4. 16–30 | Ps. 123; 124; 125; *126*<br>Hag. 1. 1–11<br>Mark 8. 11–21 |
| | Gw | | | |

# September 2015

| | | | Sunday Principal Service / Weekday Eucharist | Third Service / Morning Prayer |
|---|---|---|---|---|
| **1** | Tu | *Giles of Provence, Hermit, c. 710* | 1 Thess. 5. 1–6, 9–11<br>Ps. 27. 1–8<br>Luke 4. 31–37 | Ps. *132*; 133<br>Hag. 1.12 – 2.9<br>Mark 8. 22–26 |
| | G | | | |
| **2** | W | *The Martyrs of Papua New Guinea, 1901 and 1942* | Col. 1. 1–8<br>Ps. 34. 11–18<br>Luke 4. 38–end | Ps. 119. 153–end<br>Hag. 2. 10–end<br>Mark 8.27 – 9.1 |
| | G | | | |
| **3** | Th | Gregory the Great, Bishop of Rome, Teacher, 604<br>Com. Teacher          *or*<br>*also* 1 Thess. 2. 3–8 | Col. 1. 9–14<br>Ps. 98. 1–5<br>Luke 5. 1–11 | Ps. *143*; 146<br>Zech. 1. 1–17<br>Mark 9. 2–13 |
| | Gw | | | |

| Second Service Evening Prayer | Calendar and Holy Communion | | Morning Prayer | Evening Prayer |
|---|---|---|---|---|
| | **THE TWELFTH SUNDAY AFTER TRINITY** | | | |
| Ps. 116 (or 116. 10–end)<br>Exod. 4.27 – 5.1<br>Heb. 13. 16–21<br>*Gospel: Luke 13. 10–17*<br>*or First EP of Bartholomew*<br>Ps. 97<br>Isa. 61. 1–9<br>2 Cor. 6. 1–10<br><br>**R ct** | Exod. 34. 29–end<br>Ps. 34. 1–10<br>2 Cor. 3. 4–9<br>Mark 7. 31–37 | **G** | Ps. 115<br>Jonah ch. 2<br>or Ecclus. 3. 17–29<br>Rev. ch. 1 | Ps. 116<br>(or 116. 10–end)<br>Exod. 4.27 – 5.1<br>Heb. 13. 16–21<br>*or First EP of*<br>*Bartholomew*<br>Ps. 97<br>Isa. 61. 1–9<br>2 Cor. 6. 1–10<br>**R ct** |
| | **BARTHOLOMEW THE APOSTLE** | | | |
| *EP:* Ps. 91; 116<br>Ecclus. 39. 1–10<br>or Deut. 18. 15–19<br>Matt. 10. 1–22 | Gen. 28. 10–17<br>Ps. 15<br>Acts 5. 12–16<br>Luke 22. 24–30 | **R** | (Ps. 86; 117)<br>Isa. 43. 8–13<br>John 1. 43–end | (Ps. 91; 116)<br>Ecclus. 39. 1–10<br>or Deut. 18. 15–19<br>Matt. 10. 1–22 |
| Ps. 107†<br>2 Sam. 12. 1–25<br>Acts 9. 1–19a | | **G** | Mic. 7. 8–end<br>Mark 7. 1–13 | 2 Sam. 12. 1–25<br>Acts 9. 1–19a |
| Ps. 119. 129–152<br>2 Sam. 15. 1–12<br>Acts 9. 19b–31 | | **G** | Hab. 1. 1–11<br>Mark 7. 14–23 | 2 Sam. 15. 1–12<br>Acts 9. 19b–31 |
| Ps. 114; *116*; 117<br>2 Sam. 15. 13–end<br>Acts 9. 32–end | | **G** | Hab. 1.12 – 2.5<br>Mark 7. 24–30 | 2 Sam. 15. 13–end<br>Acts 9. 32–end |
| Ps. *130*; 131; 137<br>2 Sam. 16. 1–14<br>Acts 10. 1–16 | **Augustine, Bishop of Hippo, 430**<br>Com. Doctor | **Gw** | Hab. 2. 6–end<br>Mark 7. 31–end | 2 Sam. 16. 1–14<br>Acts 10. 1–16 |
| Ps. 118<br>2 Sam. 17. 1–23<br>Acts 10. 17–33<br>**ct** | **The Beheading of John the Baptist**<br>2 Chron. 24. 17–21<br>Ps. 92. 11–end<br>Heb. 11.32 – 12.2<br>Matt. 14. 1–12 | **Gr** | Hab. 3. 2–19a<br>Mark 8. 1–10 | 2 Sam. 17. 1–23<br>Acts 10. 17–33<br><br>**ct** |
| | **THE THIRTEENTH SUNDAY AFTER TRINITY** | | | |
| Ps. 119. 1–16 (or 9–16)<br>Exod. 12. 21–27<br>Matt. 4.23 – 5.20 | Lev. 19. 13–18<br>Ps. 74. 20–end<br>Gal. 3. 16–22<br>or Heb. 13. 1–6<br>Luke 10. 23b–37 | **G** | Ps. 119. 17–40<br>Jonah 3. 1–9<br>or Ecclus. 11. [7–18]<br>19–28<br>Rev. 3. 14–end | Ps. 119. 1–16<br>(or 9–16)<br>Exod. 12. 21–27<br>Matt. 4.23 – 5.20 |
| Ps. *127*; 128; 129<br>2 Sam. 18. 1–18<br>Acts 10. 34–end | | **G** | Hag. 1. 1–11<br>Mark 8. 11–21 | 2 Sam. 18. 1–18<br>Acts 10. 34–end |
| Ps. (134); *135*<br>2 Sam. 18.19 – 19.8a<br>Acts 11. 1–18 | **Giles of Provence, Hermit, c. 710**<br>Com. Abbot | **Gw** | Hag. 1.12 – 2.9<br>Mark 8. 22–26 | 2 Sam. 18.19 – 19.8a<br>Acts 11. 1–18 |
| Ps. 136<br>2 Sam. 19. 8b–23<br>Acts 11. 19–end | | **G** | Hag. 2. 10–end<br>Mark 8.27 – 9.1 | 2 Sam. 19. 8b–23<br>Acts 11. 19–end |
| Ps. *138*; 140; 141<br>2 Sam. 19. 24–end<br>Acts 12. 1–17 | | **G** | Zech. 1. 1–17<br>Mark 9. 2–13 | 2 Sam. 19. 24–end<br>Acts 12. 1–17 |

# September 2015

| | | | Sunday Principal Service / Weekday Eucharist | Third Service / Morning Prayer |
|---|---|---|---|---|

| **4** | F | *Birinus, Bishop of Dorchester (Oxon), Apostle of Wessex, 650\** | | |
| | | | Col. 1. 15–20 | Ps. 142; **144** |
| | | | Ps. 89. 19b–28 | Zech. 1.18 – 2.end |
| | G | | Luke 5. 33–end | Mark 9. 14–29 |

| **5** | Sa | | Col. 1. 21–23 | Ps. 147 |
| | | | Ps. 117 | Zech. ch. 3 |
| | G | | Luke 6. 1–5 | Mark 9. 30–37 |

| **6** | S | THE FOURTEENTH SUNDAY AFTER TRINITY (**Proper 18**) | | |
| | | *Track 1* | *Track 2* | |
| | | Prov. 22. 1–2, 8–9, 22–23 | Isa. 35. 4–7a | Ps. 119. 57–72 |
| | | Ps. 125 | Ps. 146 | Jonah 3.10 – 4.11 |
| | | James 2. 1–10 [11–13] 14–17 | James 2. 1–10 [11–13] 14–17 | or Ecclus. 27.30 – 28.9 |
| | G | Mark 7. 24–end | Mark 7. 24–end | Rev. 8. 1–5 |

| **7** DEL 23 | M | | | |
| | | | Col. 1.24 – 2.3 | Ps. **1**; 2; 3 |
| | | | Ps. 62. 1–7 | Zech. ch. 4 |
| | G | | Luke 6. 6–11 | Mark 9. 38–end |

| **8** | Tu | **The Birth of the Blessed Virgin Mary\*\*** | | |
| | | Com. BVM | *or* Col. 2. 6–15 | Ps. **5**; 6; (8) |
| | | | Ps. 8 | Zech. 6. 9–end |
| | Gw | | Luke 6. 12–19 | Mark 10. 1–16 |

| **9** | W | *Charles Fuge Lowder, Priest, 1880* | | |
| | | | Col. 3. 1–11 | Ps. 119. 1–32 |
| | | | Ps. 15 | Zech. ch. 7 |
| | G | | Luke 6. 20–26 | Mark 10. 17–31 |

| **10** | Th | | Col. 3. 12–17 | Ps. 14; **15**; 16 |
| | | | Ps. 149. 1–5 | Zech. 8. 1–8 |
| | G | | Luke 6. 27–38 | Mark 10. 32–34 |

| **11** | F | | 1 Tim. 1. 1–2, 12–14 | Ps. 17; **19** |
| | | | Ps. 16 | Zech. 8. 9–end |
| | G | | Luke 6. 39–42 | Mark 10. 35–45 |

| **12** | Sa | | 1 Tim. 1. 15–17 | Ps. 20; 21; **23** |
| | | | Ps. 113 | Zech. 9. 1–12 |
| | G | | Luke 6. 43–end | Mark 10. 46–end |

| **13** | S | THE FIFTEENTH SUNDAY AFTER TRINITY (**Proper 19**) | | |
| | | *Track 1* | *Track 2* | |
| | | Prov. 1. 20–33 | Isa. 50. 4–9a | Ps. 119. 105–120 |
| | | Ps. 19 (or 19. 1–6) | Ps. 116. 1–8 | Isa. 44.24 – 45.8 |
| | | or Canticle: Wisd. 7.26 – 8.1 | James 3. 1–12 | Rev. 12. 1–12 |
| | | James 3. 1–12 | Mark 8. 27–end | |
| | | Mark 8. 27–end | | |
| | G | | | |

| **14** DEL 24 | M | HOLY CROSS DAY | | |
| | | | Num. 21. 4–9 | MP: Ps. 2; 8; 146 |
| | | | Ps. 22. 23–28 | Gen. 3. 1–15 |
| | | | Phil. 2. 6–11 | John 12. 27–36a |
| | R | | John 3. 13–17 | |

| **15** | Tu | **Cyprian, Bishop of Carthage, Martyr, 258** | | |
| | | Com. Martyr | *or* 1 Tim. 3. 1–13 | Ps. 32; **36** |
| | | esp. 1 Pet. 4. 12–end | Ps. 101 | Zech. 11. 4–end |
| | Gr | also Matt. 18. 18–22 | Luke 7. 11–17 | Mark 11. 12–26 |

\*Cuthbert may be celebrated on 4 September instead of 20 March.
\*\*The Blessed Virgin Mary may be celebrated on 8 September instead of 15 August.

| Second Service Evening Prayer | Calendar and Holy Communion | | Morning Prayer | Evening Prayer |
|---|---|---|---|---|
| Ps. 145 2 Sam. 23. 1–7 Acts 12. 18–end | | G | Zech. 1.18 – 2.end Mark 9. 14–29 | 2 Sam. 23. 1–7 Acts 12. 18–end |
| Ps. *148*; 149; 150 2 Sam. ch. 24 Acts 13. 1–12 ct | | G | Zech. ch. 3 Mark 9. 30–37 | 2 Sam. ch. 24 Acts 13. 1–12 ct |
| | THE FOURTEENTH SUNDAY AFTER TRINITY | | | |
| Ps. 119. 41–56 (or 49–56) Exod. 14. 5–end Matt. 6. 1–18 | 2 Kings 5. 9–16 Ps. 118. 1–9 Gal. 5. 16–24 Luke 17. 11–19 | G | Ps. 119. 57–72 Jonah 3.10 – 4.11 or Ecclus. 27.30 – 28.9 Rev. 8. 1–5 | Ps. 119. 41–56 (or 49–56) Exod. 14. 5–end Matt. 6. 1–18 |
| Ps. *4*; 7 1 Kings 1. 5–31 Acts 13. 13–43 | **Evurtius, Bishop of Orleans, 4th century** Com. Bishop | Gw | Zech. ch. 4 Mark 9. 38–end | 1 Kings 1. 5–31 Acts 13. 13–43 |
| Ps. *9*; 10† 1 Kings 1.32 – 2.4, 10–12 Acts 13.44 – 14.7 | **The Nativity of the Blessed Virgin Mary** Gen. 3. 9–15 Ps. 45. 11–18 Rom. 5. 12–17 Luke 11. 27–28 | Gw | Zech. 6. 9–end Mark 10. 1–16 | 1 Kings 1.32 – 2.4, 10–12 Acts 13.44 – 14.7 |
| Ps. *11*; 12; 13 1 Kings ch. 3 Acts 14. 8–end | | G | Zech. ch. 7 Mark 10. 17–31 | 1 Kings ch. 3 Acts 14. 8–end |
| Ps. 18† 1 Kings 4.29 – 5.12 Acts 15. 1–21 | | G | Zech. 8. 1–8 Mark 10. 32–34 | 1 Kings 4.29 – 5.12 Acts 15. 1–21 |
| Ps. 22 1 Kings 6. 1, 11–28 Acts 15. 22–35 | | G | Zech. 8. 9–end Mark 10. 35–45 | 1 Kings 6. 1, 11–28 Acts 15. 22–35 |
| Ps. *24*; 25 1 Kings 8. 1–30 Acts 15.36 – 16.5 ct | | G | Zech. 9. 1–12 Mark 10. 46–end | 1 Kings 8. 1–30 Acts 15.36 – 16.5 ct |
| | THE FIFTEENTH SUNDAY AFTER TRINITY | | | |
| Ps. 119. 73–88 (or 73–80) Exod. 18. 13–26 Matt. 7. 1–14 or First EP of Holy Cross Day Ps. 66 Isa. 52.13 – 53.end Eph. 2. 11–end R ct | Josh. 24. 14–25 Ps. 92. 1–6 Gal. 6. 11–end Matt. 6. 24–end | G | Ps. 119. 105–120 Isa. 44.24 – 45.8 Rev. 12. 1–12 | Ps. 119. 73–88 (or 73–80) Exod. 18. 13–26 Matt. 7. 1–14 |
| EP: Ps. 110; 150 Isa. 63. 1–16 1 Cor. 1. 18–25 | **Holy Cross Day** To celebrate Holy Cross as a festival, see *Common Worship* provision. Num. 21. 4–9 Ps. 67 1 Cor. 1. 17–25 John 12. 27–33 | Gr | Zech. ch. 10 Mark 11. 1–11 | 1 Kings 8. 31–62 Acts 16. 6–24 |
| Ps. 33 1 Kings 8.63 – 9.9 Acts 16. 25–end | | G | Zech. 11. 4–end Mark 11. 12–26 | 1 Kings 8.63 – 9.9 Acts 16. 25–end |

# September 2015

| | | Sunday Principal Service<br>Weekday Eucharist | Third Service<br>Morning Prayer |
|---|---|---|---|

**16** W — **Ninian, Bishop of Galloway, Apostle of the Picts, c. 432**
*Edward Bouverie Pusey, Priest, Tractarian, 1882*

| | | | |
|---|---|---|---|
| | Com. Missionary | *or* | I Tim. 3. 14–end | Ps. 34 |
| | *esp.* Acts 13. 46–49 | | Ps. 111. 1–5 | Zech. 12. 1–10 |
| Gw | Mark 16. 15–end | | Luke 7. 31–35 | Mark 11. 27–end |

**17** Th — **Hildegard, Abbess of Bingen, Visionary, 1179**

| | | | |
|---|---|---|---|
| | Com. Religious | *or* | I Tim. 4. 12–end | Ps. 37† |
| | *also* I Cor. 2. 9–13 | | Ps. 111. 6–end | Zech. ch. 13 |
| Gw | Luke 10. 21–24 | | Luke 7. 36–end | Mark 12. 1–12 |

**18** F

| | | |
|---|---|---|
| | I Tim. 6. 2b–12 | Ps. 31 |
| | Ps. 49. 1–9 | Zech. 14. 1–11 |
| G | Luke 8. 1–3 | Mark 12. 13–17 |

**19** Sa — *Theodore of Tarsus, Archbishop of Canterbury, 690*

| | | |
|---|---|---|
| | I Tim. 6. 13–16 | Ps. 41; **42**; 43 |
| | Ps. 100 | Zech. 14. 12–end |
| G | Luke 8. 4–15 | Mark 12. 18–27 |

**20** S — **THE SIXTEENTH SUNDAY AFTER TRINITY (Proper 20)**

| Track I | Track 2 | |
|---|---|---|
| Prov. 31. 10–end | Wisd. 1.16 – 2.1, 12–22 | Ps. 119. 153–end |
| Ps. I | *or* Jer. 11. 18–20 | Isa. 45. 9–22 |
| James 3.13 – 4.3, 7–8a | Ps. 54 | Rev. 14. 1–5 |
| Mark 9. 30–37 | James 3.13 – 4.3, 7–8a | |
| | Mark 9. 30–37 | |

G

**21** M — **MATTHEW, APOSTLE AND EVANGELIST**
DEL 25

| | | |
|---|---|---|
| | Prov. 3. 13–18 | *MP:* Ps. 49; 117 |
| | Ps. 119. 65–72 | I Kings 19. 15–end |
| | 2 Cor. 4. 1–6 | 2 Tim. 3. 14–end |
| R | Matt. 9. 9–13 | |

**22** Tu

| | | |
|---|---|---|
| | Ezra 6. 7–8, 12, 14–20 | Ps. **48**; 52 |
| | Ps. 124 | Ecclus. 1. 11–end |
| | Luke 8. 19–21 | *or* Ezek. 1.15 – 2.2 |
| G | | Mark 12. 35–end |

**23** W — Ember Day*

| | | |
|---|---|---|
| | Ezra 9. 5–9 | Ps. 119. 57–80 |
| | *Canticle:* Song of Tobit | Ecclus. ch. 2 |
| G *or* R | *or* Ps. 103. 1–6 | *or* Ezek. 2.3 – 3.11 |
| | Luke 9. 1–6 | Mark 13. 1–13 |

**24** Th

| | | |
|---|---|---|
| | Hag. 1. 1–8 | Ps. 56; **57**; (63†) |
| | Ps. 149. 1–5 | Ecclus. 3. 17–29 |
| | Luke 9. 7–9 | *or* Ezek. 3. 12–end |
| G | | Mark 13. 14–23 |

**25** F — **Lancelot Andrewes, Bishop of Winchester, Spiritual Writer, 1626**
Ember Day*
*Sergei of Radonezh, Russian Monastic Reformer, Teacher, 1392*

| | | | |
|---|---|---|---|
| | Com. Bishop | *or* | Hag. 1.15b – 2.9 | Ps. **51**; 54 |
| | *esp.* Isa. 6. 1–8 | | Ps. 43 | Ecclus. 4. 11–28 |
| | | | Luke 9. 18–22 | *or* Ezek. ch. 8 |
| Gw *or* Rw | | | | Mark 13. 24–31 |

**26** Sa — Ember Day*
*Wilson Carlile, Founder of the Church Army, 1942*

| | | |
|---|---|---|
| | Zech. 2. 1–5, 10–11 | Ps. 68 |
| | Ps. 125 | Ecclus. 4.29 – 6.1 |
| | *or Canticle:* Jer. 31. 10–13 | *or* Ezek. ch. 9 |
| G *or* R | Luke 9. 43b–45 | Mark 13. 32–end |

*For Ember Day provision, see p. 11.

| Second Service Evening Prayer | Calendar and Holy Communion | | Morning Prayer | Evening Prayer |
|---|---|---|---|---|
| Ps. 119. 33–56<br>I Kings 10. 1–25<br>Acts 17. 1–15 | Ember Day<br>Ember CEG<br><br>G | | Zech. 12. 1–10<br>Mark 11. 27–end | I Kings 10. 1–25<br>Acts 17. 1–15 |
| Ps. 39; **40**<br>I Kings 11. 1–13<br>Acts 17. 16–end | **Lambert, Bishop of Maastricht, Martyr, 709**<br>Com. Martyr<br><br>Gr | | Zech. ch. 13<br>Mark 12. 1–12 | I Kings 11. 1–13<br>Acts 17. 16–end |
| Ps. 35<br>I Kings 11. 26–end<br>Acts 18. 1–21 | Ember Day<br>Ember CEG<br><br>G | | Zech. 14. 1–11<br>Mark 12. 13–17 | I Kings 11. 26–end<br>Acts 18. 1–21 |
| Ps. 45; **46**<br>I Kings 12. 1–24<br>Acts 18.22 – 19.7<br>ct | Ember Day<br>Ember CEG<br><br>G | | Zech. 14. 12–end<br>Mark 12. 18–27 | I Kings 12. 1–24<br>Acts 18.22 – 19.7<br><br>ct |
| Ps. 119. 137–152<br>(or 137–144)<br>Exod. 19. 10–end<br>Matt. 8. 23–end<br>or First EP of Matthew<br>Ps. 34<br>Isa. 33. 13–17<br>Matt. 6. 19–end<br>**R** ct | THE SIXTEENTH SUNDAY AFTER TRINITY<br>I Kings 17. 17–end<br>Ps. 102. 12–17<br>Eph. 3. 13–end<br>Luke 7. 11–17<br><br><br><br>G | | Ps. 119. 153–end<br>Isa. 45. 9–22<br>Rev. 14. 1–5 | Ps. 119. 137–152<br>(or 137–144)<br>Exod. 19. 10–end<br>Matt. 8. 23–end<br>or First EP of Matthew<br>Ps. 34<br>Prov. 3. 3–18<br>Matt. 6. 19–end<br>**R** ct |
| EP: Ps. 119. 33–40, 89–96<br>Eccles. 5. 4–12<br>Matt. 19. 16–end | MATTHEW, APOSTLE AND EVANGELIST<br>Isa. 33. 13–17<br>Ps. 119. 65–72<br>2 Cor. 4. 1–6<br>Matt. 9. 9–13 | R | (Ps. 49; 117)<br>I Kings 19. 15–end<br>2 Tim. 3. 14–end | (Ps. 119. 33–40,<br>89–96)<br>Eccles. 5. 4–12<br>Matt. 19. 16–end |
| Ps. 50<br>I Kings 13. 11–end<br>Acts 19. 21–end | G | | Ecclus. 1. 11–end<br>or Ezek. 1.15 – 2.2<br>Mark 12. 35–end | I Kings 13. 11–end<br>Acts 19. 21–end |
| Ps. **59**; 60; (67)<br>I Kings ch. 17<br>Acts 20. 1–16 | G | | Ecclus. ch. 2<br>or Ezek. 2.3 – 3.11<br>Mark 13. 1–13 | I Kings ch. 17<br>Acts 20. 1–16 |
| Ps. 61; **62**; 64<br>I Kings 18. 1–20<br>Acts 20. 17–end | G | | Ecclus. 3. 17–29<br>or Ezek. 3. 12–end<br>Mark 13. 14–23 | I Kings 18. 1–20<br>Acts 20. 17–end |
| Ps. 38<br>I Kings 18. 21–end<br>Acts 21. 1–16 | G | | Ecclus. 4. 11–28<br>or Ezek. ch. 8<br>Mark 13. 24–31 | I Kings 18. 21–end<br>Acts 21. 1–16 |
| Ps. 65; **66**<br>I Kings ch. 19<br>Acts 21. 17–36<br>ct | **Cyprian, Bishop of Carthage, Martyr, 258**<br>Com. Martyr<br><br>Gr | | Ecclus. 4.29 – 6.1<br>or Ezek. ch. 9<br>Mark 13. 32–end | I Kings ch. 19<br>Acts 21. 17–36<br><br>ct |

# September 2015

| | | Sunday Principal Service<br>Weekday Eucharist | Third Service<br>Morning Prayer |
|---|---|---|---|
| **27** | S | THE SEVENTEENTH SUNDAY AFTER TRINITY **(Proper 21)** | |
| | | *Track 1*        *Track 2* | |
| | | Esther 7. 1–6, 9–10; 9. 20–22    Num. 11. 4–6, 10–16, 24–29 | Ps. 122 |
| | | Ps. 124        Ps. 19. 7–end | Isa. 48. 12–end |
| | | James 5. 13–end      James 5. 13–end | Luke 11. 37–end |
| | G | Mark 9. 38–end      Mark 9. 38–end | |
| **28**<br>DEL 26 | M | Zech. 8. 1–8 | Ps. 71 |
| | | Ps. 102. 12–22 | Ecclus. 6. 14–end |
| | | Luke 9. 46–50 | or Ezek. 10. 1–19 |
| | | | Mark 14. 1–11 |
| | G | | |
| **29** | Tu | MICHAEL AND ALL ANGELS | |
| | | Gen. 28. 10–17 | MP: Ps. 34; 150 |
| | | or Rev. 12. 7–12 | Tobit 12. 6–end |
| | | Ps. 103. 19–end | or Dan. 12. 1–4 |
| | | Rev. 12. 7–12 | Acts 12. 1–11 |
| | | or Heb. 1. 5–end | |
| | W | John 1. 47–end | |
| **30** | W | *Jerome, Translator of the Scriptures, Teacher, 420* | |
| | | Neh. 2. 1–8 | Ps. 77 |
| | | Ps. 137. 1–6 | Ecclus. 10. 6–8, 12–24 |
| | | Luke 9. 57–end | or Ezek. 12. 1–16 |
| | G | | Mark 14. 26–42 |

# October 2015

| | | | |
|---|---|---|---|
| **1** | Th | *Remigius, Bishop of Rheims, Apostle of the Franks, 533; Anthony Ashley Cooper, Earl of Shaftesbury, Social Reformer, 1885* | |
| | | Neh. 8. 1–12 | Ps. 78. 1–39† |
| | | Ps. 19. 7–11 | Ecclus. 11. 7–28 |
| | | Luke 10. 1–12 | or Ezek. 12. 17–end |
| | G | | Mark 14. 43–52 |
| **2** | F | | Ps. 55 |
| | | Baruch 1. 15–end | Ecclus. 14.20 – 15.10 |
| | | or Deut. 31. 7–13 | or Ezek. 13. 1–16 |
| | | Ps. 79. 1–9 | Mark 14. 53–65 |
| | G | Luke 10. 13–16 | |
| **3** | Sa | *George Bell, Bishop of Chichester, Ecumenist, Peacemaker, 1958* | |
| | | Baruch 4. 5–12, 27–29 | Ps. **76**; 79 |
| | | or Josh. 22. 1–6 | Ecclus. 15. 11–end |
| | | Ps. 69. 33–37 | or Ezek. 14. 1–11 |
| | | Luke 10. 17–24 | Mark 14. 66–end |
| | G | | |
| **4** | S | THE EIGHTEENTH SUNDAY AFTER TRINITY **(Proper 22)** | |
| | | *Track 1*        *Track 2* | |
| | | Job 1. 1; 2. 1–10      Gen. 2. 18–24 | Ps. 123; 124 |
| | | Ps. 26        Ps. 8 | Isa. 49. 13–23 |
| | | Heb. 1. 1–4; 2. 5–12    Heb. 1. 1–4; 2. 5–12 | Luke 12. 1–12 |
| | G | Mark 10. 2–16      Mark 10. 2–16 | |
| | | *or, if observed as Dedication Festival:* | |
| | | Gen. 28. 11–18 | MP: Ps. 48; 150 |
| | | or Rev. 21. 9–14 | Hag. 2. 6–9 |
| | | Ps. 122 | Heb. 10. 19–25 |
| | | 1 Pet. 2. 1–10 | |
| | ))) | John 10. 22–29 | |

| Second Service Evening Prayer | Calendar and Holy Communion | Morning Prayer | Evening Prayer |
|---|---|---|---|
| | **THE SEVENTEENTH SUNDAY AFTER TRINITY** | | |
| Ps. 120; 121<br>Exod. ch. 24<br>Matt. 9. 1–8 | Prov. 25. 6–14<br>Ps. 33. 6–12<br>Eph. 4. 1–6<br>G  Luke 14. 1–11 | Ps. 132<br>Isa. 48. 12–end<br>Luke 11. 37–end | Ps. 120; 121<br>Exod. ch. 24<br>Matt. 9. 1–8 |
| Ps. **72**; 75<br>1 Kings ch. 21<br>Acts 21.37 – 22.21<br>or First EP of Michael<br>and All Angels<br>Ps. 91<br>2 Kings 6. 8–17<br>Matt. 18. 1–6, 10<br>**W ct** | G | Ecclus. 6. 14–end<br>or Ezek. 10. 1–19<br>Mark 14. 1–11 | 1 Kings ch. 21<br>Acts 21.37 – 22.21<br>or First EP of Michael<br>and All Angels<br>(Ps. 91)<br>2 Kings 6. 8–17<br>John 1. 47–51<br><br>**W ct** |
| EP: Ps. 138; 148<br>Dan. 10. 4–end<br>Rev. ch. 5 | **MICHAEL AND ALL ANGELS**<br>Dan. 10. 10–19a<br>Ps. 103. 17–22<br>Rev. 12. 7–12<br>Matt. 18. 1–10<br><br>W | (Ps. 34; 150)<br>Tobit 12. 6–end<br>or Dan. 12. 1–4<br>Acts 12. 1–11 | (Ps. 138; 148)<br>Gen. 28. 10–17<br>Rev. ch. 5 |
| Ps. 119. 81–104<br>1 Kings 22. 29–45<br>Acts 23. 12–end | **Jerome, Translator of the Scriptures, Teacher, 420**<br>Com. Doctor<br><br>Gw | Ecclus. 10. 6–8, 12–24<br>or Ezek. 12. 1–16<br>Mark 14. 26–42 | 1 Kings 22. 29–45<br>Acts 23. 12–end |
| | | | |
| Ps. 78. 40–end†<br>2 Kings 1. 2–17<br>Acts 24. 1–23 | **Remigius, Bishop of Rheims, Apostle of the Franks, 533**<br>Com. Bishop<br><br>Gw | Ecclus. 11. 7–28<br>or Ezek. 12. 17–end<br>Mark 14. 43–52 | 2 Kings 1. 2–17<br>Acts 24. 1–23 |
| Ps. 69<br>2 Kings 2. 1–18<br>Acts 24.24 – 25.12 | G | Ecclus. 14.20 – 15.10<br>or Ezek. 13. 1–16<br>Mark 14. 53–65 | 2 Kings 2. 1–18<br>Acts 24.24 – 25.12 |
| Ps. 81; **84**<br>2 Kings 4. 1–37<br>Acts 25. 13–end<br>ct<br>or First EP of Dedication<br>Festival<br>Ps. 24<br>2 Chron. 7. 11–16<br>John 4. 19–29<br>⟨⟩ ct | G | Ps. **76**; 79<br>Ecclus. 15. 11–end<br>or Ezek. 14. 1–11<br>Mark 14. 66–end | Ps. 81; **84**<br>2 Kings 4. 1–37<br>Acts 25. 13–end<br>ct<br>or First EP of<br>Dedication Festival<br>Ps. 24<br>2 Chron. 7. 11–16<br>John 4. 19–29<br>⟨⟩ ct |
| | **THE EIGHTEENTH SUNDAY AFTER TRINITY** | | |
| Ps. 125; 126<br>Josh. 3. 7–end<br>Matt. 10. 1–22 | Deut. 6. 4–9<br>Ps. 122<br>1 Cor. 1. 4–8<br>G  Matt. 22. 34–end | Ps. 123; 124<br>Isa. 49. 13–23<br>Luke 12. 1–12 | Ps. 125; 126<br>Josh. 3. 7–end<br>Matt. 10. 1–22 |
| EP: Ps. 132<br>Jer. 7. 1–11<br>Luke 19. 1–10 | *or, if observed as Dedication Festival:*<br>2 Chron. 7. 11–16<br>Ps. 122<br>1 Cor. 3. 9–17<br>or 1 Pet. 2. 1–5<br>Matt. 21. 12–16<br>⟨⟩  or John 10. 22–29 | Ps. 48; 150<br>Hag. 2. 6–9<br>Heb. 10. 19–25 | Ps. 132<br>Jer. 7. 1–11<br>Luke 19. 1–10 |

# October 2015

| | Sunday Principal Service / Weekday Eucharist | Third Service / Morning Prayer |
|---|---|---|

**5**  M  DEL 27  G

Jonah 1.1 – 2.2, 10
Canticle: Jonah 2. 2–4, 7
or Ps. 69. 1–6
Luke 10. 25–37

Ps. **80**; 82
Ecclus. 16. 17–end
or Ezek. 14. 12–end
Mark 15. 1–15

---

**6**  Tu  Gr

**William Tyndale, Translator of the Scriptures, Reformation Martyr, 1536**
Com. Martyr    or    Jonah ch. 3
also Prov. 8. 4–11           Ps. 130
2 Tim. 3. 12–end            Luke 10. 38–end

Ps. 87; **89. 1–18**
Ecclus. 17. 1–24
or Ezek. 18. 1–20
Mark 15. 16–32

---

**7**  W  G

Jonah ch. 4
Ps. 86. 1–9
Luke 11. 1–4

Ps. 119. 105–128
Ecclus. 18. 1–14
or Ezek. 18. 21–32
Mark 15. 33–41

---

**8**  Th  G

Mal. 3.13 – 4.2a
Ps. 1
Luke 11. 5–13

Ps. 90; **92**
Ecclus. 19. 4–17
or Ezek. 20. 1–20
Mark 15. 42–end

---

**9**  F  G

*Denys, Bishop of Paris, and his Companions, Martyrs, c. 250; Robert Grosseteste, Bishop of Lincoln, Philosopher, Scientist, 1253*

Joel 1. 13–15; 2. 1–2
Ps. 9. 1–7
Luke 11. 15–26

Ps. **88**; (95)
Ecclus. 19. 20–end
or Ezek. 20. 21–38
Mark 16. 1–8

---

**10**  Sa  Gw

**Paulinus, Bishop of York, Missionary, 644**
*Thomas Traherne, Poet, Spiritual Writer, 1674*
Com. Missionary    or    Joel 3. 12–end
esp. Matt. 28. 16–end      Ps. 97. 1, 8–end
Luke 11. 27–28

Ps. 96; **97**; 100
Ecclus. 21. 1–17
or Ezek. 24. 15–end
Mark 16. 9–end

---

**11**  S  G

THE NINETEENTH SUNDAY AFTER TRINITY (**Proper 23**)

| Track 1 | Track 2 | |
|---|---|---|
| Job 23. 1–9, 16–end | Amos 5. 6–7, 10–15 | Ps. 129; 130 |
| Ps. 22. 1–15 | Ps. 90. 12–end | Isa. 50. 4–10 |
| Heb. 4. 12–end | Heb. 4. 12–end | Luke 13. 22–30 |
| Mark 10. 17–31 | Mark 10. 17–31 | |

---

**12**  M  DEL 28  Gw

**Wilfrid of Ripon, Bishop, Missionary, 709**
*Elizabeth Fry, Prison Reformer, 1845; Edith Cavell, Nurse, 1915*
Com. Missionary    or    Rom. 1. 1–7
esp. Luke 5. 1–11          Ps. 98
also 1 Cor. 1. 18–25      Luke 11. 29–32

Ps. **98**; 99; 101
Ecclus. 22. 6–22
or Ezek. 28. 1–19
John 13. 1–11

---

**13**  Tu  Gw

**Edward the Confessor, King of England, 1066**
Com. Saint    or    Rom. 1. 16–25
also 2 Sam. 23. 1–5     Ps. 19. 1–4
1 John 4. 13–16          Luke 11. 37–41

Ps. **106**†; (or 103)
Ecclus. 22.27 – 23.15
or Ezek. 33. 1–20
John 13. 12–20

---

**14**  W  G

Rom. 2. 1–11
Ps. 62. 1–8
Luke 11. 42–46

Ps. 110; **111**; 112
Ecclus. 24. 1–22
or Ezek. 33. 21–end
John 13. 21–30

---

**15**  Th  Gw

**Teresa of Avila, Teacher, 1582**
Com. Teacher    or    Rom. 3. 21–30
also Rom. 8. 22–27      Ps. 130
Luke 11. 47–end

Ps. 113; **115**
Ecclus. 24. 23–end
or Ezek. 34. 1–16
John 13. 31–end

---

**16**  F  G

*Nicholas Ridley, Bishop of London, and Hugh Latimer, Bishop of Worcester, Reformation Martyrs, 1555*

Rom. 4. 1–8
Ps. 32
Luke 12. 1–7

Ps. 139
Ecclus. 27.30 – 28.9
or Ezek. 34. 17–end
John 14. 1–14

| Second Service Evening Prayer | | Calendar and Holy Communion | Morning Prayer | Evening Prayer |
|---|---|---|---|---|
| Ps. *85*; 86<br>2 Kings ch. 5<br>Acts 26. 1–23 | G | | Ecclus. 16. 17–end<br>or Ezek. 14. 12–end<br>Mark 15. 1–15 | 2 Kings ch. 5<br>Acts 26. 1–23 |
| Ps. 89. 19–end<br>2 Kings 6. 1–23<br>Acts 26. 24–end | Gr | **Faith of Aquitaine, Martyr, c. 304**<br>Com. Virgin Martyr | Ecclus. 17. 1–24<br>or Ezek. 18. 1–20<br>Mark 15. 16–32 | 2 Kings 6. 1–23<br>Acts 26. 24–end |
| Ps. *91*; 93<br>2 Kings 9. 1–16<br>Acts 27. 1–26 | G | | Ecclus. 18. 1–14<br>or Ezek. 18. 21–32<br>Mark 15. 33–41 | 2 Kings 9. 1–16<br>Acts 27. 1–26 |
| Ps. 94<br>2 Kings 9. 17–end<br>Acts 27. 27–end | G | | Ecclus. 19. 4–17<br>or Ezek. 20. 1–20<br>Mark 15. 42–end | 2 Kings 9. 17–end<br>Acts 27. 27–end |
| Ps. 102<br>2 Kings 12. 1–19<br>Acts 28. 1–16 | Gr | **Denys, Bishop of Paris, Martyr, c. 250**<br>Com. Martyr | Ecclus. 19. 20–end<br>or Ezek. 20. 21–38<br>Mark 16. 1–8 | 2 Kings 12. 1–19<br>Acts 28. 1–16 |
| Ps. 104<br>2 Kings 17. 1–23<br>Acts 28. 17–end<br>ct | G | | Ecclus. 21. 1–17<br>or Ezek. 24. 15–end<br>Mark 16. 9–end | 2 Kings 17. 1–23<br>Acts 28. 17–end<br>ct |
| Ps. 127; [128]<br>Josh. 5.13 – 6.20<br>Matt. 11. 20–end | G | THE NINETEENTH SUNDAY AFTER TRINITY<br>Gen. 18. 23–32<br>Ps. 141. 1–9<br>Eph. 4. 17–end<br>Matt. 9. 1–8 | Ps. 129; 130<br>Isa. 50. 4–10<br>Luke 13. 22–30 | Ps. 127; [128]<br>Josh. 5.13 – 6.20<br>Matt. 11. 20–end |
| Ps. **105**† (or 103)<br>2 Kings 17. 24–end<br>Phil. 1. 1–11 | G | | Ecclus. 22. 6–22<br>or Ezek. 28. 1–19<br>John 13. 1–11 | 2 Kings 17. 24–end<br>Phil. 1. 1–11 |
| Ps. **107**†<br>2 Kings 18. 1–12<br>Phil. 1. 12–end | Gw | **Edward the Confessor, King of England, 1066, translated 1163**<br>Com. Saint | Ecclus. 22.27 – 23.15<br>or Ezek. 33. 1–20<br>John 13. 12–20 | 2 Kings 18. 1–12<br>Phil. 1. 12–end |
| Ps. 119. 129–152<br>2 Kings 18. 13–end<br>Phil. 2. 1–13 | G | | Ecclus. 24. 1–22<br>or Ezek. 33. 21–end<br>John 13. 21–30 | 2 Kings 18. 13–end<br>Phil. 2. 1–13 |
| Ps. 114; *116*; 117<br>2 Kings 19. 1–19<br>Phil. 2. 14–end | G | | Ecclus. 24. 23–end<br>or Ezek. 34. 1–16<br>John 13. 31–end | 2 Kings 19. 1–19<br>Phil. 2. 14–end |
| Ps. *130*; 131; 137<br>2 Kings 19. 20–36<br>Phil. 3.1 – 4.1 | G | | Ecclus. 27.30 – 28.9<br>or Ezek. 34. 17–end<br>John 14. 1–14 | 2 Kings 19. 20–36<br>Phil. 3.1 – 4.1 |

# October 2015

| | | Sunday Principal Service<br>Weekday Eucharist | Third Service<br>Morning Prayer |
|---|---|---|---|

| | Sa | **Ignatius, Bishop of Antioch, Martyr, c. 107** | |
|**17**| | Com. Martyr *or* Rom. 4. 13, 16–18 | Ps. 120; *121*; 122 |
| | | *also* Phil. 3. 7–12    Ps. 105. 6–10, 41–44 | Ecclus. 28. 14–end |
| | | John 6. 52–58    Luke 12. 8–12 | or Ezek. 36. 16–36 |
| | | | John 14. 15–end |

| | Gr | | |
|**18**| S | LUKE THE EVANGELIST (or transferred to 19 October) | |
| | | Isa. 35. 3–6 | MP: Ps. 145; 146 |
| | | or Acts 16. 6–12a | Isa. ch. 55 |
| | | Ps. 147. 1–7 | Luke 1. 1–4 |
| | R | 2 Tim. 4. 5–17 | |
| | | Luke 10. 1–9 | |
| | | *or, for The Twentieth Sunday after Trinity (Proper 24):* | |
| | | *Track 1*    *Track 2* | |
| | | Job 38. 1–7 [34–end]    Isa. 53. 4–end | Ps. 133; 134; 137. 1–6 |
| | | Ps. 104. 1–10, 26, 35c (or 1–10)    Ps. 91. 9–end | Isa. 54. 1–14 |
| | | Heb. 5. 1–10    Heb. 5. 1–10 | Luke 13. 31–end |
| | G | Mark 10. 35–45    Mark 10. 35–45 | |

| | M | **Henry Martyn, Translator of the Scriptures, Missionary in India and Persia, 1812** | |
|**19**| | Com. Missionary    *or* Rom. 4. 20–end | Ps. 123; 124; 125; *126* |
| DEL 29 | | *esp.* Mark 16. 15–end    Canticle: Benedictus 1–6 | Ecclus. 31. 1–11 |
| | | *also* Isa. 55. 6–11    Luke 12. 13–21 | or Ezek. 37. 1–14 |
| | Gw | | John 15. 1–11 |

| | Tu | | |
|**20**| | Rom. 5. 12, 15, 17–end | Ps. *132*; 133 |
| | | Ps. 40. 7–12 | Ecclus. 34. 9–end |
| | G | Luke 12. 35–38 | or Ezek. 37. 15–end |
| | | | John 15. 12–17 |

| | W | | |
|**21**| | Rom. 6. 12–18 | Ps. 119. 153–end |
| | | Ps. 124 | Ecclus. ch. 35 |
| | G | Luke 12. 39–48 | or Ezek. 39. 21–end |
| | | | John 15. 18–end |

| | Th | | |
|**22**| | Rom. 6. 19–end | Ps. *143*; 146 |
| | | Ps. 1 | Ecclus. 37. 7–24 |
| | G | Luke 12. 49–53 | or Ezek. 43. 1–12 |
| | | | John 16. 1–15 |

| | F | | |
|**23**| | Rom. 7. 18–end | Ps. 142; *144* |
| | | Ps. 119. 33–40 | Ecclus. 38. 1–14 |
| | G | Luke 12. 54–end | or Ezek. 44. 4–16 |
| | | | John 16. 16–22 |

| | Sa | | |
|**24**| | Rom. 8. 1–11 | Ps. 147 |
| | | Ps. 24. 1–6 | Ecclus. 38. 24–end |
| | G | Luke 13. 1–9 | or Ezek. 47. 1–12 |
| | | | John 16. 23–end |

| | S | THE LAST SUNDAY AFTER TRINITY **(Proper 25)**\* | |
|**25**| | *Track 1*    *Track 2* | |
| | | Job 42. 1–6, 10–end    Jer. 31. 7–9 | Ps. 119. 89–104 |
| | | Ps. 34. 1–8, 19–end (or 1–8)    Ps. 126 | Isa. 59. 9–20 |
| | | Heb. 7. 23–end    Heb. 7. 23–end | Luke 14. 1–14 |
| | G | Mark 10. 46–end    Mark 10. 46–end | |
| | | *or, if being observed as Bible Sunday:* | |
| | | Isa. 55. 1–11 | Ps. 119. 89–104 |
| | | Ps. 19. 7–end | Isa. 45. 22–end |
| | | 2 Tim. 3.14 – 4.5 | Matt. 24. 30–35 |
| | G | John 5. 36b–end | or Luke 14. 1–14 |

\*If the Dedication Festival is kept on this Sunday, use the provision given on 3 and 4 October.

| Second Service Evening Prayer | Calendar and Holy Communion | Morning Prayer | Evening Prayer |
|---|---|---|---|
| | **Etheldreda, Abbess of Ely, 679** | | |
| Ps. 118 | Com. Abbess | Ecclus. 28. 14–end | 2 Kings ch. 20 |
| 2 Kings ch. 20 | | or Ezek. 36. 16–36 | Phil. 4. 2–end |
| Phil. 4. 2–end | | John 14. 15–end | ct |
| ct | | | |
| or First EP of Luke | | | or First EP of Luke |
| Ps. 33 | | | (Ps. 33) |
| Hos. 6. 1–3 | | | Hos. 6. 1–3 |
| 2 Tim. 3. 10–end | | | 2 Tim. 3. 10–end |
| **R** ct | Gw | | **R** ct |
| | LUKE THE EVANGELIST (or transferred to 19 October) | | |
| EP: Ps. 103 | Isa. 35. 3–6 | Ps. 145; 146 | Ps. 103 |
| Ecclus. 38. 1–14 | Ps. 147. 1–6 | Isa. ch. 55 | Ecclus. 38. 1–14 |
| or Isa. 61. 1–6 | 2 Tim. 4. 5–15 | Luke 1. 1–4 | or Isa. 61. 1–6 |
| Col. 4. 7–end | Luke 10. 1–9 | | Col. 4. 7–end |
| | **R** or Luke 7. 36–end | | |
| | or, for The Twentieth Sunday after Trinity: | | |
| Ps. 141 | Prov. 9. 1–6 | Ps. 133; 134; 137. 1–6 | Ps. 142 |
| Josh. 14. 6–14 | Ps. 145. 15–end | Isa. 54. 1–14 | Josh. 14. 6–14 |
| Matt. 12. 1–21 | Eph. 5. 15–21 | Luke 13. 31–end | Matt. 12. 1–21 |
| | G Matt. 22. 1–14 | | |
| Ps. *127*; 128; 129 | | Ecclus. 31. 1–11 | 2 Kings 21. 1–18 |
| 2 Kings 21. 1–18 | | or Ezek. 37. 1–14 | 1 Tim. 1. 1–17 |
| 1 Tim. 1. 1–17 | | John 15. 1–11 | |
| | G | | |
| Ps. (134); *135* | | Ecclus. 34. 9–end | 2 Kings 22.1 – 23.3 |
| 2 Kings 22.1 – 23.3 | | or Ezek. 37. 15–end | 1 Tim. 1.18 – 2.end |
| 1 Tim. 1.18 – 2.end | | John 15. 12–17 | |
| | G | | |
| Ps. 136 | | Ecclus. ch. 35 | 2 Kings 23. 4–25 |
| 2 Kings 23. 4–25 | | or Ezek. 39. 21–end | 1 Tim. ch. 3 |
| 1 Tim. ch. 3 | | John 15. 18–end | |
| | G | | |
| Ps. *138*; 140; 141 | | Ecclus. 37. 7–24 | 2 Kings 23.36 – 24.17 |
| 2 Kings 23.36 – 24.17 | | or Ezek. 43. 1–12 | 1 Tim. ch. 4 |
| 1 Tim. ch. 4 | | John 16. 1–15 | |
| | G | | |
| Ps. 145 | | Ecclus. 38. 1–14 | 2 Kings 24.18 – 25.12 |
| 2 Kings 24.18 – 25.12 | | or Ezek. 44. 4–16 | 1 Tim. 5. 1–16 |
| 1 Tim. 5. 1–16 | | John 16. 16–22 | |
| | G | | |
| Ps. *148*; 149; 150 | | Ecclus. 38. 24–end | 2 Kings 25. 22–end |
| 2 Kings 25. 22–end | | or Ezek. 47. 1–12 | 1 Tim. 5. 17–end |
| 1 Tim. 5. 17–end | | John 16. 23–end | |
| ct | G | | ct |
| | THE TWENTY-FIRST SUNDAY AFTER TRINITY | | |
| Ps. 119. 121–136 | Gen. 32. 24–29 | Ps. 119. 89–104 | Ps. 119. 121–136 |
| Eccles. chs 11 and 12 | Ps. 90. 1–12 | Isa. 59. 9–20 | Eccles. chs 11 and 12 |
| 2 Tim. 2. 1–7 | Eph. 6. 10–20 | Luke 14. 1–14 | 2 Tim. 2. 1–7 |
| Gospel: Luke 18. 9–14 | John 4. 46b–end | | |
| | | | |
| Ps. 119. 1–16 | | | |
| 2 Kings ch. 22 | | | |
| Col. 3. 12–17 | | | |
| Gospel: Luke 4. 14–30 | G | | |

# October 2015

| | | Sunday Principal Service / Weekday Eucharist | | Third Service / Morning Prayer |
|---|---|---|---|---|

**October 2015**

Sunday Principal Service
Weekday Eucharist

Third Service
Morning Prayer

---

**26** M

DEL 30

Gw

**Alfred the Great, King of the West Saxons, Scholar, 899**
*Cedd, Abbot of Lastingham, Bishop of the East Saxons, 664\**
Com. Saint            *or*    Rom. 8. 12–17
*also* 2 Sam. 23. 1–5            Ps. 68. 1–6, 19
John 18. 33–37            Luke 13. 10–17

Ps. *1*; 2; 3
Ecclus. 39. 1–11
*or* Eccles. ch. 1
John 17. 1–5

---

**27** Tu

Rom. 8. 18–25
Ps. 126
Luke 13. 18–21

Ps. *5*; 6; (8)
Ecclus. 39. 13–end
*or* Eccles. ch. 2
John 17. 6–19

---

G

---

**28** W

R

SIMON AND JUDE, APOSTLES

Isa. 28. 14–16
Ps. 119. 89–96
Eph. 2. 19–end
John 15. 17–end

*MP*: Ps. 116; 117
Wisd. 5. 1–16
*or* Isa. 45. 18–end
Luke 6. 12–16

---

**29** Th

Gr

**James Hannington, Bishop of Eastern Equatorial Africa, Martyr in Uganda, 1885**
Com. Martyr            *or*    Rom. 8. 31–end
*esp.* Matt. 10. 28–39            Ps. 109. 20–26, 29–30
Luke 13. 31–end

Ps. 14; *15*; 16
Ecclus. 43. 1–12
*or* Eccles. 3.16 – 4.end
John 18. 1–11

---

**30** F

G

Rom. 9. 1–5
Ps. 147. 13–end
Luke 14. 1–6

Ps. 17; *19*
Ecclus. 43. 13–end
*or* Eccles. ch. 5
John 18. 12–27

---

**31** Sa

G

*Martin Luther, Reformer, 1546*

Rom. 11. 1–2, 11–12, 25–29
Ps. 94. 14–19
Luke 14. 1, 7–11

Ps. 20; 21; *23*
Ecclus. 44. 1–15
*or* Eccles. ch. 6
John 18. 28–end

---

# November 2015

**1** S

𝔴

ALL SAINTS' DAY

Wisd. 3. 1–9
*or* Isa. 25. 6–9
Ps. 24. 1–6
Rev. 21. 1–6a
John 11. 32–44

*MP*: Ps. 15; 84; 149
Isa. ch. 35
Luke 9. 18–27

---

**2** M

DEL 31

Rp *or* Gp

**Commemoration of the Faithful Departed (All Souls' Day)**
Lam. 3. 17–26, 31–33            *or*    Rom. 11. 29–end
*or* Wisd. 3. 1–9            Ps. 69. 31–37
Ps. 23            Luke 14. 12–14
*or* Ps. 27. 1–6, 16–end
Rom. 5. 5–11
*or* 1 Pet. 1. 3–9
John 5. 19–25
*or* John 6. 37–40

Ps. *2*; 146
*alt.* Ps. 27; *30*
Isa. 1. 1–20
Matt. 1. 18–end

---

**3** Tu

Rw *or* Gw

**Richard Hooker, Priest, Anglican Apologist, Teacher, 1600**
*Martin of Porres, Friar, 1639*
Com. Teacher            *or*    Rom. 12. 5–16
*esp.* John 16. 12–15            Ps. 131
*also* Ecclus. 44. 10–15            Luke 14. 15–24

Ps. *5*; 147. 1–12
*alt.* Ps. 32; *36*
Isa. 1. 21–end
Matt. 2. 1–15

---

\*Chad may be celebrated with Cedd on 26 October instead of 2 March.

| Second Service Evening Prayer | Calendar and Holy Communion | Morning Prayer | Evening Prayer |
|---|---|---|---|
| Ps. *4*; 7<br>Judith ch. 4<br>*or* Exod. 22. 21–27; 23. 1–17<br>1 Tim. 6. 1–10<br><br>G | | Ecclus. 39. 1–11<br>*or* Eccles. ch. 1<br>John 17. 1–5 | Judith ch. 4<br>*or* Exod. 22. 21–27;<br>23. 1–17<br>1 Tim. 6. 1–10 |
| Ps. *9*; 10†<br>Judith 5.1 – 6.4<br>*or* Exod. 29.38 – 30.16<br>1 Tim. 6. 11–end<br>*or First EP of Simon and Jude*<br>Ps. 124; 125; 126<br>Deut. 32. 1–4<br>John 14. 15–26<br>**R ct**<br>G | | Ecclus. 39. 13–end<br>*or* Eccles. ch. 2<br>John 17. 6–19 | Judith 5.1 – 6.4<br>*or* Exod. 29.38 – 30.16<br>1 Tim. 6. 11–end<br>*or First EP of Simon<br>and Jude*<br>(Ps. 124; 125; 126)<br>Deut. 32. 1–4<br>John 14. 15–26<br>**R ct** |
| *EP*: Ps. 119. 1–16<br>1 Macc. 2. 42–66<br>*or* Jer. 3. 11–18<br>Jude 1–4, 17–end | **SIMON AND JUDE, APOSTLES**<br>Isa. 28. 9–16<br>Ps. 116. 11–end<br>Jude 1–8<br>*or* Rev. 21. 9–14<br>John 15. 17–end<br>R | (Ps. 119. 89–96)<br>Wisd. 5. 1–16<br>*or* Isa. 45. 18–end<br>Luke 6. 12–16 | (Ps. 119. 1–16)<br>1 Macc. 2. 42–66<br>*or* Jer. 3. 11–18<br>Eph. 2. 19–end |
| Ps. 18†<br>Judith 7. 19–end<br>*or* Lev. ch. 9<br>2 Tim. 1.15 – 2.13<br><br>G | | Ecclus. 43. 1–12<br>*or* Eccles. 3.16 – 4.end<br>John 18. 1–11 | Judith 7. 19–end<br>*or* Lev. ch. 9<br>2 Tim. 1.15 – 2.13 |
| Ps. 22<br>Judith 8. 9–end<br>*or* Lev. 16. 2–24<br>2 Tim. 2. 14–end<br><br>G | | Ecclus. 43. 13–end<br>*or* Eccles. ch. 5<br>John 18. 12–27 | Judith 8. 9–end<br>*or* Lev. 16. 2–24<br>2 Tim. 2. 14–end |
| *First EP of All Saints*<br>Ps. 1; 5<br>Ecclus. 44. 1–15<br>*or* Isa. 40. 27–end<br>Rev. 19. 6–10<br>Ⱳ **ct**<br>G | | Ecclus. 44. 1–15<br>*or* Eccles. ch. 6<br>John 18. 28–end | *First EP of All Saints*<br>Ps. 1; 5<br>Ecclus. 44. 1–15<br>*or* Isa. 40. 27–end<br>Rev. 19. 6–10<br>Ⱳ **ct** |
| *EP*: Ps. 148; 150<br>Isa. 65. 17–end<br>Heb. 11.32 – 12.2<br><br>Ⱳ | **ALL SAINTS' DAY**<br>Isa. 66. 20–23<br>Ps. 33. 1–5<br>Rev. 7. 2–4 [5–8] 9–12<br>Matt. 5. 1–12 | Ps. 15; 84; 149<br>Isa. ch. 35<br>Luke 9. 18–27 | Ps. 148; 150<br>Isa. 65. 17–end<br>Heb. 11.32 – 12.2 |
| Ps. *92*; 96; 97<br>*alt.* Ps. 26; **28**; 29<br>Dan. ch. 1<br>Rev. ch. 1<br><br><br><br><br>G | To celebrate All Souls' Day, see *Common Worship* provision.<br>Isa. 1. 1–20<br>Matt. 1. 18–end | | Dan. ch. 1<br>Rev. ch. 1 |
| 98; 99; *100*<br>*alt.* Ps. 33<br>Dan. 2. 1–24<br>Rev. 2. 1–11<br>G | | Isa. 1. 21–end<br>Matt. 2. 1–15 | Dan. 2. 1–24<br>Rev. 2. 1–11 |

# November 2015

| | | Sunday Principal Service<br>Weekday Eucharist | Third Service<br>Morning Prayer |
|---|---|---|---|
| **4** | W | Rom. 13. 8–10<br>Ps. 112<br>Luke 14. 25–33 | Ps. *9*; 147. 13–end<br>*alt.* Ps. 34<br>Isa. 2. 1–11 |
| | R *or* G | | Matt. 2. 16–end |
| **5** | Th | Rom. 14. 7–12<br>Ps. 27. 14–end<br>Luke 15. 1–10 | Ps. 11; *15*; 148<br>*alt.* Ps. 37†<br>Isa. 2. 12–end |
| | R *or* G | | Matt. ch. 3 |
| **6** | F | *Leonard, Hermit, 6th century; William Temple, Archbishop of Canterbury, Teacher, 1944* | |
| | | Rom. 15. 14–21<br>Ps. 98<br>Luke 16. 1–8 | Ps. *16*; 149<br>*alt.* Ps. 31<br>Isa. 3. 1–15 |
| | R *or* G | | Matt. 4. 1–11 |
| **7** | Sa | **Willibrord of York, Bishop, Apostle of Frisia, 739**<br>Com. Missionary<br>*esp.* Isa. 52. 7–10<br>Matt. 28. 16–end | *or* Rom. 16. 3–9, 16, 22–end<br>Ps. 145. 1–7<br>Luke 16. 9–15 | Ps. *18. 31–end*; 150<br>*alt.* Ps. 41; *42*; 43<br>Isa. 4.2 – 5.7 |
| | Rw *or* Gw | | Matt. 4. 12–22 |
| **8** | S | THE THIRD SUNDAY BEFORE ADVENT<br>(Remembrance Sunday) | |
| | | Jonah 3. 1–5, 10<br>Ps. 62. 5–end<br>Heb. 9. 24–end<br>Mark 1. 14–20 | Ps. 136<br>Mic. 4. 1–5<br>Phil. 4. 6–9 |
| | R *or* G | | |
| **9**<br>DEL 32 | M | *Margery Kempe, Mystic, c. 1440* | |
| | | Wisd. 1. 1–7<br>*or* Titus 1. 1–9<br>Ps. 139. 1–9<br>*or* Ps. 24. 1–6<br>Luke 17. 1–6 | Ps. 19; *20*<br>*alt.* Ps. 44<br>Isa. 5. 8–24<br>Matt. 4.23 – 5.12 |
| | R *or* G | | |
| **10** | Tu | **Leo the Great, Bishop of Rome, Teacher, 461**<br>Com. Teacher<br>*also* 1 Pet. 5. 1–11 | *or* Wisd. 2.23 – 3.9<br>*or* Titus 2. 1–8, 11–14<br>Ps. 34. 1–6<br>*or* Ps. 37. 3–5, 30–32<br>Luke 17. 7–10 | Ps. *21*; 24<br>*alt.* Ps. *48*; 52<br>Isa. 5. 25–end<br>Matt. 5. 13–20 |
| | Rw *or* Gw | | |
| **11** | W | **Martin, Bishop of Tours, c. 397**<br>Com. Bishop<br>*also* 1 Thess. 5. 1–11<br>Matt. 25. 34–40 | *or* Wisd. 6. 1–11<br>*or* Titus 3. 1–7<br>Ps. 82<br>*or* Ps. 23<br>Luke 17. 11–19 | Ps. *23*; 25<br>*alt.* Ps. 119. 57–80<br>Isa. ch. 6<br>Matt. 5. 21–37 |
| | Rw *or* Gw | | |
| **12** | Th | Wisd. 7.22 – 8.1<br>*or* Philemon 7–20<br>Ps. 119. 89–96<br>*or* Ps. 146. 4–end<br>Luke 17. 20–25 | Ps. *26*; 27<br>*alt.* Ps. 56; *57*; (63†)<br>Isa. 7. 1–17<br>Matt. 5. 38–end |
| | R *or* G | | |
| **13** | F | **Charles Simeon, Priest, Evangelical Divine, 1836**<br>Com. Pastor<br>*esp.* Mal. 2. 5–7<br>*also* Col. 1. 3–8<br>Luke 8. 4–8 | *or* Wisd. 13. 1–9<br>*or* 2 John 4–9<br>Ps. 19. 1–4<br>*or* Ps. 119. 1–8<br>Luke 17. 26–end | Ps. 28; *32*<br>*alt.* Ps. *51*; 54<br>Isa. 8. 1–15<br>Matt. 6. 1–18 |
| | Rw *or* Gw | | |
| **14** | Sa | *Samuel Seabury, first Anglican Bishop in North America, 1796* | |
| | | Wisd. 18. 14–16; 19. 6–9<br>*or* 3 John 5–8<br>Ps. 105. 1–5, 35–42<br>*or* Ps. 112<br>Luke 18. 1–8 | Ps. 33<br>*alt.* Ps. 68<br>Isa. 8.16 – 9.7<br>Matt. 6. 19–end |
| | R *or* G | | |

| Second Service Evening Prayer | Calendar and Holy Communion | Morning Prayer | Evening Prayer |
|---|---|---|---|
| Ps. 111; *112*; 116<br>*alt*. Ps. 119. 33–56<br>Dan. 2. 25–end<br>Rev. 2. 12–end<br><br>G | | Isa. 2. 1–11<br>Matt. 2. 16–end | Dan. 2. 25–end<br>Rev. 2. 12–end |
| Ps. 118<br>*alt*. Ps. 39; *40*<br>Dan. 3. 1–18<br>Rev. 3. 1–13<br><br>G | | Isa. 2. 12–end<br>Matt. ch. 3 | Dan. 3. 1–18<br>Rev. 3. 1–13 |
| Ps. 137; 138; *143*<br>*alt*. Ps. 35<br>Dan. 3. 19–end<br>Rev. 3. 14–end<br><br>Gw | **Leonard, Hermit, 6th century**<br>Com. Abbot | Isa. 3. 1–15<br>Matt. 4. 1–11 | Dan. 3. 19–end<br>Rev. 3. 14–end |
| Ps. 145<br>*alt*. Ps. 45; *46*<br>Dan. 4. 1–18<br>Rev. ch. 4<br>ct<br>G | | Isa. 4.2 – 5.7<br>Matt. 4. 12–22 | Dan. 4. 1–18<br>Rev. ch. 4<br><br>ct |
| Ps. 46; [82]<br>Isa. 10.33 – 11.9<br>John 14. [1–22] 23–29<br>G | **THE TWENTY-THIRD SUNDAY AFTER TRINITY**<br>Isa. 11. 1–10<br>Ps. 44. 1–9<br>Phil. 3. 17–end<br>Matt. 22. 15–22 | Ps. 136<br>Mic. 4. 1–5<br>Phil. 4. 6–9 | Ps. 144<br>Isa. 10.33 – 11.9<br>John 14. [1–22] 23–29 |
| Ps. 34<br>*alt*. Ps. *47*; 49<br>Dan. 4. 19–end<br>Rev. ch. 5<br><br>G | | Isa. 5. 8–24<br>Matt. 4.23 – 5.12 | Dan. 4. 19–end<br>Rev. ch. 5 |
| Ps. 36; *40*<br>*alt*. Ps. 50<br>Dan. 5. 1–12<br>Rev. ch. 6<br><br>G | | Isa. 5. 25–end<br>Matt. 5. 13–20 | Dan. 5. 1–12<br>Rev. ch. 6 |
| Ps. 37<br>*alt*. Ps. *59*; 60; (67)<br>Dan. 5. 13–end<br>Rev. 7. 1–4, 9–end<br><br>Gw | **Martin, Bishop of Tours, c. 397**<br>Com. Bishop | Isa. ch. 6<br>Matt. 5. 21–37 | Dan. 5. 13–end<br>Rev. 7. 1–4, 9–end |
| Ps. 42; *43*<br>*alt*. Ps. 61; *62*; 64<br>Dan. ch. 6<br>Rev. ch. 8<br><br>G | | Isa. 7. 1–17<br>Matt. 5. 38–end | Dan. ch. 6<br>Rev. ch. 8 |
| Ps. 31<br>*alt*. Ps. 38<br>Dan. 7. 1–14<br>Rev. 9. 1–12<br><br>Gw | **Britius, Bishop of Tours, 444**<br>Com. Bishop | Isa. 8. 1–15<br>Matt. 6. 1–18 | Dan. 7. 1–14<br>Rev. 9. 1–12 |
| Ps. 84; *86*<br>*alt*. Ps. 65; *66*<br>Dan. 7. 15–end<br>Rev. 9. 13–end<br>ct<br>G | | Isa. 8.16 – 9.7<br>Matt. 6. 19–end | Dan. 7. 15–end<br>Rev. 9. 13–end<br><br>ct |

# November 2015

Sunday Principal Service
Weekday Eucharist

Third Service
Morning Prayer

---

**15** S    THE SECOND SUNDAY BEFORE ADVENT

Dan. 12. 1–3
Ps. 16
Heb. 10. 11–14 [15–18] 19–25
Mark 13. 1–8

Ps. 96
1 Sam. 9.27 – 10.2a;
10. 17–26
Matt. 13. 31–35

R or G

---

**16** M    **Margaret, Queen of Scotland, Philanthropist, Reformer of the Church, 1093**

DEL 33    *Edmund Rich of Abingdon, Archbishop of Canterbury, 1240*

Com. Saint                          or    1 Macc. 1. 10–15, 41–43,          Ps. 46; **47**
*also* Prov. 3. 31. 10–12, 20, 26–end       54–57, 62–64                     *alt.* Ps. 71
1 Cor. 12.13 – 13.3                        *or* Rev. 1. 1–4; 2. 1–5          Isa. 9.8 – 10.4
Matt. 25. 34–end                           Ps. 79. 1–5                      Matt. 7. 1–12
                                           *or* Ps. 1
Rw *or* Gw                                 Luke 18. 35–end

---

**17** Tu    **Hugh, Bishop of Lincoln, 1200**

Com. Bishop                         or    2 Macc. 6. 18–end                Ps. 48; **52**
*also* 1 Tim. 6. 11–16                     *or* Rev. 3. 1–6, 14–31          *alt.* Ps. 73
                                           Ps. 11                          Isa. 10. 5–19
                                           *or* Ps. 15                     Matt. 7. 13–end
Rw *or* Gw                                 Luke 19. 1–10

---

**18** W    **Elizabeth of Hungary, Princess of Thuringia, Philanthropist, 1231**

Com. Saint                          or    2 Macc. 7. 1, 20–31             Ps. **56**; 57
*esp.* Matt. 25. 31–end                    *or* Rev. ch. 4                 *alt.* Ps. 77
*also* Prov. 31. 10–end                    Ps. 116. 10–end                Isa. 10. 20–32
                                           *or* Ps. 150                    Matt. 8. 1–13
Rw *or* Gw                                 Luke 19. 11–28

---

**19** Th    **Hilda, Abbess of Whitby, 680**

*Mechtild, Béguine of Magdeburg, Mystic, 1280*

Com. Religious                      or    1 Macc. 2. 15–29                Ps. 61; **62**
*esp.* Isa. 61.10 – 62.5                   *or* Rev. 5. 1–10               *alt.* Ps. 78. 1–39†
                                           Ps. 129                         Isa. 10.33 – 11.9
                                           *or* Ps. 149. 1–5              Matt. 8. 14–22
Rw *or* Gw                                 Luke 19. 41–44

---

**20** F    **Edmund, King of the East Angles, Martyr, 870**

*Priscilla Lydia Sellon, a Restorer of the Religious Life in the Church of England, 1876*

Com. Martyr                         or    1 Macc. 4. 36–37, 52–59        Ps. **63**; 65
*also* Prov. 20. 28; 21. 1–4, 7            *or* Rev. 10. 8–11             *alt.* Ps. 55
                                           Ps. 122                         Isa. 11.10 – 12.end
                                           *or* Ps. 119. 65–72           Matt. 8. 23–end
R *or* Gr                                  Luke 19. 45–48

---

**21** Sa

1 Macc. 6. 1–13                Ps. 78. 1–39
*or* Rev. 11. 4–12             *alt.* Ps. **76**; 79
Ps. 124                         Isa. 13. 1–13
*or* Ps. 144. 1–9              Matt. 9. 1–17
Luke 20. 27–40

R *or* G

---

**22** S    CHRIST THE KING
The Sunday Next Before Advent

Dan. 7. 9–10, 13–14            *MP*: Ps. 29; 110
Ps. 93                          Isa. 32. 1–8
Rev. 1. 4b–8                   Rev. 3. 7–end
R *or* W                                   John 18. 33–37

---

**23** M    **Clement, Bishop of Rome, Martyr, c. 100**

DEL 34    Com. Martyr                 or    Dan. 1. 1–6, 8–20              Ps. 92; **96**
*also* Phil. 3.17 – 4.3                    *Canticle*: Bless the Lord     *alt.* Ps. **80**; 82
Matt. 16. 13–19                            Luke 21. 1–4                   Isa. 14. 3–20
R *or* Gr                                                                 Matt. 9. 18–34

| Second Service Evening Prayer | Calendar and Holy Communion | Morning Prayer | Evening Prayer |
|---|---|---|---|
| Ps. 95<br>Dan. 3. [1–12] 13–end<br>Matt. 13. 24–30, 36–43 | THE TWENTY-FOURTH SUNDAY AFTER TRINITY<br>Isa. 55. 6–11<br>Ps. 85. 1–7<br>Col. 1. 3–12<br>Matt. 9. 18–26<br><br>G | Ps. 96<br>1 Sam. 9.27 – 10.2a;<br>10. 17–26<br>Matt. 13. 31–35 | Ps. 95<br>Dan. 3. [1–12]<br>13–end<br>Matt. 13. 24–30,<br>36–43 |
| Ps. 70; **71**<br>alt. Ps. **72**; 75<br>Dan. 8. 1–14<br>Rev. ch. 10 | G | Isa. 9.8 – 10.4<br>Matt. 7. 1–12 | Dan. 8. 1–14<br>Rev. ch. 10 |
| Ps. **67**; 72<br>alt. Ps. 74<br>Dan. 8. 15–end<br>Rev. 11. 1–14 | **Hugh, Bishop of Lincoln, 1200**<br>Com. Bishop<br><br>Gw | Isa. 10. 5–19<br>Matt. 7. 13–end | Dan. 8. 15–end<br>Rev. 11. 1–14 |
| Ps. 73<br>alt. Ps. 119. 81–104<br>Dan. 9. 1–19<br>Rev. 11. 15–end | G | Isa. 10. 20–32<br>Matt. 8. 1–13 | Dan. 9. 1–19<br>Rev. 11. 15–end |
| Ps. 74; **76**<br>alt. Ps. 78. 40–end†<br>Dan. 9. 20–end<br>Rev. ch. 12 | G | Isa. 10.33 – 11.9<br>Matt. 8. 14–22 | Dan. 9. 20–end<br>Rev. ch. 12 |
| Ps. 77<br>alt. Ps. 69<br>Dan. 10.1 – 11.1<br>Rev. 13. 1–10 | **Edmund, King of the East Angles, Martyr, 870**<br>Com. Martyr<br><br>Gr | Isa. 11.10 – 12.end<br>Matt. 8. 23–end | Dan. 10.1 – 11.1<br>Rev. 13. 1–10 |
| Ps. 78. 40–end<br>alt. Ps. 81; **84**<br>Dan. ch. 12<br>Rev. 13. 11–end<br>**ct**<br>or First EP of Christ the King<br>Ps. 99; 100<br>Isa. 10.33 – 11.9<br>1 Tim. 6. 11–16<br>**R** or **W ct** | G | Isa. 13. 1–13<br>Matt. 9. 1–17 | Dan. ch. 12<br>Rev. 13. 11–end<br><br><br><br><br><br>ct |
| EP: Ps. 72 (or 72. 1–7)<br>Dan. ch. 5<br>John 6. 1–15 | THE SUNDAY NEXT BEFORE ADVENT<br>To celebrate Christ the King, see *Common Worship* provision.<br>Jer. 23. 5–8<br>Ps. 85. 8–end<br>Col. 1. 13–20<br>John 6. 5–14<br>G | Ps. 29; 110<br>Isa. 32. 1–8<br>Rev. 3. 7–end | Ps. 72 (or 72. 1–7)<br>Dan. ch. 5<br>Rev. 1. 4b–8 |
| Ps. **80**; 81<br>alt. Ps. **85**; 86<br>Isa. 40. 1–11<br>Rev. 14. 1–13 | **Clement, Bishop of Rome, Martyr, c. 100**<br>Com. Martyr<br><br>Gr | Isa. 14. 3–20<br>Matt. 9. 18–34 | Isa. 40. 1–11<br>Rev. 14. 1–13 |

# November 2015

| | | Sunday Principal Service<br>Weekday Eucharist | Third Service<br>Morning Prayer |
|---|---|---|---|
| **24** | Tu | Dan. 2. 31–45<br>*Canticle:* Benedicite 1–3<br>Luke 21. 5–11 | Ps. **97**; 98; 100<br>*alt.* Ps. 87; **89**. *1–18*<br>Isa. ch. 17 |
| | R *or* G | | Matt. 9.35 – 10.15 |
| **25** | W | *Catherine of Alexandria, Martyr, 4th century; Isaac Watts, Hymn Writer, 1748* | |
| | | Dan. 5. 1–6, 13–14, 16–17,<br>23–28<br>*Canticle:* Benedicite 4–5<br>Luke 21. 12–19 | Ps. 110; 111; **112**<br>*alt.* Ps. 119. 105–128<br>Isa. ch. 19 |
| | R *or* G | | Matt. 10. 16–33 |
| **26** | Th | Dan. 6. 12–end<br>*Canticle:* Benedicite 6–8a<br>Luke 21. 20–28 | Ps. **125**; 126; 127; 128<br>*alt.* Ps. 90; **92**<br>Isa. 21. 1–12 |
| | R *or* G | | Matt. 10.34 – 11.1 |
| **27** | F | Dan. 7. 2–14<br>*Canticle:* Benedicite 8b–10a<br>Luke 21. 29–33 | Ps. 139<br>*alt.* Ps. **88**; (95)<br>Isa. 22. 1–14 |
| | R *or* G | | Matt. 11. 2–19 |
| **28** | Sa | Dan. 7. 15–27<br>*Canticle:* Benedicite 10b–end<br>Luke 21. 34–36 | Ps. 145<br>*alt.* Ps. 96; **97**; 100<br>Isa. ch. 24 |
| | R *or* G | | Matt. 11. 20–end |
| **29** | S | **THE FIRST SUNDAY OF ADVENT**<br>CW Year C begins | |
| | | Jer. 33. 14–16<br>Ps. 25. 1–9<br>1 Thess. 3. 9–end<br>Luke 21. 25–36 | Ps. 44<br>Isa. 51. 4–11<br>Rom. 13. 11–end |
| | P | | |
| **30** | M | **ANDREW THE APOSTLE** | |
| | | Isa. 52. 7–10<br>Ps. 19. 1–6<br>Rom. 10. 12–18<br>Matt. 4. 18–22 | MP: Ps. 47; 147. 1–12<br>Ezek. 47. 1–12<br>*or* Ecclus. 14. 20–end<br>John 12. 20–32 |
| | R | | |

# December 2015

| | | | | |
|---|---|---|---|---|
| **1** | Tu | *Charles de Foucauld, Hermit in the Sahara, 1916*<br>Daily Eucharistic Lectionary Year 2 begins | | |
| | | | Isa. 11. 1–10<br>Ps. 72. 1–4, 18–19<br>Luke 10. 21–24 | Ps. **80**; 82<br>*alt.* Ps. **5**; 6; (8)<br>Isa. 26. 1–13 |
| | P | | | Matt. 12. 22–37 |
| **2** | W | | Isa. 25. 6–10a<br>Ps. 23<br>Matt. 15. 29–37 | Ps. 5; **7**<br>*alt.* Ps. 119. 1–32<br>Isa. 28. 1–13 |
| | P | | | Matt. 12. 38–end |
| **3** | Th | *Francis Xavier, Missionary, Apostle of the Indies, 1552* | | |
| | | | Isa. 26. 1–6<br>Ps. 118. 18–27a<br>Matt. 7. 21, 24–27 | Ps. **42**; 43<br>*alt.* Ps. 14; **15**; 16<br>Isa. 28. 14–end |
| | P | | | Matt. 13. 1–23 |
| **4** | F | *John of Damascus, Monk, Teacher, c. 749; Nicholas Ferrar, Deacon, Founder of the Little Gidding Community, 1637* | | |
| | | | Isa. 29. 17–end<br>Ps. 27. 1–4, 16–17<br>Matt. 9. 27–31 | Ps. **25**; 26<br>*alt.* Ps. 17; **19**<br>Isa. 29. 1–14 |
| | P | | | Matt. 13. 24–43 |

| Second Service Evening Prayer | | Calendar and Holy Communion | Morning Prayer | Evening Prayer |
|---|---|---|---|---|
| Ps. 99; *101*<br>*alt.* Ps. 89. 19–end<br>Isa. 40. 12–26<br>Rev. 14.14 – 15.end | G | | Isa. ch. 17<br>Matt. 9.35 – 10.15 | Isa. 40. 12–26<br>Rev. 14.14 – 15.end |
| Ps. 121; *122*; 123; 124<br>*alt.* Ps. *91*; 93<br>Isa. 40.27 – 41.7<br>Rev. 16. 1–11 | Gr | **Catherine of Alexandria, Martyr, 4th century**<br>Com. Virgin Martyr | Isa. ch. 19<br>Matt. 10. 16–33 | Isa. 40.27 – 41.7<br>Rev. 16. 1–11 |
| Ps. 131; 132; *133*<br>*alt.* Ps. 94<br>Isa. 41. 8–20<br>Rev. 16. 12–end | G | | Isa. 21. 1–12<br>Matt. 10.34 – 11.1 | Isa. 41. 8–20<br>Rev. 16. 12–end |
| Ps. *146*; 147<br>*alt.* Ps. 102<br>Isa. 41.21 – 42.9<br>Rev. ch. 17 | G | | Isa. 22. 1–14<br>Matt. 11. 2–19 | Isa. 41.21 – 42.9<br>Rev. ch. 17 |
| Ps. 148; 149; *150*<br>*alt.* Ps. 104<br>Isa. 42. 10–17<br>Rev. ch. 18<br>**P ct** | G | | Isa. ch. 24<br>Matt. 11. 20–end | Isa. 42. 10–17<br>Rev. ch. 18<br>**P ct** |
| Ps. 9 (*or* 9. 1–8)<br>Joel 3. 9–end<br>Rev. 14.13 – 15.4<br>*Gospel:* John 3. 1–17<br>*or First EP of Andrew*<br>*the Apostle*<br>Ps. 48<br>Isa. 49. 1–9a<br>1 Cor. 4. 9–16<br>**R ct** | P | THE FIRST SUNDAY IN ADVENT<br>Advent 1 Collect until Christmas Eve<br>Mic. 4. 1–4, 6–7<br>Ps. 25. 1–9<br>Rom. 13. 8–14<br>Matt. 21. 1–13 | Ps. 44<br>Isa. 51. 4–11<br>Rom. 13. 11–end | Ps. 9 (*or* 9. 1–8)<br>Joel 3. 9–end<br>Rev. 14.13 – 15.4<br>*or First EP of Andrew*<br>*the Apostle*<br>Ps. 48<br>Isa. 49. 1–9a<br>1 Cor. 4. 9–16<br>**R ct** |
| EP: Ps. 87; 96<br>Zech. 8. 20–end<br>John 1. 35–42 | R | ANDREW THE APOSTLE<br>Zech. 8. 20–end<br>Ps. 92. 1–5<br>Rom. 10. 9–end<br>Matt. 4. 18–22 | (Ps. 47; 147. 1–12)<br>Ezek. 47. 1–12<br>*or* Ecclus. 14. 20–end<br>John 12. 20–32 | (Ps. 87; 96)<br>Isa. 52. 7–10<br>John 1. 35–42 |
| Ps. *74*; 75<br>*alt.* Ps. *9*; 10†<br>Isa. 43. 1–13<br>Rev. ch. 20 | P | | Isa. 26. 1–13<br>Matt. 12. 22–37 | Isa. 43. 1–13<br>Rev. ch. 20 |
| Ps. 76; *77*<br>*alt.* Ps. *11*; 12; 13<br>Isa. 43. 14–end<br>Rev. 21. 1–8 | P | | Isa. 28. 1–13<br>Matt. 12. 38–end | Isa. 43. 14–end<br>Rev. 21. 1–8 |
| Ps. *40*; 46<br>*alt.* Ps. 18†<br>Isa. 44. 1–8<br>Rev. 21. 9–21 | P | | Isa. 28. 14–end<br>Matt. 13. 1–23 | Isa. 44. 1–8<br>Rev. 21. 9–21 |
| Ps. 16; *17*<br>*alt.* Ps. 22<br>Isa. 44. 9–23<br>Rev. 21.22 – 22.5 | P | | Isa. 29. 1–14<br>Matt. 13. 24–43 | Isa. 44. 9–23<br>Rev. 21.22 – 22.5 |

# December 2015

| | | Sunday Principal Service<br>Weekday Eucharist | Third Service<br>Morning Prayer |
|---|---|---|---|
| **5** | Sa | Isa. 30. 19–21, 23–26<br>Ps. 146. 4–9<br>Matt. 9.35 – 10.1, 6–8 | Ps. **9**; (10)<br>alt. Ps. 20; 21; **23**<br>Isa. 29. 15–end |
| | P | | Matt. 13. 44–end |
| **6** | S    THE SECOND SUNDAY OF ADVENT | Baruch ch. 5<br>or Mal. 3. 1–4<br>Canticle: Benedictus<br>Phil. 1. 3–11 | Ps. 80<br>Isa. 64. 1–7<br>Matt. 11. 2–11 |
| | P | Luke 3. 1–6 | |
| **7** | M | **Ambrose, Bishop of Milan, Teacher, 397**<br>Com. Teacher          or<br>also Isa. 41. 9b–13<br>Luke 22. 24–30 | Isa. ch. 35<br>Ps. 85. 7–end<br>Luke 5. 17–26 | Ps. 44<br>alt. Ps. 27; **30**<br>Isa. 30. 1–18 |
| | Pw | | Matt. 14. 1–12 |
| **8** | Tu | **The Conception of the Blessed Virgin Mary**<br>Com. BVM          or | Isa. 40. 1–11<br>Ps. 96. 1, 10–end<br>Matt. 18. 12–14 | Ps. **56**; 57<br>alt. Ps. 32; **36**<br>Isa. 30. 19–end |
| | Pw | | Matt. 14. 13–end |
| **9** | W | Ember Day* | Isa. 40. 25–end<br>Ps. 103. 8–13<br>Matt. 11. 28–end | Ps. **62**; 63<br>alt. Ps. 34<br>Isa. ch. 31 |
| | P | | Matt. 15. 1–20 |
| **10** | Th | | Isa. 41. 13–20<br>Ps. 145. 1, 8–13<br>Matt. 11. 11–15 | Ps. 53; **54**; 60<br>alt. Ps. 37†<br>Isa. ch. 32 |
| | P | | Matt. 15. 21–28 |
| **11** | F | Ember Day* | Isa. 48. 17–19<br>Ps. 1<br>Matt. 11. 16–19 | Ps. 85; **86**<br>alt. Ps. 31<br>Isa. 33. 1–22 |
| | P | | Matt. 15. 29–end |
| **12** | Sa | Ember Day* | Ecclus. 48. 1–4, 9–11<br>or 2 Kings 2. 9–12<br>Ps. 80. 1–4, 18–19<br>Matt. 17. 10–13 | Ps. 145<br>alt. Ps. 41; **42**; 43<br>Isa. ch. 35 |
| | P | | Matt. 16. 1–12 |
| **13** | S    THE THIRD SUNDAY OF ADVENT | Zeph. 3. 14–end<br>Canticle: Isa. 12. 2–end<br>or Ps. 146. 4–end<br>Phil. 4. 4–7 | Ps. 12; 14<br>Isa. 25. 1–9<br>1 Cor. 4. 1–5 |
| | P | Luke 3. 7–18 | |
| **14** | M | **John of the Cross, Poet, Teacher, 1591**<br>Com. Teacher          or<br>esp. 1 Cor. 2. 1–10<br>also John 14. 18–23 | Num. 24. 2–7, 15–17<br>Ps. 25. 3–8<br>Matt. 21. 23–27 | Ps. 40<br>alt. Ps. 44<br>Isa. 38. 1–8, 21–22 |
| | Pw | | Matt. 16. 13–end |
| **15** | Tu | | Zeph. 3. 1–2, 9–13<br>Ps. 34. 1–6, 21–22<br>Matt. 21. 28–32 | Ps. **70**; 74<br>alt. Ps. **48**; 52<br>Isa. 38. 9–20 |
| | P | | Matt. 17. 1–13 |
| **16** | W | | Isa. 45. 6b–8, 18, 21b–end<br>Ps. 85. 7–end<br>Luke 7. 18b–23 | Ps. **75**; 96<br>alt. Ps. 119. 57–80<br>Isa. ch. 39 |
| | P | | Matt. 17. 14–21 |

*For Ember Day provision, see p. 11.

| Second Service Evening Prayer | | Calendar and Holy Communion | Morning Prayer | Evening Prayer |
|---|---|---|---|---|
| Ps. **27**; 28<br>alt. Ps. **24**; 25<br>Isa. 44.24 – 45.13<br>Rev. 22. 6–end<br>ct | P | | Isa. 29. 15–end<br>Matt. 13. 44–end | Isa. 44.24 – 45.13<br>Rev. 22. 6–end<br><br>ct |
| Ps. **75**; [76]<br>Isa. 40. 1–11<br>Luke 1. 1–25 | P | **THE SECOND SUNDAY IN ADVENT**<br>2 Kings 22. 8–10; 23. 1–3<br>Ps. 50. 1–6<br>Rom. 15. 4–13<br>Luke 21. 25–33 | Ps. 40<br>Isa. 64. 1–7<br>Luke 3. 1–6 | Ps. 75; [76]<br>Mal. 3. 1–4<br>Luke 1. 1–25 |
| Ps. **144**; 146<br>alt. Ps. 26; **28**; 29<br>Isa. 45. 14–end<br>1 Thess. ch. 1 | P | | Isa. 30. 1–18<br>Matt. 14. 1–12 | Isa. 45. 14–end<br>1 Thess. ch. 1 |
| Ps. **11**; 12; 13<br>alt. Ps. 33<br>Isa. ch. 46<br>1 Thess. 2. 1–12 | Pw | **The Conception of the Blessed Virgin Mary**<br> | Isa. 30. 19–end<br>Matt. 14. 13–end | Isa. ch. 46<br>1 Thess. 2. 1–12 |
| Ps. **10**; 14<br>alt. Ps. 119. 33–56<br>Isa. ch. 47<br>1 Thess. 2. 13–end | P | | Isa. ch. 31<br>Matt. 15. 1–20 | Isa. ch. 47<br>1 Thess. 2. 13–end |
| Ps. 73<br>alt. Ps. 39; **40**<br>Isa. 48. 1–11<br>1 Thess. ch. 3 | P | | Isa. ch. 32<br>Matt. 15. 21–28 | Isa. 48. 1–11<br>1 Thess. ch. 3 |
| Ps. 82; **90**<br>alt. Ps. 35<br>Isa. 48. 12–end<br>1 Thess. 4. 1–12 | P | | Isa. 33. 1–22<br>Matt. 15. 29–end | Isa. 48. 12–end<br>1 Thess. 4. 1–12 |
| Ps. 93; **94**<br>alt. Ps. 45; **46**<br>Isa. 49. 1–13<br>1 Thess. 4. 13–end<br>ct | P | | Isa. ch. 35<br>Matt. 16. 1–12 | Isa. 49. 1–13<br>1 Thess. 4. 13–end<br><br>ct |
| Ps. 50. 1–6; 62 (or 50. 1–6)<br>Isa. ch. 35<br>Luke 1. 57–66 [67–end] | P | **THE THIRD SUNDAY IN ADVENT**<br>Isa. ch. 35<br>Ps. 80. 1–7<br>1 Cor. 4. 1–5<br>Matt. 11. 2–10 | Ps. 12; 14<br>Isa. 25. 1–9<br>Luke 3. 7–18 | Ps. 62<br>Zeph. 3. 14–end<br>Luke 1. 57–66<br>[67–end] |
| Ps. 25; **26**<br>alt. Ps. **47**; 49<br>Isa. 49. 14–25<br>1 Thess. 5. 1–11 | P | | Isa. 38. 1–8, 21–22<br>Matt. 16. 13–end | Isa. 49. 14–25<br>1 Thess. 5. 1–11 |
| Ps. **50**; 54<br>alt. Ps. 50<br>Isa. ch. 50<br>1 Thess. 5. 12–end | P | | Isa. 38. 9–20<br>Matt. 17. 1–13 | Isa. ch. 50<br>1 Thess. 5. 12–end |
| Ps. 25; **82**<br>alt. Ps. **59**; 60; (67)<br>Isa. 51. 1–8<br>2 Thess. ch. 1 | P | O Sapientia<br>Ember Day<br>Ember CEG | Isa. ch. 39<br>Matt. 17. 14–21 | Isa. 51. 1–8<br>2 Thess. ch. 1 |

# December 2015

| | | | Sunday Principal Service<br>Weekday Eucharist | Third Service<br>Morning Prayer |
|---|---|---|---|---|
| **17** | Th | O Sapientia*<br>*Eglantyne Jebb, Social Reformer, Founder of 'Save the Children', 1928* | Gen. 49. 2, 8–10<br>Ps. 72. 1–5, 18–19<br>Matt. 1. 1–17 | Ps. **76**; 97<br>*alt*. Ps. 56; **57**; (63†) |
| | P | | | Zeph. 1.1 – 2.3<br>Matt. 17. 22–end |
| **18** | F | | Jer. 23. 5–8<br>Ps. 72. 1–2, 12–13, 18–end<br>Matt. 1. 18–24 | Ps. 77; **98**<br>*alt*. Ps. **51**; 54 |
| | P | | | Zeph. 3. 1–13<br>Matt. 18. 1–20 |
| **19** | Sa | | Judg. 13. 2–7, 24–end<br>Ps. 71. 3–8<br>Luke 1. 5–25 | Ps. 144; **146**<br>Zeph. 3. 14–end |
| | P | | | Matt. 18. 21–end |
| **20** | S | THE FOURTH SUNDAY OF ADVENT | Mic. 5. 2–5a<br>*Canticle*: Magnificat<br>*or* Ps. 80. 1–8<br>Heb. 10. 5–10<br>Luke 1. 39–45 [46–55] | Ps. 144<br>Isa. 32. 1–8<br>Rev. 22. 6–end |
| | P | | | |
| **21** | M** | | Zeph. 3. 14–18<br>Ps. 33. 1–4, 11–12, 20–end<br>Luke 1. 39–45 | Ps. **121**; 122; 123<br>Mal. 1. 1, 6–end |
| | P | | | Matt. 19. 1–12 |
| **22** | Tu | | 1 Sam. 1. 24–end<br>Ps. 113<br>Luke 1. 46–56 | Ps. **124**; 125; 126; 127<br>Mal. 2. 1–16 |
| | P | | | Matt. 19. 13–15 |
| **23** | W | | Mal. 3. 1–4; 4. 5–end<br>Ps. 25. 3–9<br>Luke 1. 57–66 | Ps. 128; 129; **130**; 131<br>Mal. 2.17 – 3.12 |
| | P | | | Matt. 19. 16–end |
| **24** | Th | CHRISTMAS EVE | *Morning Eucharist*<br>2 Sam. 7. 1–5, 8–11, 16<br>Ps. 89. 2, 19–27<br>Acts 13. 16–26<br>Luke 1. 67–79 | Ps. **45**; 113<br>Mal. 3.13 – 4.end<br>Matt. 23. 1–12 |
| | P | | | |
| **25** | F | **CHRISTMAS DAY**<br>*Any of the following sets of readings may be used on the evening of Christmas Eve and on Christmas Day. Set III should be used at some service during the celebration.* | *I*<br>Isa. 9. 2–7<br>Ps. 96<br>Titus 2. 11–14<br>Luke 2. 1–14 [15–20] | MP: Ps. **110**; 117<br>Isa. 62. 1–5<br>Matt. 1. 18–end |
| | | | *II*<br>Isa. 62. 6–end<br>Ps. 97<br>Titus 3. 4–7<br>Luke 2. [1–7] 8–20 | |
| | ⫸ | | *III*<br>Isa. 52. 7–10<br>Ps. 98<br>Heb. 1. 1–4 [5–12]<br>John 1. 1–14 | |

| Second Service Evening Prayer | | Calendar and Holy Communion | Morning Prayer | Evening Prayer |
|---|---|---|---|---|
| Ps. 44 *alt.* Ps. 61; *62*; 64 Isa. 51. 9–16 2 Thess. ch. 2 | P | | Zeph. 1.1 – 2.3 Matt. 17. 22–end | Isa. 51. 9–16 2 Thess. ch. 2 |
| Ps. 49 *alt.* Ps. 38 Isa. 51. 17–end 2 Thess. ch. 3 | P | Ember Day Ember CEG | Zeph. 3. 1–13 Matt. 18. 1–20 | Isa. 51. 17–end 2 Thess. ch. 3 |
| Ps. 10; *57* Isa. 52. 1–12 Jude ct | P | Ember Day Ember CEG | Zeph. 3. 14–end Matt. 18. 21–end | Isa. 52. 1–12 Jude ct |
| Ps. 123; [131] Isa. 10.33 – 11.10 Matt. 1. 18–end | P | THE FOURTH SUNDAY IN ADVENT Isa. 40. 1–9 Ps. 145. 17–end Phil. 4. 4–7 John 1. 19–28 | Ps. 144 Isa. 32. 1–8 Rev. 22. 6–end | Ps. 123; [131] Isa. 10.33 – 11.10 Matt. 1. 18–end *or First EP of Thomas* Ps. 27 Isa. ch. 35 Heb. 10.35 – 11.1 **R** ct |
| Ps. 80; *84* Isa. 52.13 – 53.end 2 Pet. 1. 1–15 | R | THOMAS THE APOSTLE Job 42. 1–6 Ps. 139. 1–11 Eph. 2. 19–end John 20. 24–end | (Ps. 92; 146) 2 Sam. 15. 17–21 *or Ecclus.* ch. 2 John 11. 1–16 | (Ps. 139) Hab. 2. 1–4 1 Pet. 1. 3–12 |
| Ps. 24; *48* Isa. ch. 54 2 Pet. 1.16 – 2.3 | P | | Mal. 2. 1–16 Matt. 19. 13–15 | Isa. ch. 54 2 Pet. 1.16 – 2.3 |
| Ps. 89. 1–37 Isa. ch. 55 2 Pet. 2. 4–end | P | | Mal. 2.17 – 3.12 Matt. 19. 16–end | Isa. ch. 55 2 Pet. 2. 4–end |
| Ps. 85 Zech. ch. 2 Rev. 1. 1–8 | P | CHRISTMAS EVE Collect (1) Christmas Eve (2) Advent 1 Mic. 5. 2–5a Ps. 24 Titus 3. 3–7 Luke 2. 1–14 | Mal. 3.13 – 4.end Matt. 23. 1–12 | Zech. ch. 2 Rev. 1. 1–8 |
| | | **CHRISTMAS DAY** | | |
| *EP:* Ps. 8 Isa. 65. 17–25 Phil. 2. 5–11 *or Luke 2. 1–20 if it has not been used at the principal service of the day* | | Isa. 9. 2–7 Ps. 98 Heb. 1. 1–12 John 1. 1–14 | Ps. 110; 117 Isa. 62. 1–5 Matt. 1. 18–end | Ps. 8 Isa. 65. 17–25 Phil. 2. 5–11 *or Luke 2. 1–20* |

# December 2015

| | Sunday Principal Service / Weekday Eucharist | Third Service / Morning Prayer |
|---|---|---|

| | | Sunday Principal Service<br>Weekday Eucharist | Third Service<br>Morning Prayer |
|---|---|---|---|
| **26** Sa | STEPHEN, DEACON, FIRST MARTYR<br>*The reading from Acts must be used<br>as either the first or second reading<br>at the Eucharist.* | 2 Chron. 24. 20–22<br>*or* Acts 7. 51–end<br>Ps. 119. 161–168<br>Acts 7. 51–end<br>*or* Gal. 2. 16b–20<br>Matt. 10. 17–22 | *MP*: Ps. *13*; 31. 1–8; 150<br>Jer. 26. 12–15<br>Acts ch. 6 |
| R | | | |
| **27** S | JOHN, APOSTLE AND EVANGELIST (or transferred to 29th) | Exod. 33. 7–11a<br>Ps. 117<br>1 John ch. 1<br>John 21. 19b–end | *MP*: Ps. *21*; 147. 13–end<br>Exod. 33. 12–end<br>1 John 2. 1–11 |
| W | | | |
| | *or, for The First Sunday of Christmas:* | 1 Sam. 2. 18–20, 26<br>Ps. 148 (*or* 148. 7–end)<br>Col. 3. 12–17<br>Luke 2. 41–end | Ps. 105. 1–11<br>Isa. 41.21 – 42.1<br>1 John 1. 1–7 |
| W | | | |
| **28** M | THE HOLY INNOCENTS | Jer. 31. 15–17<br>Ps. 124<br>1 Cor. 1. 26–29<br>Matt. 2. 13–18 | *MP*: Ps. *36*; 146<br>Baruch 4. 21–27<br>*or* Gen. 37. 13–20<br>Matt. 18. 1–10 |
| R | | | |
| **29** Tu | **Thomas Becket, Archbishop of Canterbury, Martyr, 1170\***<br>(For John, Apostle and Evangelist, see provision on 27th.)<br>Com. Martyr      *or*<br>*esp.* Matt. 10. 28–33<br>Wr     *also* Ecclus. 51. 1–8 | 1 John 2. 3–11<br>Ps. 96. 1–4<br>Luke 2. 22–35 | Ps. *19*; 20<br>Jonah ch. 1<br>Col. 1. 1–14 |
| **30** W<br>W | | 1 John 2. 12–17<br>Ps. 96. 7–10<br>Luke 2. 36–40 | Ps. 111; 112; *113*<br>Jonah ch. 2<br>Col. 1. 15–23 |
| **31** Th | *John Wyclif, Reformer, 1384* | 1 John 2. 18–21<br>Ps. 96. 1, 11–end<br>John 1. 1–18 | Ps. 102<br>Jonah chs 3 & 4<br>Col. 1.24 – 2.7 |
| W | | | |

\*Thomas Becket may be celebrated on 7 July instead of 29 December.

| Second Service Evening Prayer | | Calendar and Holy Communion | Morning Prayer | Evening Prayer |
|---|---|---|---|---|
| EP: Ps. 57; *86* Gen. 4. 1–10 Matt. 23. 34–end | | STEPHEN, DEACON, FIRST MARTYR Collect (1) Stephen (2) Christmas 2 Chron. 24. 20–22 Ps. 119. 161–168 Acts 7. 55–end | (Ps. 13; 31. 1–8; 150) Jer. 26. 12–15 Acts ch. 6 | (Ps. 57; 86) Gen. 4. 1–10 Matt. 10. 17–22 |
| | R | Matt. 23. 34–end | | |
| EP: Ps. 97 Isa. 6. 1–8 1 John 5. 1–12 | | JOHN, APOSTLE AND EVANGELIST (or transferred to 29th) Collect (1) John (2) Christmas Exod. 33. 18–end Ps. 92. 11–end 1 John ch. 1 | Ps. 21; 147. 13–end Exod. 33. 7–11a 1 John 2. 1–11 | Ps. 97 Isa. 6. 1–8 1 John 5. 1–12 |
| | W | John 21. 19b–end | | |
| Ps. 132 Isa. ch. 61 Gal. 3.27 – 4.7 or Luke 2. 15–21 | | *or, for The Sunday after Christmas Day* Isa. 62. 10–12 Ps. 45. 1–7 Gal. 4. 1–7 | Ps. 105. 1–11 Isa. 41.21 – 42.1 1 John 1. 1–7 | Ps. 132 Isa. ch. 61 Luke 2. 15–21 |
| | W | Matt. 1. 18–end | | |
| EP: Ps. 123; *128* Isa. 49. 14–25 Mark 10. 13–16 | | THE HOLY INNOCENTS Collect (1) Innocents (2) Christmas Jer. 31. 10–17 Ps. 123 Rev. 14. 1–5 | (Ps. 36; 146) Baruch 4. 21–27 or Gen. 37. 13–20 Matt. 18. 1–10 | (Ps. 124; 128) Isa. 49. 14–25 Mark 10. 13–16 |
| | R | Matt. 2. 13–18 | | |
| Ps. 131; *132* Isa. 57. 15–end John 1. 1–18 | W | | Jonah ch. 1 Col. 1. 1–14 | Isa. 57. 15–end John 1. 1–18 |
| Ps. *65*; 84 Isa. 59. 1–15a John 1. 19–28 | W | | Jonah ch. 2 Col. 1. 15–23 | Isa. 59. 1–15a John 1. 19–28 |
| Ps. *90*; 148 Isa. 59. 15b–end John 1. 29–34 or First EP of The Naming of Jesus Ps. 148 Jer. 23. 1–6 Col. 2. 8–15 ct | W | Silvester, Bishop of Rome, 335 Com. Bishop | Jonah chs 3 & 4 Col. 1.24 – 2.7 | Isa. 59. 15b–end John 1. 29–34 or First EP of The Circumcision of Christ (Ps. 148) Jer. 23. 1–6 Col. 2. 8–15 ct |

## The *Common Worship* Additional Weekday Lectionary

The Additional Weekday Lectionary provides two readings on a one-year cycle for each day (except for Sundays, Principal Feasts and Holy Days, Festivals and Holy Week). They 'stand alone' and are intended particularly for use in those churches and cathedrals that attract occasional rather than regular congregations. The Additional Weekday Lectionary has been designed to complement rather than replace the existing Weekday Lectionary. Thus a church with a regular congregation in the morning and a congregation made up mainly of visitors in the evening would continue to use the Weekday Lectionary in the morning but might choose to use this Additional Weekday Lectionary for Evening Prayer.

Psalms are not provided, since the Weekday Lectionary already offers a variety of approaches with regard to psalmody. This Lectionary is not intended for use at the Eucharist; the Daily Eucharistic Lectionary is already authorized for that purpose.

On Sundays, Principal Feasts, other Principal Holy Days, Festivals, and in Holy Week, where no readings are provided in this table, the lectionary provision in the main part of this volume should be used.

| Date | | Old Testament | New Testament |
|---|---|---|---|
| **November 2014** | | | |
| 30 | S | THE FIRST SUNDAY OF ADVENT | |
| **December 2014** | | | |
| 1 | M | ANDREW (transferred from 30th) | |
| 2 | Tu | Zeph. 3. 14–end | 1 Thess. 4. 13–end |
| 3 | W | Isa. 65.17 – 66.2 | Matt. 24. 1–14 |
| 4 | Th | Mic. 5. 2–5a | John 3. 16–21 |
| 5 | F | Isa. 66. 18–end | Luke 13. 22–30 |
| 6 | Sa | Mic. 7. 8–15 | Rom. 15.30 – 16.7, 25–end |
| 7 | S | THE SECOND SUNDAY OF ADVENT | |
| 8 | M | Jer. 7. 1–11 | Phil. 4. 4–9 |
| 9 | Tu | Dan. 7. 9–14 | Matt. 24. 15–28 |
| 10 | W | Amos 9. 11–end | Rom. 13. 8–14 |
| 11 | Th | Jer. 23. 5–8 | Mark 11. 1–11 |
| 12 | F | Jer. 33. 14–22 | Luke 21. 25–36 |
| 13 | Sa | Zech. 14. 4–11 | Rev. 22. 1–7 |
| 14 | S | THE THIRD SUNDAY OF ADVENT | |
| 15 | M | Isa. 40. 1–11 | Matt. 3. 1–12 |
| 16 | Tu | Lam. 3. 22–33 | 1 Cor. 1. 1–9 |
| 17 | W | Ecclus. 24. 1–9 *or* Prov. 6. 22–31 | 1 Cor. 2. 1–13 |
| 18 | Th | Exod. 3. 1–6 | Acts 7. 20–36 |
| 19 | F | Isa. 11. 1–9 | Rom. 15. 7–13 |
| 20 | Sa | Isa. 22. 21–23 | Rev. 3. 7–13 |
| 21 | S | THE FOURTH SUNDAY OF ADVENT | |
| 22 | M | Jer. 30. 7–11a | Acts 4. 1–12 |
| 23 | Tu | Isa. 7. 10–15 | Matt. 1. 18–23 |
| 24 | W | *At Evening Prayer the readings for Christmas Eve are used. At other services the following readings are used:* | |
| | | Isa. 29. 13–18 | 1 John 4. 7–16 |
| 25 | Th | **CHRISTMAS DAY** | |
| 26 | F | STEPHEN | |
| 27 | Sa | JOHN THE EVANGELIST | |
| 28 | S | THE HOLY INNOCENTS (THE FIRST SUNDAY OF CHRISTMAS) | |
| 29 | M | *Where The Holy Innocents is celebrated on Sunday 28 December:* | |
| | | Mic. 1. 1–4; 2. 12–13 | Luke 2. 1–7 |
| | | *or The Holy Innocents* | |
| 30 | Tu | Isa. 9. 2–7 | John 8. 12–20 |
| 31 | W | Eccles. 3. 1–13 | Rev. 21. 1–8 |
| **January 2015** | | | |
| 1 | Th | **THE NAMING AND CIRCUMCISION OF JESUS** | |
| 2 | F | Isa. 66. 6–14 | Matt. 12. 46–50 |
| 3 | Sa | Deut. 6. 4–15 | John 10. 31–end |
| 4 | S | THE SECOND SUNDAY OF CHRISTMAS (*or The Epiphany*) | |
| 5 | M | *At Evening Prayer the readings for the Eve of the Epiphany are used. At other services the following readings are used:* | |
| | | Isa. ch. 12 | 2 Cor. 2. 12–end |
| | | *Where, for pastoral reasons, The Epiphany is celebrated on Sunday 4 January, the following readings are used:* | |
| | | Deut. 6.4–15 | John 10.31–end |

| Date | | Old Testament | New Testament |
|---|---|---|---|
| 6 | Tu | **THE EPIPHANY** | |
| | | *Where, for pastoral reasons, The Epiphany is celebrated on Sunday 4 January, the following readings are used:* | |
| | | Isa. 63.7–16 | Gal. 2.23 – 4.7 |
| 7 | W | Gen. 25. 19–end | Eph. 1. 1–6 |
| 8 | Th | Joel 2. 28–end | Eph. 1. 7–14 |
| 9 | F | Prov. 8. 12–21 | Eph. 1. 15–end |
| 10 | Sa | *At Evening Prayer the readings for the Eve of the Baptism of Christ are used. At other services the following readings are used:* | |
| | | Gen. 19. 15–29 | Eph. 2. 1–10 |
| 11 | S | THE BAPTISM OF CHRIST (THE FIRST SUNDAY OF EPIPHANY) | |
| 12 | M | Isa. 41. 14–20 | John 1. 29–34 |
| 13 | Tu | Exod. 17. 1–7 | Acts 8. 26–end |
| 14 | W | Exod. 15. 1–19 | Col. 2. 8–15 |
| 15 | Th | Zech. 6. 9–15 | 1 Pet. 2. 4–10 |
| 16 | F | Isa. 51. 7–16 | Gal. 6. 14–18 |
| 17 | Sa | Lev. 16. 11–22 | Heb. 10. 19–25 |
| 18 | S | THE SECOND SUNDAY OF EPIPHANY | |
| 19 | M | 1 Kings. 17. 8–16 | Mark 8. 1–10 |
| 20 | Tu | 1 Kings 19. 1–9a | Mark 1. 9–15 |
| 21 | W | 1 Kings 19. 9b–18 | Mark 9. 2–13 |
| 22 | Th | Lev. 11. 1–8, 13–19, 41–45 | Acts 10. 9–16 |
| 23 | F | Isa. 49. 8–13 | Acts 10. 34–43 |
| 24 | Sa | Gen. 35. 1–15 | Acts 10. 44–end |
| 25 | S | CONVERSION OF PAUL (THE THIRD SUNDAY OF EPIPHANY) | |
| 26 | M | *When the Conversion of Paul is celebrated on Sunday 25 January* | |
| | | Ezek. 37. 15–end | John 17. 1–19 |
| | | *or Conversion of Paul* | |
| 27 | Tu | Ezek. 20. 39–44 | John 17. 20–end |
| 28 | W | Neh. 2. 1–10 | Rom. 12. 1–8 |
| 29 | Th | Deut. 26. 16–end | Rom. 14. 1–9 |
| 30 | F | Lev. 19. 9–28 | Rom. 15. 1–7 |
| 31 | Sa | Jer. 33. 1–11 | 1 Pet. 5. 5b–end |
| **February 2015** | | | |
| 1 | S | THE FOURTH SUNDAY OF EPIPHANY (*or The Presentation*) | |
| | | *The alternative readings for Monday are used if the Presentation is observed on Sunday 1 February.* | |
| 2 | M | **THE PRESENTATION** or | |
| | | Jonah ch. 3 | 2 Cor. 5. 11–21 |
| 3 | Tu | Prov. 4. 10–end | Matt. 5. 13–20 |
| 4 | W | Isa. 61. 1–9 | Luke 7. 18–30 |
| 5 | Th | Isa. 52. 1–12 | Matt. 10. 1–15 |
| 6 | F | Isa. 56. 1–8 | Matt. 28. 16–end |
| 7 | Sa | Hab. 2.1–4 | Rev. 14. 1–7 |
| 8 | S | THE SECOND SUNDAY BEFORE LENT | |
| 9 | M | Isa. 61. 1–9 | Mark 6. 1–13 |
| 10 | Tu | Isa. 52. 1–10 | Rom. 10. 5–21 |
| 11 | W | Isa. 52.13 – 53.6 | Rom. 15. 14–21 |
| 12 | Th | Isa. 53. 4–12 | 2 Cor. 4. 1–10 |
| 13 | F | Zech. 8. 16–end | Matt. 10. 1–15 |
| 14 | Sa | Jer. 1. 4–10 | Matt. 10. 16–22 |
| 15 | S | THE SUNDAY NEXT BEFORE LENT | |
| 16 | M | 2 Kings 2. 13–22 | 3 John |

| Date | | Old Testament | New Testament |
|---|---|---|---|
| 17 | Tu | Judges 14. 5–17 | Rev. 10. 4–11 |
| 18 | W | **ASH WEDNESDAY** | |
| 19 | Th | Gen. 2. 7–end | Heb. 2. 5–end |
| 20 | F | Gen. 4. 1–12 | Heb. 4. 12–end |
| 21 | Sa | 2 Kings 22. 11–end | Heb. 5. 1–10 |
| 22 | S | THE FIRST SUNDAY OF LENT | |
| 23 | M | Gen. 6. 11–end; 7. 11–16 | Luke 4. 14–21 |
| 24 | Tu | Deut. 31. 7–13 | 1 John 3. 1–10 |
| 25 | W | Gen. 11. 1–9 | Matt. 24. 15–28 |
| 26 | Th | Gen. 13. 1–13 | 1 Pet. 2. 13–end |
| 27 | F | Gen. 21. 1–8 | Luke 9. 18–27 |
| 28 | Sa | Gen. 32. 22–32 | 2 Pet. 1. 10–end |

## March 2015

| Date | | Old Testament | New Testament |
|---|---|---|---|
| 1 | S | THE SECOND SUNDAY OF LENT | |
| 2 | M | 1 Chron. 21. 1–17 | 1 John 2. 1–8 |
| 3 | Tu | Zech. ch. 3 | 2 Pet. 2. 1–10a |
| 4 | W | Job 1. 1–22 | Luke 21.34 – 22.6 |
| 5 | Th | 2 Chron. 29. 1–11 | Mark 11. 15–19 |
| 6 | F | Exod. 19. 1–9a | 1 Pet. 1. 1–9 |
| 7 | Sa | Exod. 19. 9b–19 | Acts 7. 44–50 |
| 8 | S | THE THIRD SUNDAY OF LENT | |
| 9 | M | Josh. 4. 1–13 | Luke 9. 1–11 |
| 10 | Tu | Exod. 15. 22–27 | Heb. 10. 32–end |
| 11 | W | Gen. 9. 8–17 | 1 Pet. 3. 18–end |
| 12 | Th | Dan. 12. 5–end | Mark 13. 21–end |
| 13 | F | Num. 20. 1–13 | 1 Cor. 10. 23–end |
| 14 | Sa | Isa. 43. 14–end | Heb. 3. 1–15 |
| 15 | S | THE FOURTH SUNDAY OF LENT (Mothering Sunday) | |
| 16 | M | 2 Kings 24.18 – 25.7 | 1 Cor. 15. 20–34 |
| 17 | Tu | Jer. 13. 12–19 | Acts 13. 26–35 |
| 18 | W | Jer. 13. 20–27 | 1 Pet. 1.17 – 2.3 |
| 19 | Th | JOSEPH OF NAZARETH | |
| 20 | F | Jer. 17. 1–14 | Luke 6. 17–26 |
| 21 | Sa | Ezra ch. 1 | 2 Cor. 1. 12–19 |
| 22 | S | THE FIFTH SUNDAY OF LENT **(Passiontide begins)** | |
| 23 | M | Joel 2. 12–17 | 2 John |
| 24 | Tu | Isa. 58. 1–11 | Mark 10. 32–45 |
| 25 | W | **THE ANNUNCIATION** | |
| 26 | Th | Jer. 9. 17–22 | Luke 13. 31–35 |
| 27 | F | Lam. 5. 1–3, 19–22 | John 12. 20–26 |
| 28 | Sa | Job 17. 6–end | John 12. 27–36 |
| 29 | S | PALM SUNDAY | |
| | | HOLY WEEK | |

## April 2015

| Date | | Old Testament | New Testament |
|---|---|---|---|
| 5 | S | **EASTER DAY** | |
| 6 | M | Isa. 54. 1–14 | Rom. 1. 1–7 |
| 7 | Tu | Isa. 51. 1–11 | John 5. 19–29 |
| 8 | W | Isa. 26. 1–19 | John 20. 1–10 |
| 9 | Th | Isa. 43. 14–21 | Rev. 1. 4–end |
| 10 | F | Isa. 42. 10–17 | 1 Thess. 5. 1–11 |
| 11 | Sa | Job 14. 1–14 | John 21. 1–14 |
| 12 | S | THE SECOND SUNDAY OF EASTER | |
| 13 | M | Ezek. 1. 22–end | Rev. ch. 4 |
| 14 | Tu | Prov. 8. 1–11 | Acts 16. 6–15 |
| 15 | W | Hos. 5.15 – 6.6 | 1 Cor. 15. 1–11 |
| 16 | Th | Jonah ch. 2 | Mark 4. 35–end |
| 17 | F | Gen. 6. 9–end | 1 Pet. 3. 8–end |
| 18 | Sa | 1 Sam. 2. 1–8 | Matt. 28. 8–15 |
| 19 | S | THE THIRD SUNDAY OF EASTER | |
| 20 | M | Exod. 24. 1–11 | Rev. ch. 5 |
| 21 | Tu | Lev. 19. 9–18, 32–end | Matt. 5. 38–end |
| 22 | W | Gen. 3. 8–21 | 1 Cor. 15. 12–28 |
| 23 | Th | GEORGE | |
| 24 | F | Neh. 9. 6–17 | Rom. 5. 12–end |
| 25 | Sa | MARK | |
| 26 | S | THE FOURTH SUNDAY OF EASTER | |

| Date | | Old Testament | New Testament |
|---|---|---|---|
| 27 | M | Jer. 31. 10–17 | Rev. 7. 9–end |
| 28 | Tu | Job 31. 13–23 | Matt. 7. 1–12 |
| 29 | W | Gen. 2. 4b–9 | 1 Cor. 15. 35–49 |
| 30 | Th | Prov. 28. 3–end | Mark 10. 17–31 |

## May 2015

| Date | | Old Testament | New Testament |
|---|---|---|---|
| 1 | F | PHILIP AND JAMES | |
| 2 | Sa | 1 Chron. 29. 10–13 | Luke 24. 13–35 |
| 3 | S | THE FIFTH SUNDAY OF EASTER | |
| 4 | M | Gen. 15. 1–18 | Rom. 4. 13–end |
| 5 | Tu | Deut. 8. 1–10 | Matt. 6. 19–end |
| 6 | W | Hos. 13. 4–14 | 1 Cor. 15. 50–end |
| 7 | Th | Exod. 3. 1–15 | Mark 12. 18–27 |
| 8 | F | Ezek. 36. 33–end | Rom. 8. 1–11 |
| 9 | Sa | Isa. 38. 9–20 | Luke 24. 33–end |
| 10 | S | THE SIXTH SUNDAY OF EASTER | |
| 11 | M | Prov. 4. 1–13 | Phil. 2. 1–11 |
| 12 | Tu | Isa. 32. 12–end | Rom. 5. 1–11 |
| 13 | W | *At Evening Prayer the readings for the Eve of Ascension Day are used. At other services the following readings are used:* | |
| | | Isa. 43. 1–13 | Titus 2.11 – 3.8 |
| 14 | Th | **ASCENSION DAY** | |
| 15 | F | MATTHIAS | |
| | | *Where Matthias is celebrated on 24 February:* | |
| | | Exod. 35.30 – 36.1 | Gal. 5. 13–end |
| 16 | Sa | Num. 11. 16–17, 24–29 | 1 Cor. ch. 2 |
| 17 | S | THE SEVENTH SUNDAY OF EASTER (Sunday after Ascension Day) | |
| 18 | M | Num. 27. 15–end | 1 Cor. ch. 3 |
| 19 | Tu | 1 Sam. 10. 1–10 | 1 Cor. 12. 1–13 |
| 20 | W | 1 Kings 19. 1–18 | Matt. 13–end |
| 21 | Th | Ezek. 11. 14–20 | Matt. 9.35 – 10.20 |
| 22 | F | Ezek. 36. 22–28 | Matt. 12. 22–32 |
| 23 | Sa | *At Evening Prayer the readings for the Eve of Pentecost are used. At other services the following readings are used:* | |
| | | Mic. 3. 1–8 | Eph. 6. 10–20 |
| 24 | S | **PENTECOST** (Whit Sunday) | |
| 25 | M | Gen. 12. 1–9 | Rom. 4. 13–end |
| 26 | Tu | Gen. 13. 1–12 | Rom. 12. 9–end |
| 27 | W | Gen. ch. 15 | Rom. 4. 1–8 |
| 28 | Th | Gen. 22. 1–18 | Heb. 11. 8–19 |
| 29 | F | Isa. 51. 1–8 | John 8. 48–end |
| 30 | Sa | *At Evening Prayer the readings for the Eve of Trinity Sunday are used. At other services the following readings are used:* | |
| | | Ecclus. 44. 19–23 or Josh. 2. 1–15 | James 2. 14–26 |
| 31 | S | **TRINITY SUNDAY** | |

## June 2015

| Date | | Old Testament | New Testament |
|---|---|---|---|
| 1 | M | THE VISITATION | |
| | | *Where The Visitation is celebrated on 2 July:* | |
| | | Exod. 2. 1–10 | Heb. 11. 23–31 |
| 2 | Tu | Exod. 2. 11–end | Acts 7. 17–29 |
| 3 | W | Exod. 3. 1–12 | Acts 7. 30–38 |
| 4 | Th | *Day of Thanksgiving for the Institution of the Holy Communion (Corpus Christi), or, where Corpus Christi is celebrated as a Lesser Festival:* | |
| | | Exod. 6. 1–13 | John 9. 24–38 |
| 5 | F | Exod. 34. 1–10 | Mark 7. 1–13 |
| 6 | Sa | Exod. 34. 27–end | 2 Cor. 3. 7–end |
| 7 | S | THE FIRST SUNDAY AFTER TRINITY | |
| 8 | M | Gen. 37. 1–11 | Rom. 11. 9–21 |
| 9 | Tu | Gen. 41. 15–40 | Mark 13. 1–13 |
| 10 | W | Gen. 42. 17–end | Matt. 18. 1–14 |
| 11 | Th | BARNABAS | |
| 12 | F | Gen. 47. 1–12 | 1 Thess. 5. 12–end |

| Date | | Old Testament | New Testament |
|---|---|---|---|
| 13 | Sa | Gen. 50. 4–21 | Luke 15. 11–end |
| 14 | S | THE SECOND SUNDAY AFTER TRINITY | |
| 15 | M | Isa. ch. 32 | James 3. 13–end |
| 16 | Tu | Prov. 3. 1–18 | Matt. 5. 1–12 |
| 17 | W | Judg. 6. 1–16 | Matt. 5. 13–24 |
| 18 | Th | Jer. 6. 9–15 | 1 Tim. 2. 1–6 |
| 19 | F | 1 Sam. 16. 14–end | John 14. 15–end |
| 20 | Sa | Isa. 6. 1–9 | Rev. 19. 9–end |
| 21 | S | THE THIRD SUNDAY AFTER TRINITY | |
| 22 | M | Exod. 13. 13b–end | Luke 15. 1–10 |
| 23 | Tu | Prov. 1. 20–end | James 5. 13–end |
| 24 | W | THE BIRTH OF JOHN THE BAPTIST | |
| 25 | Tu | Isa. 57. 14–end | John 13. 1–17 |
| 26 | F | Jer. 15. 15–end | Luke 16. 19–31 |
| 27 | Sa | Isa. 25. 1–9 | Acts 2. 22–33 |
| 28 | S | THE FOURTH SUNDAY AFTER TRINITY | |
| 29 | M | PETER AND PAUL | |
| 30 | Tu | Prov. 6. 6–19 | Luke 4. 1–14 |

**July 2015**

| | | | |
|---|---|---|---|
| 1 | W | Isa. 24. 1–15 | 1 Cor. 6. 1–11 |
| 2 | Th | Job ch. 7 | Matt. 7. 21–29 |
| 3 | F | THOMAS | |
| | | Where Thomas is celebrated on 21 December: | |
| | | Jer. 20. 7–end | Matt. 27. 27–44 |
| 4 | Sa | Job ch. 28 | Heb. 11.32 – 12.2 |
| 5 | S | THE FIFTH SUNDAY AFTER TRINITY | |
| 6 | M | Exod. 32. 1–14 | Col. 3. 1–11 |
| 7 | Tu | Prov. 9. 1–12 | 2 Thess. 2.13 – 3.5 |
| 8 | W | Isa. 26. 1–9 | Rom. 8. 12–27 |
| 9 | Th | Jer. 8.18 – 9.6 | John 13. 21–35 |
| 10 | F | 2 Sam. 5. 1–12 | Matt. 27. 45–56 |
| 11 | Sa | Hos. 11. 1–11 | Matt. 28. 1–7 |
| 12 | S | THE SIXTH SUNDAY AFTER TRINITY | |
| 13 | M | Exod. 40. 1–16 | Luke 14. 15–24 |
| 14 | Tu | Prov. 11. 1–12 | Mark 12. 38–44 |
| 15 | W | Isa. 33. 2–10 | Phil. 1. 1–11 |
| 16 | Th | Job ch. 38 | Luke 18. 1–14 |
| 17 | F | Job 42. 1–6 | John 3. 1–15 |
| 18 | Sa | Eccles. 9. 1–11 | Heb. 1. 1–9 |
| 19 | S | THE SEVENTH SUNDAY AFTER TRINITY | |
| 20 | M | Num. 23. 1–12 | 1 Cor. 1. 10–17 |
| 21 | Tu | Prov. 12. 1–12 | Gal. 3. 1–14 |
| 22 | W | MARY MAGDALENE | |
| 23 | Th | Hos. ch. 14 | John 15. 1–17 |
| 24 | F | 2 Sam. 18. 18–end | Matt. 27. 57–66 |
| 25 | Sa | JAMES | |
| 26 | S | THE EIGHTH SUNDAY AFTER TRINITY | |
| 27 | M | Joel 3. 16–21 | Mark 4. 21–34 |
| 28 | Tu | Prov. 12. 13–end | John 1. 43–51 |
| 29 | W | Isa. 55. 8–end | 2 Tim. 2. 8–19 |
| 30 | Th | Isa. 38. 1–8 | Mark 5. 21–43 |
| 31 | F | Jer. 14. 1–9 | Luke 8. 4–15 |

**August 2015**

| | | | |
|---|---|---|---|
| 1 | Sa | Eccles. 5. 10–19 | 1 Tim. 6. 6–16 |
| 2 | S | THE NINTH SUNDAY AFTER TRINITY | |
| 3 | M | Josh. 1. 1–9 | 1 Cor. 9. 19–end |
| 4 | Tu | Prov. 15. 1–11 | Gal. 2. 15–end |
| 5 | W | Isa. 49. 1–7 | 1 John 1 |
| 6 | Th | THE TRANSFIGURATION | |
| 7 | F | Isa. 59. 8–end | Mark 15. 6–20 |
| 8 | Sa | Zech. 7.8 – 8.8 | Luke 20. 27–40 |
| 9 | S | THE TENTH SUNDAY AFTER TRINITY | |
| 10 | M | Judg. 13. 1–23 | Luke 10. 38–42 |
| 11 | Tu | Prov. 15. 15–end | Matt. 15. 21–28 |
| 12 | W | Isa. 45. 1–7 | Eph. 4. 1–16 |
| 13 | Th | Jer. 16. 1–5 | Luke 12. 35–48 |

| Date | | Old Testament | New Testament |
|---|---|---|---|
| 14 | F | Jer. 18. 1–11 | Heb. 1. 1–9 |
| 15 | Sa | THE BLESSED VIRGIN MARY | |
| | | When the Blessed Virgin Mary is celebrated on 8 September: | |
| | | Jer. 26. 1–19 | Eph. 3. 1–13 |
| 16 | S | THE ELEVENTH SUNDAY AFTER TRINITY | |
| 17 | M | Ruth 2. 1–13 | Luke 10. 25–37 |
| 18 | Tu | Prov. 16. 1–11 | Phil. 3. 4b–end |
| 19 | W | Deut. 11. 1–21 | 2 Cor. 9. 6–end |
| 20 | Th | Ecclus. ch. 2 or | John 16. 1–15 |
| | | Eccles. 2. 12–25 | |
| 21 | F | Obad. 1–10 | John 19. 1–16 |
| 22 | Sa | 2 Kings 2. 11–14 | Luke 24. 36–end |
| 23 | S | THE TWELFTH SUNDAY AFTER TRINITY | |
| 24 | M | BARTHOLOMEW | |
| 25 | Tu | Prov. 17. 1–15 | Luke 7. 1–17 |
| 26 | W | Jer. 5. 20–end | 2 Pet. 3. 8–end |
| 27 | Th | Dan. 2. 1–23 | Luke 10. 1–20 |
| 28 | F | Dan. 3. 1–28 | Rev. ch. 15 |
| 29 | Sa | Dan. ch. 6 | Phil. 2. 14–24 |
| 30 | S | THE THIRTEENTH SUNDAY AFTER TRINITY | |
| 31 | M | 2 Sam. 7. 4–17 | 2 Cor. 5. 1–10 |

**September 2015**

| | | | |
|---|---|---|---|
| 1 | Tu | Prov. 18. 10–21 | Rom. 14. 10–end |
| 2 | W | Judg. 4. 1–10 | Rom. 1. 8–17 |
| 3 | Th | Isa. 49. 14–end | John 16. 16–24 |
| 4 | F | Job 9. 1–24 | Mark 15. 21–32 |
| 5 | Sa | Exod. 19. 1–9 | John 20. 11–18 |
| 6 | S | THE FOURTEENTH SUNDAY AFTER TRINITY | |
| 7 | M | Hag. ch. 1 | Mark 7. 9–23 |
| 8 | Tu | Prov. 21. 1–18 | Mark 6. 30–44 |
| 9 | W | Hos. 11. 1–11 | 1 John 4. 9–end |
| 10 | Th | Lam. 3. 34–48 | Rom. 7. 14–end |
| 11 | F | 2 Kings 19. 4–18 | 1 Thess. ch. 3 |
| 12 | Sa | Ecclus. 4. 1–28 or | 2 Tim. 3. 10–end |
| | | Deut. 29. 2–15 | |
| 13 | S | THE FIFTEENTH SUNDAY AFTER TRINITY | |
| 14 | M | HOLY CROSS DAY | |
| 15 | Tu | Prov. 8. 1–11 | Luke 6. 39–end |
| 16 | W | Prov. 2. 1–15 | Col. 1. 9–20 |
| 17 | Th | Baruch 3. 14–end or | John 1. 1–18 |
| | | Gen. 1. 1–13 | |
| 18 | F | Ecclus. 1. 1–20 or | 1 Cor. 1. 18–end |
| | | Deut. 7. 7–16 | |
| 19 | Sa | Wisd. 9. 1–12 or Jer. 1. 4–10 | Luke 2. 41–end |
| 20 | S | THE SIXTEENTH SUNDAY AFTER TRINITY | |
| 21 | M | MATTHEW | |
| 22 | Tu | Ruth 4. 7–17 | Luke 2. 25–38 |
| 23 | W | 2 Kings 4. 1–7 | John 2. 1–11 |
| 24 | Th | 2 Kings 4. 25b–37 | Mark 3. 19b–35 |
| 25 | F | Judith 8. 9–17, 28–36 or | John 19. 25b–30 |
| | | Ruth 1. 1–18 | |
| 26 | Sa | Exod. 15. 19–27 | Acts 1. 6–14 |
| 27 | S | THE SEVENTEENTH SUNDAY AFTER TRINITY | |
| 28 | M | Exod. 19. 16–end | Heb. 12. 18–end |
| 29 | Tu | MICHAEL AND ALL ANGELS | |
| 30 | W | 1 Chron. 29. 10–19 | Col. 3. 12–17 |

**October 2015**

| | | | |
|---|---|---|---|
| 1 | Th | Neh. 8. 1–12 | 1 Cor. 14. 1–12 |
| 2 | F | Isa. 1. 10–17 | Mark 12. 28–34 |
| 3 | Sa | Dan. 6. 6–23 | Rev. 12. 7–12 |
| 4 | S | THE EIGHTEENTH SUNDAY AFTER TRINITY | |
| 5 | M | 2 Sam. 22. 4–7, 17–20 | Heb. 7.26 – 8.6 |
| 6 | Tu | Prov. 22. 17–end | 2 Cor. 12. 1–10 |
| 7 | W | Hos. ch. 14 | James 2. 14–26 |
| 8 | Th | Isa. 24. 1–15 | John 16. 25–33 |

| Date | Old Testament | New Testament |
| --- | --- | --- |
| 9 F | Jer. 14. 1–9 | Luke 23. 44–56 |
| 10 Sa | Zech. 8. 14–end | John 20. 19–end |
| 11 S | THE NINETEENTH SUNDAY AFTER TRINITY | |
| 12 M | I Kings 3. 3–14 | I Tim. 3.14 – 4.8 |
| 13 Tu | Prov. 27. 11–end | Gal. 6. 1–10 |
| 14 W | Isa. 51. 1–6 | 2 Cor. 1. 1–11 |
| 15 Th | Ecclus. 18. 1–14 or Job ch. 26 | I Cor. 11. 17–end |
| 16 F | Ecclus. 28. 2–12 or Job 19. 21–end | Mark 15. 33–47 |
| 17 Sa | Isa. 44. 21–end | John 21. 15–end |
| 18 S | LUKE (THE TWENTIETH SUNDAY AFTER TRINITY) | |
| 19 M | Where Luke is celebrated on Sunday 18 October: I Kings 6. 2–10 or Luke | John 12. 1–11 |
| 20 Tu | Prov. 31. 10–end | Luke 10. 38–42 |
| 21 W | Jonah ch. 1 | Luke 5. 1–11 |
| 22 Th | Exod. 12. 1–20 | I Thess. 4. 1–12 |
| 23 F | Isa. ch. 64 | Matt. 27. 45–56 |
| 24 Sa | 2 Sam. 7. 18–end | Acts 2. 22–33 |
| 25 S | THE LAST SUNDAY AFTER TRINITY | |
| 26 M | Isa. 42. 14–21 | Luke 1. 5–25 |
| 27 Tu | I Sam. 4. 12–end | Luke 1. 57–end |
| 28 W | SIMON AND JUDE | |
| 29 Th | Isa. ch. 35 | Matt. 11. 2–19 |
| 30 F | 2 Sam. 11. 1–17 | Matt. 14. 1–12 |
| 31 Sa | At Evening Prayer the readings for the Eve of All Saints are used. At other services the following readings are used: Isa. 43. 15–21 | Acts 19. 1–10 |

## November 2015

| Date | Old Testament | New Testament |
| --- | --- | --- |
| 1 S | ALL SAINTS' DAY | |
| 2 M | Esther 3. 1–11; 4. 7–17 | Matt. 18. 1–10 |
| 3 Tu | Ezek. 18. 21–end | Matt. 18. 12–20 |
| 4 W | Prov. 3. 27–end | Matt. 18. 21–end |
| 5 Th | Exod. 23. 1–9 | Matt. 19. 1–15 |
| 6 F | Prov. 3. 13–18 | Matt. 19. 16–end |
| 7 Sa | Deut. 28. 1–6 | Matt. 20. 1–16 |
| 8 S | THE THIRD SUNDAY BEFORE ADVENT | |
| 9 M | Isa. 40. 21–end | Rom. 11. 25–end |
| 10 Tu | Ezek. 34. 20–end | John 10. 1–18 |
| 11 W | Lev. 26. 3–13 | Titus 2. 1–10 |
| 12 Th | Hos. 6. 1–6 | Matt. 9. 9–13 |
| 13 F | Mal. ch. 4 | John 4. 5–26 |
| 14 Sa | Mic. 6. 6–8 | Col. 3. 12–17 |
| 15 S | THE SECOND SUNDAY BEFORE ADVENT | |
| 16 M | Mic. 7. 1–7 | Matt. 10. 24–39 |
| 17 Tu | Hab. 3. 1–19a | I Cor. 4. 9–16 |
| 18 W | Zech. 8. 1–13 | Mark 13. 3–8 |
| 19 Th | Zech. 10. 6–end | I Pet. 5. 1–11 |
| 20 F | Mic. 4. 1–5 | Luke 9. 28–36 |

| Date | Old Testament | New Testament |
| --- | --- | --- |
| 21 Sa | At Evening Prayer the readings for the Eve of Christ the King are used. At other services the following readings are used: Exod. 16. 1–21 | John 6. 3–15 |
| 22 S | CHRIST THE KING (The Sunday next before Advent) | |
| 23 M | Jer. 30. 1–3, 10–17 | Rom. 12. 9–21 |
| 24 Tu | Jer. 30. 18–24 | John 10. 22–30 |
| 25 W | Jer. 31. 1–9 | Matt. 15. 21–31 |
| 26 Th | Jer. 31. 10–17 | Matt. 16. 13–end |
| 27 F | Jer. 31. 31–37 | Heb. 10. 11–18 |
| 28 Sa | Isa. 51.17 – 52.2 | Eph. 5. 1–20 |
| 29 S | THE FIRST SUNDAY OF ADVENT | |
| 30 M | ANDREW | |

## December 2015

| Date | Old Testament | New Testament |
| --- | --- | --- |
| 1 Tu | Zeph. 3. 14–end | I Thess. 4. 13–end |
| 2 W | Isa. 65.17 – 66.2 | Matt. 24. 1–14 |
| 3 Th | Mic. 5. 2–5a | John 3. 16–21 |
| 4 F | Isa. 66. 18–end | Luke 13. 22–30 |
| 5 Sa | Mic. 7. 8–15 | Rom. 15.30 – 16.7, 25–end |
| 6 S | THE SECOND SUNDAY OF ADVENT | |
| 7 M | Jer. 7. 1–11 | Phil. 4. 4–9 |
| 8 Tu | Dan. 7. 9–14 | Matt. 24. 15–28 |
| 9 W | Amos 9. 11–end | Rom. 13. 8–14 |
| 10 Th | Jer. 23. 5–8 | Mark 11. 1–11 |
| 11 F | Jer. 33. 14–22 | Luke 21. 25–36 |
| 12 Sa | Zech. 14. 4–11 | Rev. 22. 1–7 |
| 13 S | THE THIRD SUNDAY OF ADVENT | |
| 14 M | Isa. 40. 1–11 | Matt. 3. 1–12 |
| 15 Tu | Lam. 3. 22–33 | I Cor. 1. 1–9 |
| 16 W | Joel 3. 9–16 | Matt. 24. 29–35 |
| 17 Th | Ecclus. 24. 1–9 or Prov. 6. 22–31 | I Cor. 2. 1–13 |
| 18 F | Exod. 3. 1–6 | Acts 7. 20–36 |
| 19 Sa | Isa. 11. 1–9 | Rom. 15. 7–13 |
| 20 S | THE FOURTH SUNDAY OF ADVENT | |
| 21 M | Num. 24. 15b–19 | Rev. 22. 10–21 |
| 22 Tu | Jer. 30. 7–11a | Acts 4. 1–12 |
| 23 W | Isa. 7. 10–15 | Matt. 1. 18–23 |
| 24 Th | At Evening Prayer the readings for Christmas Eve are used. At other services the following readings are used: Isa. 29. 13–18 | I John 4. 7–16 |
| 25 F | CHRISTMAS DAY | |
| 26 Sa | STEPHEN | |
| 27 S | JOHN THE EVANGELIST (THE FIRST SUNDAY OF CHRISTMAS) | |
| 28 M | THE HOLY INNOCENTS | |
| 29 Tu | Mic. 1. 1–4; 2. 12–13 or John the Evangelist | Luke 2. 1–7 |
| 30 W | Isa. 9. 2–7 | John 8. 12–20 |
| 31 Th | Eccles. 3. 1–13 | Rev. 21. 1–8 |

# CALENDAR 2015

## JANUARY
| Su | M | Tu | W | Th | F | Sa |
|---|---|---|---|---|---|---|
|  |  |  |  | 1 | 2 | 3 |
| $X^2$ 4 | 5 | $E$ 6 | 7 | 8 | 9 | 10 |
| $B$ 11 | 12 | 13 | 14 | 15 | 16 | 17 |
| $E^2$ 18 | 19 | 20 | 21 | 22 | 23 | 24 |
| $E^3$ 25 | 26 | 27 | 28 | 29 | 30 | 31 |

## FEBRUARY
| Su | M | Tu | W | Th | F | Sa |
|---|---|---|---|---|---|---|
| $E^4$ 1 | $Pr$ 2 | 3 | 4 | 5 | 6 | 7 |
| 8 | 9 | 10 | 11 | 12 | 13 | 14 |
| 15 | 16 | 17 | $A$ 18 | 19 | 20 | 21 |
| $L^1$ 22 | 23 | 24 | 25 | 26 | 27 | 28 |

## MARCH
| Su | M | Tu | W | Th | F | Sa |
|---|---|---|---|---|---|---|
| $L^2$ 1 | 2 | 3 | 4 | 5 | 6 | 7 |
| $L^3$ 8 | 9 | 10 | 11 | 12 | 13 | 14 |
| $L^4$ 15 | 16 | 17 | 18 | 19 | 20 | 21 |
| $L^5$ 22 | 23 | 24 | $An$ 25 | 26 | 27 | 28 |
| $P$ 29 | 30 | 31 |  |  |  |  |

## APRIL
| Su | M | Tu | W | Th | F | Sa |
|---|---|---|---|---|---|---|
|  |  |  | 1 | $M$ 2 | $G$ 3 | 4 |
| $E$ 5 | 6 | 7 | 8 | 9 | 10 | 11 |
| $E^2$ 12 | 13 | 14 | 15 | 16 | 17 | 18 |
| $E^3$ 19 | 20 | 21 | 22 | 23 | 24 | 25 |
| $E^4$ 26 | 27 | 28 | 29 | 30 |  |  |

## MAY
| Su | M | Tu | W | Th | F | Sa |
|---|---|---|---|---|---|---|
|  |  |  |  |  | 1 | 2 |
| $E^5$ 3 | 4 | 5 | 6 | 7 | 8 | 9 |
| $E^6$ 10 | 11 | 12 | 13 | $A$ 14 | 15 | 16 |
| $E^7$ 17 | 18 | 19 | 20 | 21 | 22 | 23 |
| $W$ 24 | 25 | 26 | 27 | 28 | 29 | 30 |
| $T$ 31 |  |  |  |  |  |  |

## JUNE
| Su | M | Tu | W | Th | F | Sa |
|---|---|---|---|---|---|---|
|  | 1 | 2 | 3 | 4 | 5 | 6 |
| $T^1$ 7 | 8 | 9 | 10 | 11 | 12 | 13 |
| $T^2$ 14 | 15 | 16 | 17 | 18 | 19 | 20 |
| $T^3$ 21 | 22 | 23 | 24 | 25 | 26 | 27 |
| $T^4$ 28 | 29 | 30 |  |  |  |  |

## JULY
| Su | M | Tu | W | Th | F | Sa |
|---|---|---|---|---|---|---|
|  |  |  | 1 | 2 | 3 | 4 |
| $T^5$ 5 | 6 | 7 | 8 | 9 | 10 | 11 |
| $T^6$ 12 | 13 | 14 | 15 | 16 | 17 | 18 |
| $T^7$ 19 | 20 | 21 | 22 | 23 | 24 | 25 |
| $T^8$ 26 | 27 | 28 | 29 | 30 | 31 |  |

## AUGUST
| Su | M | Tu | W | Th | F | Sa |
|---|---|---|---|---|---|---|
|  |  |  |  |  |  | 1 |
| $T^9$ 2 | 3 | 4 | 5 | 6 | 7 | 8 |
| $T^{10}$ 9 | 10 | 11 | 12 | 13 | 14 | 15 |
| $T^{11}$ 16 | 17 | 18 | 19 | 20 | 21 | 22 |
| $T^{12}$ 23 | 24 | 25 | 26 | 27 | 28 | 29 |
| $T^{13}$ 30 | 31 |  |  |  |  |  |

## SEPTEMBER
| Su | M | Tu | W | Th | F | Sa |
|---|---|---|---|---|---|---|
|  |  | 1 | 2 | 3 | 4 | 5 |
| $T^{14}$ 6 | 7 | 8 | 9 | 10 | 11 | 12 |
| $T^{15}$ 13 | 14 | 15 | 16 | 17 | 18 | 19 |
| $T^{16}$ 20 | 21 | 22 | 23 | 24 | 25 | 26 |
| $T^{17}$ 27 | 28 | 29 | 30 |  |  |  |

## OCTOBER
| Su | M | Tu | W | Th | F | Sa |
|---|---|---|---|---|---|---|
|  |  |  |  | 1 | 2 | 3 |
| $T^{18}$ 4 | 5 | 6 | 7 | 8 | 9 | 10 |
| $T^{19}$ 11 | 12 | 13 | 14 | 15 | 16 | 17 |
| $T^{20}$ 18 | 19 | 20 | 21 | 22 | 23 | 24 |
| $T^{-}$ 25 | 26 | 27 | 28 | 29 | 30 | 31 |

## NOVEMBER
| Su | M | Tu | W | Th | F | Sa |
|---|---|---|---|---|---|---|
| $AS$ 1 | 2 | 3 | 4 | 5 | 6 | 7 |
| $A^{-3}$ 8 | 9 | 10 | 11 | 12 | 13 | 14 |
| $A^{-2}$ 15 | 16 | 17 | 18 | 19 | 20 | 21 |
| $A^{-1}$ 22 | 23 | 24 | 25 | 26 | 27 | 28 |
| $A$ 29 | 30 |  |  |  |  |  |

## DECEMBER
| Su | M | Tu | W | Th | F | Sa |
|---|---|---|---|---|---|---|
|  |  | 1 | 2 | 3 | 4 | 5 |
| $A^2$ 6 | 7 | 8 | 9 | 10 | 11 | 12 |
| $A^3$ 13 | 14 | 15 | 16 | 17 | 18 | 19 |
| $A^4$ 20 | 21 | 22 | 23 | 24 | $X$ 25 | 26 |
| $X^1$ 27 | 28 | 29 | 30 | 31 |  |  |

**Legend (2015)**

- $A$ = Ash Wednesday, Ascension, Advent
- $A^{-}$ = Before Advent
- $A^{-4}$ = also All Saints, 2016 (if trans.)
- $A^{-1}$ = Christ the King
- $An$ = Annunciation
- $AS$ = All Saints (also Fourth Sunday before Advent, 2015)
- $B$ = Baptism
- $E$ = Epiphany, Easter
- $(E^3$ = also Conversion of Paul, 2015)
- $E^4$ = also Presentation, 2015 and 2016 (if trans.)

---

# CALENDAR 2016

## JANUARY
| Su | M | Tu | W | Th | F | Sa |
|---|---|---|---|---|---|---|
|  |  |  |  |  | 1 | 2 |
| $X^2$ 3 | 4 | 5 | $E$ 6 | 7 | 8 | 9 |
| $B$ 10 | 11 | 12 | 13 | 14 | 15 | 16 |
| $E^2$ 17 | 18 | 19 | 20 | 21 | 22 | 23 |
| $E^3$ 24 | 25 | 26 | 27 | 28 | 29 | 30 |
| $E^4$ 31 |  |  |  |  |  |  |

## FEBRUARY
| Su | M | Tu | W | Th | F | Sa |
|---|---|---|---|---|---|---|
|  | 1 | $Pr$ 2 | 3 | 4 | 5 | 6 |
| $L^{-}$ 7 | 8 | 9 | $A$ 10 | 11 | 12 | 13 |
| $L^1$ 14 | 15 | 16 | 17 | 18 | 19 | 20 |
| $L^2$ 21 | 22 | 23 | 24 | 25 | 26 | 27 |
| $L^3$ 28 | 29 |  |  |  |  |  |

## MARCH
| Su | M | Tu | W | Th | F | Sa |
|---|---|---|---|---|---|---|
|  |  | 1 | 2 | 3 | 4 | 5 |
| $L^4$ 6 | 7 | 8 | 9 | 10 | 11 | 12 |
| $L^5$ 13 | 14 | 15 | 16 | 17 | 18 | 19 |
| $P$ 20 | 21 | 22 | 23 | $M$ 24 | $G$ 25 | 26 |
| $E$ 27 | 28 | 29 | 30 | 31 |  |  |

## APRIL
| Su | M | Tu | W | Th | F | Sa |
|---|---|---|---|---|---|---|
|  |  |  |  |  | 1 | 2 |
| $E^2$ 3 | 4 | 5 | 6 | 7 | 8 | 9 |
| $E^3$ 10 | 11 | 12 | 13 | 14 | 15 | 16 |
| $E^4$ 17 | 18 | 19 | 20 | 21 | 22 | 23 |
| $E^5$ 24 | 25 | 26 | 27 | 28 | 29 | 30 |

## MAY
| Su | M | Tu | W | Th | F | Sa |
|---|---|---|---|---|---|---|
| $E^6$ 1 | 2 | 3 | 4 | $A$ 5 | 6 | 7 |
| $E^7$ 8 | 9 | 10 | 11 | 12 | 13 | 14 |
| $W$ 15 | 16 | 17 | 18 | 19 | 20 | 21 |
| $T$ 22 | 23 | 24 | 25 | 26 | 27 | 28 |
| $T^1$ 29 | 30 | 31 |  |  |  |  |

## JUNE
| Su | M | Tu | W | Th | F | Sa |
|---|---|---|---|---|---|---|
|  |  |  | 1 | 2 | 3 | 4 |
| $T^2$ 5 | 6 | 7 | 8 | 9 | 10 | 11 |
| $T^3$ 12 | 13 | 14 | 15 | 16 | 17 | 18 |
| $T^4$ 19 | 20 | 21 | 22 | 23 | 24 | 25 |
| $T^5$ 26 | 27 | 28 | 29 | 30 |  |  |

## JULY
| Su | M | Tu | W | Th | F | Sa |
|---|---|---|---|---|---|---|
|  |  |  |  |  | 1 | 2 |
| $T^6$ 3 | 4 | 5 | 6 | 7 | 8 | 9 |
| $T^7$ 10 | 11 | 12 | 13 | 14 | 15 | 16 |
| $T^8$ 17 | 18 | 19 | 20 | 21 | 22 | 23 |
| $T^9$ 24 | 25 | 26 | 27 | 28 | 29 | 30 |
| $T^{10}$ 31 |  |  |  |  |  |  |

## AUGUST
| Su | M | Tu | W | Th | F | Sa |
|---|---|---|---|---|---|---|
|  | 1 | 2 | 3 | 4 | 5 | 6 |
| $T^{11}$ 7 | 8 | 9 | 10 | 11 | 12 | 13 |
| $T^{12}$ 14 | 15 | 16 | 17 | 18 | 19 | 20 |
| $T^{13}$ 21 | 22 | 23 | 24 | 25 | 26 | 27 |
| $T^{14}$ 28 | 29 | 30 | 31 |  |  |  |

## SEPTEMBER
| Su | M | Tu | W | Th | F | Sa |
|---|---|---|---|---|---|---|
|  |  |  |  | 1 | 2 | 3 |
| $T^{15}$ 4 | 5 | 6 | 7 | 8 | 9 | 10 |
| $T^{16}$ 11 | 12 | 13 | 14 | 15 | 16 | 17 |
| $T^{17}$ 18 | 19 | 20 | 21 | 22 | 23 | 24 |
| $T^{18}$ 25 | 26 | 27 | 28 | 29 | 30 |  |

## OCTOBER
| Su | M | Tu | W | Th | F | Sa |
|---|---|---|---|---|---|---|
|  |  |  |  |  |  | 1 |
| $T^{19}$ 2 | 3 | 4 | 5 | 6 | 7 | 8 |
| $T^{20}$ 9 | 10 | 11 | 12 | 13 | 14 | 15 |
| 16 | 17 | 18 | 19 | 20 | 21 | 22 |
| 23 | 24 | 25 | 26 | 27 | 28 | 29 |
| $T^{-}$ 30 | 31 |  |  |  |  |  |

## NOVEMBER
| Su | M | Tu | W | Th | F | Sa |
|---|---|---|---|---|---|---|
|  |  | $AS$ 1 | 2 | 3 | 4 | 5 |
| $A^{-3}$ 6 | 7 | 8 | 9 | 10 | 11 | 12 |
| $A^{-2}$ 13 | 14 | 15 | 16 | 17 | 18 | 19 |
| $A^{-1}$ 20 | 21 | 22 | 23 | 24 | 25 | 26 |
| $A$ 27 | 28 | 29 | 30 |  |  |  |

## DECEMBER
| Su | M | Tu | W | Th | F | Sa |
|---|---|---|---|---|---|---|
|  |  |  |  | 1 | 2 | 3 |
| $A^2$ 4 | 5 | 6 | 7 | 8 | 9 | 10 |
| $A^3$ 11 | 12 | 13 | 14 | 15 | 16 | 17 |
| $A^4$ 18 | 19 | 20 | 21 | 22 | 23 | 24 |
| $X$ 25 | 26 | 27 | 28 | 29 | 30 | 31 |

**Legend (2016)**

- $G$ = Good Friday
- $L$ = Lent
- $L^{-}$ = Before Lent
- $P$ = Palm Sunday
- $Pr$ = Presentation
- $T$ = Trinity
- $(T^{20}$ = also Thomas, 2016)
- $(T^{26}$ = also Luke, 2015)
- $T^{-}$ = Last Sunday after Trinity
- $W$ = Pentecost (Whit Sunday)
- $X$ = Christmas
- $(X^1$ = also John, 2015)
- $X^2$ = also Epiphany, 2015 (if trans.)